Engendering Inspiration

Engendering Inspiration

Visionary Strategies
in Rilke, Lawrence, and H.D.

Helen Sword

Ann Arbor

THE UNIVERSITY OF MICHIGAN PRESS

Copyright © by the University of Michigan 1995
All rights reserved
Published in the United States of America by
The University of Michigan Press
Manufactured in the United States of America
⊛ Printed on acid-free paper

1998   1997   1996   1995   4   3   2   1

A CIP catalog record for this book is available from the British Library.

Library of Congress Cataloging-in-Publication Data

Sword, Helen.
   Engendering inspiration : visionary strategies in Rilke, Lawrence,
and H. D. / by Helen Sword.
       p.   cm.
   Includes bibliographical references (p.   ) and index.
   ISBN 0-472-10594-9 (hardcover : alk. paper)
   1. English poetry—20th century—History and criticism. 2. Rilke,
Rainer Maria, 1875–1926—Criticism and interpretation. 3. Lawrence,
D. H. (David Herbert), 1885–1930—Poetic works. 4. H. D. (Hilda
Doolittle), 1886–1961—Criticism and interpretation. 5. Difference
(Psychology) in literature. 6. Mythology, Classical, in literature.
7. Creation (Literary, artistic, etc.) 8. Prophecies in literature.
9. Sex role in literature. 10. Visions in literature.
11. Inspiration. I. Title.
PR610.S96   1995
809.1'041—dc20   95-40616
                                                                      CIP

For the sources of my inspiration:
Richard, Claire, and Peter

Contents

Acknowledgments

Poems from *The Complete Poems of D. H. Lawrence* by D. H. Lawrence, edited by V. de Sola Pinto and F. W. Roberts. Copyright © 1964, 1971 by Angelo Ravagli and C. M. Weekley, Executors of the Estate of Frieda Lawrence Ravagli. Used by permission of Viking Penguin, a division of Penguin Books USA, Inc.

"Leda" and excerpts of other poems from H.D.: *Collected Poems: 1912–1944*. Copyright © 1982 by the Estate of Hilda Doolittle. Used by permission of New Directions Publishing Corporation.

Leda and *Singing of Swans* by D. H. Lawrence. Reproduced by permission of Laurence Pollinger Ltd. and the Estate of Frieda Lawrence Ravagli.

Excerpts from unpublished manuscripts and letters by H.D. Used by permission of Perdita Schaffner and the Yale Collection of American Literature, Beinecke Rare Book and Manuscript Library, Yale University.

A version of chapter 4 originally appeared as "Orpheus and Eurydice in the Twentieth Century: Lawrence, H.D., and the Poetics of the Turn," *Twentieth Century Literature* 35, no. 4 (1989): 407–28, and is reprinted by permission. A version of chapter 5 appeared as "Leda and the Modernists," *PMLA* 107, no. 2 (1992): 305–18, and is reprinted by permission of the copyright owner, the Modern Language Association of America. Brief portions of chapter 3 appeared in "H.D.'s *Majic Ring*," *Tulsa Studies in Women's Literature* 14.2 (1995), and are reprinted by permission.

In addition, I wish to record my indebtedness to three inspiring teacher/scholars without whose influence this book might never have been written: Ralph Freedman, Sandra M. Gilbert, and Herbert Marks. For gifts of advice, information, and reassurance at various stages of the book's composition, I also thank April Alliston, Cynthia Bannon, Diana Collecott, Susan Stanford Friedman, Kristin Gager, Susan Gubar,

Marjorie Howes, Matthew Kaplan, Richard Kaye, Gayle Margherita, Adalaide Morris, Lauren Proll, Perdita Schaffner, Katherine Stern, and Susan B. Whitlock. Finally, I owe a special debt of gratitude to my family: to my mother, Lois Sword, and to the memory of my father, Charles Sword, for boundless emotional, material, and intellectual sustenance over the years; to my daughter and son, Claire Allegra and Peter Rangi, for reminding me daily what it means to be alive; and to my husband, Richard Sorrenson, for everything.

Introduction:
Engendering Inspiration

If there was
no pain, no tension, there was
no sacred word. You cannot step twice
—if I may put it this way—
into the same stream of consciousness.

—Richard Howard, "Oracles"

Demon come forth,
even if it be God I call forth
standing like a carrion,
wanting to eat me,
starting at the lips and tongue.
And me wanting to glide into his spoils,
I take bread and wine,
and the demon farts and giggles,
at my letting God out of my mouth
anonymous woman
at that anonymous altar.

—Anne Sexton, "Demon"

For poets throughout the Western literary tradition the adoption of a prophetic, visionary stance has offered a standard means to poetic authority, suggesting special selection and a privileged access to other-worldly wisdom. Paradoxically, however, prophetic poetry also implies supreme self-effacement, for to claim divine inspiration—literally, the reception of the breath, or spirit, of a god—is to admit to the suppression of one's own individual voice. "Poetic inspiration," then, is a concept steeped in oxymoronic logic: a power achieved through powerlessness, an authoritative posture maintained through abjection. Few poets would deny that poetic production (with poetry's etymological root of "making") entails a highly conscious effort; "A line will take us hours maybe," as W. B. Yeats famously complains. All the same, Wordsworthian notions of lyric poetry as a powerful "influx of feeling" or "spontaneous overflow" persist in the language and thought of our culture.[1]

Transposed into gendered terms, the paradoxes of inspiration become even more acute. Female writers, for whom tradition and authority have always been inherently problematic issues, do not lack for visionary role models; indeed, prophecy has been one of the few vehicles by which female seers such as the Pythia, Cassandra, and the Old Testament prophetesses have attained a priestly stature approaching that of their male counterparts. All too often, however, female prophecy devolves from entrancement—a god's literal entrance into, and possession of, a woman's mind and body—rather than from an active penetration of male power structures. Moreover, if prophecy burdens women with the very stereotypes it seeks to overcome, the paradox cuts both ways: male prophecy, too, enacts a conflict between traditional gender roles. The male poet who lays claim to divine inspiration must cultivate and affirm precisely those traits of passivity, receptivity, and self-denial from which generations of female writers have struggled to disassociate themselves. He can attain the spiritual authority of the prophet, in other words, only by submitting to a certain self-feminization.

Nowhere has this prophetic paradox resonated more freely or intensely than in the poetry of the modernist era, a period marked, like the prophetic mode itself, by conflicts between authority and influence, between tradition and innovation, between perceived notions of feminity (as women began to enter previously male spheres of endeavor in increasingly large numbers) and masculinity (as men, in turn, reacted to the threat posed by women's disturbance of the social status quo). The mere persistence of the prophetic paradigm throughout the modernist period may, to be sure, seem like a paradox in its own right; studies of prophetic elements in poetry are more likely to focus on Dante, Spenser, Milton, or the English and German Romantics (Blake, Hölderlin, Wordsworth, Coleridge) than on the angst-ridden, alienated literary generation that came of age during the first half of the twentieth century.[2] Yet it was, no doubt, modernism's very emphasis on irony and spiritual disenchantment that triggered, in turn, a compensatory longing for otherworldly insight and spiritual fulfillment. In addition, Freudian psychology provided early-twentieth-century poets with a new and compelling vocabulary for describing the workings of poetic inspiration, as writers increasingly directed their anxieties of author-ship away from such sacred external entities as God, Nature, and the Muses and toward that powerful internal Other identified by Freud as the unconscious. Poetic conflicts between interiority and exteriority, subject and object, and self and Other are not, of course, unique to mod-ernism. It is surely no accident, however, that they should have become especially intense in an age made so deeply and self-consciously aware, in the words of Arthur Rimbaud, that "Je est un autre" (qtd. in Perloff 60–61).

The three writers on whom this study focuses continuously sought to define and manipulate that Other—variously figured by Rilke as an inner female self, by Lawrence as an irascible but dynamic male demon, and by H.D. as an intuition-affirming oracle linked both to Apollo and Athene—through their writing and especially their poetry. Yet they were by no means alone among their modernist contempo-raries in their preoccupation with the sources, the forms, and the gen-der of inspiration. Other poets who were engaged with similar issues included W. B. Yeats, whose feminization of visionary experience I will discuss briefly in chapter 5; Else Lasker-Schüler, whose inspiring Other takes forms ranging from God to mother to male lover to androgynous playmate; Stefan George, who constructed his prophetic/poetic "new Reich" around a self-consciously male aesthetic; Paul Valéry, whose characterization of inspiration as a procreative interchange between *"forme"* and *"fond"* (form and essence) translates readily into gendered terms (*Oeuvres* 1332); William Carlos Williams, who declared in an early poem that "it is the woman in us that makes us write" (*Poems* 17) and whose epic *Paterson* revolves around the poet's search for a mysti-cal, inspiring feminine principle, "the radiant gist" (109); Robert Graves, whose "White Goddess" functions for the male poet as an infi-nitely desirable yet infinitely dangerous muse; and even T. S. Eliot, whose *Waste Land* both feminizes and devalues vatic functions even while it betrays a nostalgic desire for vatic power. Of course, more twentieth-century poets than can even be mentioned here, from Hart Crane, Wallace Stevens, Dylan Thomas, James Merrill, and Richard Howard to Louise Bogan, Sylvia Plath, Anne Sexton, and Adrienne Rich (to name just a few writing in English), have invoked prophetic inspiration at least occasionally, if only to treat it ironically or to bemoan their own lack of it. Others still, from Marianne Moore to

Philip Larkin, so rigidly avoid any appeal to a visionary poetics that their omission in itself testifies to the influence and importance of the prophetic paradigm.

Thus, Rilke, Lawrence, and H.D. can be regarded as representative rather than atypical in their persistent use of visionary tropes. They exemplify, however, three particularly striking ways in which inspiration has been gendered and engendered by modernist poets: Rilke genuinely believed in and strove for a feminization of the male artist, although his poetry itself would often undercut this position; Lawrence first advocated and then resisted such self-feminization, eventually evolving a misogynist poetics favoring male leadership, instead; and H.D. developed an ever-shifting variety of poetic strategies for transforming her own femaleness from a perceived liability into a source of creative power. Moreover, as contemporaries who came of poetic age in the first two decades of the twentieth century (H.D., however, would outlive Rilke and Lawrence by more than thirty years), all three typified the nomadic restlessness of their era, deserting their childhood homes—Prague, Nottingham, and Bethlehem, Pennsylvania, respectively—to range for most of their adult lives across Europe and, in Lawrence's case, the world. Although only limited intertextual influences can be traced among them (Lawrence and H.D. corresponded and exchanged manuscripts for a few years during and just after the Great War, and Rilke is known to have read and admired several of Lawrence's works [Schnack 831, 877, 956]), they shared many thematic concerns, wrote on a number of common issues, and engaged in similar programs of revisionist mythmaking. Finally, all three, though conventionally classified as modernists, have faced frequent denigration for their anti-ironic sentimentality and expressive intensity, qualities that can legitimately be celebrated as "prophetic" and "visionary" but that are all too often dismissed, instead, as "feminine."

Of course, it is possible to wax prophetic without ever having been divinely inspired; prophetic discourse, as I will use the term, denotes not only statements made as a result of direct visionary experience but also any mode of speech or writing that lays claim to prophetic authority by echoing traditionally prophetic cadences or appropriating prophetic language and imagery. Wordsworth points out in *The Excursion* that not every recipient of inspiration is capable of transforming such experience into edifying expression:

Oh! many are the Poets that are sown
By Nature; men endowed with highest gifts,
The vision and the faculty divine;
Yet wanting the accomplishment of verse.

(qtd. in Perkins 303)

Nor, conversely, is every poet who borrows from prophetic traditions necessarily endowed with "the faculty divine." Frederick Clarke Prescott draws a useful distinction between what he calls "primary" and "secondary" inspiration: "The poet [is] either a true ecstatic, or he [is] capable by a flexible assumption through conscious art, of writing as if he were inspired" (7). Primary inspiration, in other words, refers to real visions and real divine voices (and I have chosen to accept at face value poets' claims to such experiences), while secondary inspiration applies to verse that merely imitates prophetic tropes. Most prophetic poetry presumably owes more to secondary inspiration (speaking *like* a prophet) than to direct revelation (speaking *as* a prophet); indeed, even writers who have undergone actual visionary experiences seldom claim—Rilke being one important exception—that their poetry sprang on those occasions ready formed into their minds and from their pens. More typical would be someone like H.D., whose disconcerting bouts of visionary consciousness required years of recollection in relative tranquillity before she succeeded in converting them into art. In the end, after all, it was the poems rather than the visions that would earn her the epithet *prophetic*.

In Old Testament tradition the most important function of prophecy is not to foretell the future but, rather, to interpret the present: to offer, that is, "an exegesis of existence from a divine perspective" (Heschel xiv). Throughout this study, accordingly, I will use the words *prophet* and *prophetic* primarily to indicate poets' claims to otherworldly insight rather than necessarily to suggest predictive foresight.[3] Although I employ the words *prophetic* and *visionary* more or less interchangeably, however, a fine but crucial distinction must be drawn between these two revelatory modes and the traditions they represent. Visionary experience denotes a visual apprehension, a picture, an apparition, as when Ezekiel beholds "the likeness of the glory of the Lord" in the midst of a flashing cloud (Ezek. 1:1–28). Prophecy, in contrast, is a verbal pronouncement, an act not of private sight but of public speech.[4] Visionary experience is unmediated and absolute, like Emerson's transcendentalist epiphany:

> Standing on the bare ground,—my head bathed by the blithe air, and uplifted into infinite space,—all mean egotism vanishes. I become a transparent eyeball. I am nothing. I see all. The currents of the Universal Being circulate through me; I am part or parcel of God. (9)

Prophecy, on the other hand, whether it describes a divine vision or relays a divine message, is always doubly mediated, first by the prophet (who, in both Old Testament and classical lore, must often undergo elaborate preparations before he or she is deemed worthy to prophesy) and then by language itself.

"Visionary poetry," then, cannot really exist except as a form of prophecy, a visual revelation transposed into words. The visionary poet, the prophet, and the mystic all share the age-old dilemma of ineffability: How can one give utterance to an experience that is by its very nature unutterable? One possible solution to the visionary poet's conundrum can be found, according to Kinereth Meyer, in poetic language itself:

> Again, how can a poet, by definition, reach a point "after speech," if it is the poet's lot to be always *within* speech? The answer to this dilemma is to be found in figurative language. Searching for figures which will sustain both a still center and a constantly shifting periphery, the visionary poet looks for metaphors characterized by an oscillation which is often both physical and functional. . . . Though such figures . . . allow the modern poet to momentarily escape the "tyranny of the eye" . . . , visionary poems often demonstrate the precariousness of this escape. (6–7)

Modern visionary poets, in Meyer's gloss, deliberately employ metaphorical devices that will allow them access both to "a wordless unity" and to "a dwelling in the multiplicity of language" (2–3). As interpreters of visionary experience, they mediate between what Jacques Derrida calls the rabbinical mode, "which sees interpretation as an unfortunately necessary road back to an original truth," and the poetical, which self-consciously "affirms the play of interpretation" (*Writing and Difference* n. 311).

Such paradoxes of language and interpretation are by no means unique to modern poetry; they are woven into the very texture of prophecy from its earliest known manifestations, giving rise, in turn, to the kinds of gendered contradictions that I will trace in the visionary poetics of Rilke, Lawrence, and H.D. Old Testament prophecy, for instance, is frequently marked by parataxis (J. Burke 67), by repetition and stammering (Marks 5), and by disorienting shifts between first- and third-person pronouns (Kerrigan 32). Such tropes, which signal "the subject's resistance to an overwhelming influx" (Marks 2), replicate through disjunctive language the difficulties of translating visionary experience into speech. At the same time, however, as Christine Berg and Philippa Berry note in a study of seventeenth-century female prophets in England, "prophecy in its most exaggerated form—that is, in the form in which it most clearly distinguishes itself from a rational discourse—has much in common with that phenomenon described by Luce Irigaray as 'the language of the feminine' and by Julia Kristeva as the semiotic" (39). Disturbing the status quo by refusing to accommodate itself to any fixed symbolic order, prophecy becomes especially threatening when pronounced by a woman, since the very notion that a woman "could possess and transmit the word of God" introduces in turn "the awful, scarcely conceivable possibility that God might actually be a woman" (Berg and Berry 50, 52). But even when spoken by a man, prophetic discourse raises the specter of a feminized, "hysterical" male.

Old Testament prophecy is often characterized as an unwelcome ordeal (a Hebrew word meaning "burden" is also the technical term for "oracle") and even, in the Book of Jeremiah, as a kind of rape (Marks 6, 19). In classical history and literature, likewise, the gift of prophecy nearly always comes with strings attached, and the burden of prophecy is often, in effect, the burden of femininity. Cassandra, for instance, was granted the ability to prophesy only after she agreed to sleep with the god Apollo; when she revoked her promise, he added the curse that her predictions would never be believed (Graves, *Greek Myths II* 263–64). Both the gift and the burden of Cassandra's prophecy, then, devolve from her status as a sexual object. Similarly, the Delphic Pythia was said by ancient historians to have received her divine insight directly from Apollo; Plutarch records that she had to remain a virgin so that she could be physically entered by the god (Bevan 170), and in earlier Greek tradition she was even thought to undergo a kind of spiritual pregnancy:

> But the principal material means by which the oracular ecstasy at Delphi was believed by the Greeks to be induced was a kind of gas or vapour which, it was asserted, rose from a fissure in the ground beneath the Pythia and entered her womb. (157)

Virgil recounts, in the sixth book of the *Aeneid*, the struggle of the Sibyl of Cumae against Apollo, who physically invades her:

> she rages, savage, in her cavern, tries
> to drive the great god from her breast. So much
> the more, he tires out her raving mouth;
> he tames her wild heart, shapes by crushing force.
>
> (6:110–13)

In fact, classical sources are replete with accounts of women who, like the male prophets of the Old Testament, resist and bemoan their prophetic calling (Dodds 72; Oesterreich 321, 334). For them divine inspiration is clearly a painful and sometimes even deadly enterprise— a situation cynically inverted by T. S. Eliot in *The Waste Land*, which bears as its epigraph Petronius' description of the Cumaean Sibyl as a withered, caged old woman who, having asked Apollo for immortality but failed to ask for eternal youth, longs now only to die (*Poems*, 37).

This gendered model of inspiration becomes more complicated when male poets invoke a female muse, a trope that has persisted in Western literature from Hesiod through Milton to such twentieth-century poets as Wallace Stevens and James Merrill.[5] The many variations on the muse tradition, even within classical literature, provide fertile ground for modern poets' often uneasy manipulations of its possibilities. In some classical texts the Muses serve, rather like W. B. Yeats's automatistic wife, Georgie (see chap. 5), as poetic intermediaries who protect the poet from the dangers of direct inspiration. E. R. Dodds notes, for instance, that, when the Greek poet Pindar asks the Muse for an oracle, it is the Muse, and not the poet, who plays the part of the Pythia; the poet does not ask to be himself "possessed," but only to act as interpreter for the entranced Muse. And that seems to be the original relationship. Epic tradition represented the poet as deriving supernormal knowledge from the Muses, but not falling into ecstasy or being possessed by them. (82)

In other cases, however, the male poet is portrayed as a receptive, passive vessel of inspiration, as in Plato's *Phaedrus*, in which Socrates describes "the kind of madness and possession" that comes from the Muses: "It seizes on a delicate and virgin soul, awakes it, [and] sets it raving in songs and every form of poetry" (27). Even in their earliest known representations in ancient Greek literature, according to Penelope Murray, the Muses "symbolise the poet's feeling of dependence on the external: they are the personification of his inspiration" (89).

Feminist critics such as Rachel Blau DuPlessis, Alicia Ostriker, Adrienne Rich, and Mary K. DeShazer have forcefully argued that the muse tradition handicaps aspiring female poets: "This tradition of the objectified muse has made it hard for [the female poet] to transcend her Otherness and thus attain the subjectivity crucial to a strong poetic stance" (DeShazer 3). For the male poet, in contrast, DeShazer argues,

the invocation of a female muse—his particular way of naming the Other—leads ultimately to a strong sense of poetic autonomy, an identity vital to his creativity. Although the poet is typically portrayed as possessed by his muse, in reality it is he who possesses, since the act of naming is by nature hierarchical. . . . [T]he male poet's invocation of his muse is an act of appropriation and control: to produce poems, he typically consumes the female muse, absorbing her creative energy into himself. (2)

But even if, in invoking the Muses, men disempower women by turning them into symbols, they do so at the cost of admitting their own desperate need for such female symbols in order to create—an admission steeped in sexual anxiety, particularly for writers of the already anxious modernist era. As I will demonstrate in my chapters on the Orpheus and Leda myths, male modernists thus find themselves trapped within the paradoxes of two equally problematic models of inspiration: either the poet figures his source of inspiration, his muse, as a desired yet potentially dangerous female, like Eurydice in the Orpheus story; or else he takes on the feminized stance of Leda, inspired by a powerful Other figured as male.[6] Female modernists such as H.D., meanwhile, face the dilemma of whether to identify with inspiration's objects—dead Eurydice, ravished Leda—or, in defiance of virtually all Western literary tradition, with the myths' male heroes and gods.

One classical figure who manages to transcend, or at least to embrace, the gendered contradictions of prophecy is Tiresias, a male prophet who, according to Greek and Roman legend, spent seven years as a woman (Ovid, *Met.* 3.316–20). Having been struck blind by an angry Hera for revealing the secret that women enjoy sex more than men, Tiresias was later compensated by Zeus with the gift of prophecy; thus, he belongs among that familiar company of blind prophets—Homer, Oedipus, Milton—whose physical sightlessness in turn enables a deeper spiritual insight. By the time he finds his way into Eliot's *Waste Land* he has been demoted from a figure of hermaphroditic potency to one of modernist dessication and visionary ennui: "I Tiresias, though blind, throbbing between two lives, / Old man with wrinkled female breasts. . . . I Tiresias have foresuffered all" (*Poems* 43–44). Yet, even for Eliot, Tiresias remains "the most important personage in the poem," the paradigmatic seer whose prophetic power depends above all on his privileged identity as an emotional androgyne in whom "the two sexes meet" (n. 52).

This meeting of the sexes in a single figure (although Tiresias, to be sure, is serially rather than simultaneously a man and a woman) approaches the ideal of the *coincidentia oppositorum*, a primordial unity celebrated in mystical traditions throughout the world as a manifestation of divinity. Mircea Eliade notes that theories and beliefs concerning the dual-gendered nature of God serve above all to remind humankind that "the divine *Grund* can only be understood as a mystery or a paradox" (*Two and the One* 82). Yet, where prophecy, as I have argued, is an inescapably paradoxical mode of discourse, the ultimate aim of mystical experience is transcendence, a merging of "self with larger-than-self" (Leuba 1). That merging is often accomplished, like prophecy, by means of paradox: for example, through the *via negativa*—"stripping away sense experience and the products of reason . . . until the bodily senses and the mind of the believer are empty, and the soul is available to receive divine emanation" (Atkinson 40)—advocated by the sixth-century Neoplatonist Pseudo-Dionysius and pursued in various forms by such medieval Christian mystics as Walter Hilton and the anonymous author of *The Cloud of Unknowing*. The desired result of mystical union, however, is not the balancing act between divine revelation and individual expression that characterizes prophecy but, rather, a surrender that finally negates individuality altogether.

Like biblical and classical prophecy, mystical experience is frequently represented in gendered, and specifically in sexualized, terms. Female Christian mystics such as Julian of Norwich typically call themselves "the Bride of Christ" and describe their intercourse with the divine as a spiritual and sometimes even a physical union: Saint Theresa, for instance, recounts visions of an angel who "held in his hands a long golden dart, tipped with fire" that he "would plunge . . . through my heart, and push . . . down into my bowels," and Saint Marguerite Marie reports having been told by her heavenly bridegroom, "Let me do my pleasure. . . . I want you to be the plaything of my love, and you must live thus without resistance, surrendered to my desires, allowing me to gratify myself at your expense" (Leuba 144, 113–14). Male mystics, while seldom so sexually graphic, often describe their souls in similarly feminized, nubile terms: "For know thou well that all the business that Jesu maketh about a soul is for to make it a true perfect spouse to Him in the fullness and highness of love" (Walter Hilton; Knowles 115–16). To some extent, mysticism, with its sexual paradigm of longed-for union rather than of unwilled penetration, might be said to offer the optimistic solution to the prophetic poet's authoritative dilemma. Yet Rilke, Lawrence, and H.D. would all remain ambivalent about the ideal of mystical transcendence; as Lawrence remarked, with characteristic bluntness, "I don't like mysticism. It has no trousers and no trousers' seat" (*Fantasia* 17).

Leaving aside the gender implications of Lawrence's metaphor—which suggests that mysticism, having "no trousers," is essentially a feminine mode of being and deserves for that very reason to be denigrated—there are a number of other probable reasons why Rilke, Lawrence, and H.D. preferred the register of prophecy to that of mysticism. Mystical experience, like visionary experience, takes place, by definition, outside of language; thus, although mystics do frequently attempt verbal descriptions of their experiences, and although poets such as Stéphane Mallarmé have sought, conversely, to achieve through language something resembling mystical transcendence, the mystical mode is ultimately antithetical to the poet's craft. True mystical union, which leaves behind the body and all earthly concerns, must presumably take place in perfect silence, somewhere out of time. And even after the experience is over, as Saint John of the Cross explains, the soul "finds no terms, no means, no comparison whereby to render the sublimity of the wisdom and the delicacy of the spiritual feeling with which she is filled" (qtd. in James 312). Prophecy, in contrast, is grounded both in temporality and in the contingencies of language. Moreover, whereas mysticism denotes a private communion with God, prophecy, like poetry, belongs explicitly to the public sphere, its whole point being, as Milton puts it in *Paradise Lost*, to "justify the ways of God to Men" (1.22).

Needless to say, given the complex genealogies and intertextual intricacies of these two traditions, it can often be difficult to distinguish between them, even according to the rather schematic definitions that I have given here. Rilke, Lawrence, and H.D. were all acquainted with at least some aspects of mystical philosophy (H.D., in particular, was widely read in both Jewish and Christian mystical lore), and all were clearly intrigued by and in some measure attracted to the mystical ideal of primordial unity. To a certain extent, then, one can discern in their poetry a continuous and finally unresolved oscillation between the mystical and prophetic modes. For the most part, however, each of these three poets saw mystical transcendence as a suspect concept. Their best poetry holds itself open to and even fosters the kinds of oppositional tensions and gendered paradoxes that I have already described as hallmarks of the prophetic mode, celebrating contradiction and conflict as necessary components of, indeed catalysts for, visionary experience. Of course, not all self-contradictions in their work can be redeemed as sources of poetic empowerment, nor can every crippling ambivalence be resolved into a saving dialectic. Frequently, however, the paradoxes in their poetry do reflect a self-conscious poetics of paradox.

"The prophet is a sign of contradiction," notes Mario Di Cesare, for he or she disrupts the complacency and comfort of the status quo (11). Speaking in "notes one octave too high for our ears" (Heschel 10), the prophetic poet faces the proverbial curse of never being believed in his or her own country—or, worse yet, of being regarded as mad. The words *mantic* (seer) and *mania* (madness) share, after all, a common etymology, suggesting that "the association of prophecy and madness belongs to the Indo-European stock of ideas" (Dodds 70). Certainly, there have been enough "manic mantics"—visionaries whose brilliance has shaded over into pathology—to keep the stereotype alive even in fairly recent times: Christopher Smart, William Blake, Friedrich Nietzsche, to name only a few. Psychiatrist Albert Rothenberg reports, however, that clinical studies have failed to substantiate the age-old belief that there is "a connection between psychosis and genius" (6). Instead, Rothenberg has isolated what he believes to be two essential elements in creative thinking: first, what he calls the "janusian process" (named after the Roman god Janus, whose two faces look in opposite directions) and, second, the "homospatial process." In the janusian process, Rothenberg explains,

> multiple opposites or antitheses are conceived simultaneously, either as existing side by side or as equally operative, valid, or true. In an apparent defiance of logic or of physical possibility, the creative person consciously formulates the simultaneous operation of antithetical elements or factors and develops those formulations into integrated entities and creations. (15)

The homospatial process, similarly, "consists of conceiving two or more discrete entities occupying the same space, a conception leading to the articulation of new identities" (25). Although both of these processes can induce considerable intellectual tension (which might explain why "creative people who are not otherwise psychiatrically ill may show emotional and mental strain to a greater degree than healthy noncreative persons" [36]), they are not, Rothenberg asserts, particularly common among patients who have been diagnosed as mentally ill. Creativity, he argues, depends upon an active, intentional, and above all "healthy" ability to generate new ideas from paradoxical or oxymoronic processes of thought—a claim that bears out not only the poetic principles of Rilke, Lawrence, and H.D. but also the pronouncements of poets and philosophers throughout history, from Heraclitus ("In the tension of opposites all things have their being") to Goethe ("It is contradiction that makes us productive") to Blake ("Without Contraries is no progression").[7]

In addition to being associated (rightly or wrongly) with madness, prophecy is also linked, both etymologically and historically, with the genre of lyric poetry. The Latin word *vates*, for instance (from the Indo-European stem *wet-*, meaning "to blow, inspire, or spiritually arouse"), denotes both a prophet and a poet, suggesting that for the Romans the two functions were, at least in some instances, identical. The Greek Pythia is thought to have spoken her oracles primarily in rhymed hexameter—some sources report that her messages were versified by priests retained especially for that purpose (Dodd 93 n; Bevan 176)—and prophetic pronouncements in the Old Testament are often delivered, likewise, in the binary sentence structure and "high style" that many biblical scholars characterize as a form of verse (Kugel 3–5). Plutarch explicitly associates divine inspiration with the lyric mode:

> But above all, the ravishment of the spirit or that divine inspiration which is called *enthusiasmus*, casteth body, mind, voice, and all far beyond the ordinary habit; which is the cause that the furious raging priests of Bacchus . . . use rime and metre; those also who by a prophetical spirit give answer by oracle, deliver the same in verse. (qtd. in Prescott 265)

Rilke, Lawrence, and H.D., of course, all wrote prose as well as poetry; indeed, Lawrence's philosophical tracts and H.D.'s stream-of-consciousness autobiographies exhibit precisely the kind of rushing, eruptive intensity that is perhaps most frequently associated with prophetic discourse. But, as a form of speech "far beyond the ordinary habit," it is poetry that most effectively accommodates and focuses the dialectical tensions inherent to any act of prophecy.

I do not mean, however, to advocate a return to a New Critical conception of the lyric as a self-contained system of delicately balanced, intricately sustained paradoxes. For a start, my strategies of close reading and my privileging of paradoxical modes of thought owe at least as much to poststructuralist theories of language as a *mise en abîme*, an unending play of significations, as they do to New Critical notions of poems as "well-wrought urns" of stable, recoverable meaning. Moreover, in keeping with recent feminist and historicist interpretive models, my study posits literary production as a communicative act that is deeply imbedded in history, including personal history. If Rilke, Lawrence, and H.D. were all, in Wordsworth's phrase, "Poets sown by Nature," they were watered, so to speak, by culture. Accordingly, the first three chapters of this book attend not to their poetry alone but also to their letters, memoirs, prose fiction, essays, and, above all, to the various historical and biographical factors that most significantly influenced their thinking on the subjects of inspiration, creativity, and gender.

My final two chapters, however, move out of history and into the realm of myth, discussing how Rilke, Lawrence, and H.D., through their poetic retellings of the stories of Orpheus/Eurydice and Leda/Zeus, respectively, rendered these two ancient tales of gender conflict into modern metaphors—appropriately complex and paradoxical ones—for poetic inspiration. Carl Jung describes the recasting of visionary experience into myth as a manifestation of the collective unconscious, an individual poet's transposition of *"die unheimliche Paradoxie der Vision"* (the uncanny paradox of vision) into a universal discourse (111; Lieb 5). More cynically, one can discern in most of these poems an agenda that is at least as much revisionary as visionary. The most obvious function of myth is etiological: it seeks to explain the status quo by recounting a tale of origins, justifying individual action in the name of universal truth. Beyond merely serving as a vehicle for meditations on inspiration, then, revisionist mythmaking mirrors the workings of prophetic discourse itself: like prophecy, it invokes the authority of an ancient past in order to affirm its modern narrators' mandate to interpret and transform the present.

Rewriting an ancient myth is like assembling a Möbius strip: with a deft half-twist and a piece of tape, one constructs a self-contained loop that displays no beginning and no end, no distinction between oppositional surfaces.[8] The revisionist mythmaker fabricates, in other words, an illusion of original wholeness by inscribing him- or herself within a system that, although self-created, is nonetheless made to appear timeless and universal; in doing so, he or she enters the realm of the "always already." Of course, the enterprising reader or critic can always point to the tape on the Möbius strip, to the site where the myth of endless contiguity ruptures and where the point of origins, or at least of originatory grafting, is revealed. The word *myth*, after all, signifies not only a tale of eternal truth but also a made-up story or lie, thereby encompassing both mythology's claim to universality and the illusory nature of that claim. Modernist mythmakers, in fact, do not necessarily find such scrutiny unwelcome, for they are likely to regard their own appropriations of myth as iconoclastic rather than purely nostalgic or redemptive gestures. This is especially true of those writers who may feel themselves to have been slighted by mythological tradition; Alicia Ostriker points out, for instance, that, "when a woman rewrites an ancient myth, it is not because she yearns for a heroic past (when men were men, etc.). She is not Ezra Pound, and she probably knows that she is happier in the twentieth century than she would have been between the ages of Homer and Pericles, locked in the *gynaeceum*" (*Writing like a Woman* 132). Instead, women generally turn to myth in order to transform tales of female disenfranchisement into stories that affirm and celebrate female power, or, alternatively, they seek to expose sterotypically feminine traits (weakness, evil, amorality) as the historical and cultural constructs that they are rather than the biologically or divinely mandated facts that, for instance, the Genesis myth claims them to be. In either case it is seldom the goal of a female writer to locate herself unproblematically within an established cultural tradition.

But male modernists, too, frequently point to the fracturings of the mythological structures that they themselves have erected. Modernist writers of both sexes, in fact, even when they betray a nostalgic desire for unity, tradition, and resolution—the eternal, feminine "Yes" that ends Joyce's *Ulysses*, the "Shantih Shantih Shantih" that redeems Eliot's *Waste Land*—also foreground everywhere *sparagmos*, the topos of dismemberment described by Northrop Frye as "the archetypal theme of irony and satire" (192). This is certainly true of Rilke, Lawrence, and H.D., all three of whom render the Orpheus and Leda myths into specifically modernist fables of inspiration by problematizing visionary experience, by exploring sexual conflicts and shifting gender identities, by addressing the implications of violence as a cultural, historical, and linguistic force, but also, above all, by emphasizing the themes of rupture and reconstitution implicit in both myths. Orpheus, by turning toward his dead wife, Eurydice, loses her forever; later he is torn to pieces but is made whole once more through song. Leda, for her part, becomes most potent in the instant of her violation; in the familiar ideology of Yeats's "Leda and the Swan" the "broken wall" of her body in turn enables the birth of a new civilization from the ashes of Troy. Both myths serve, then, as exemplars of the central dialectic that motivates all revisionist mythmaking. They enact a constant movement between the desire for unitary wholeness and the reality of fragmentation—between, that is, the mystical and the prophetic modes.

H.D. describes the enterprise of the visionary poet as a kind of verbal alchemy:

> plunder, O poet,
> . . . .
> collect the fragments of the splintered glass
>
> and of your fire and breath,
> melt down and integrate,
>
> re-invoke, re-create
> opal, onyx, obsidian,
>
> now scattered in the shards
> men tread upon.[9]

The task of the literary critic, no less than that of the modernist poet, is one of meltdown and transformation, a reassembly and reinvocation of scattered shards of signification. Literary theorists such as Paul de Man (*Blindness and Insight*), Geoffrey Hartman (*Criticism in the Wilderness, Midrash and Literature*), and Harold Bloom (*Kabbalah and Criticism*) have gone so far as to suggest, explicitly or implicitly, that criticism itself is a visionary act; if prophecy is inspired interpretation, after all, then any work of interpretation that draws upon visionary traditions—by imitating, for instance, techniques of Christian allegorical exegesis or of Jewish midrash—becomes, by extension, a species of prophetic discourse. I make here no claims of my own to inspired wisdom or divine vision. I do seek, however—through my emphasis on modernism's visionary counterpoint, my probing of the cultural dynamics of myth, and my reading the creative process in terms of a gendered dialectic—to recognize inspiration and gender not merely as compelling thematic issues but also as the formative elements of a modernist poetics.

PART 1

Poets

Chapter 1

Rainer Maria Rilke and the Poetics of Femininity

It is so natural for me *to understand girls and women;* the deepest experience of creativity is feminine—for it is a receptive and birth-giving experience.
—R. M. Rilke, letter to a young girl, 1904

Rainer, of course, *knows* more than Otto knows,
he believes in women. But he feeds on us,
like all of them. His whole life, his art
is protected by women. Which of us could say that?
—Adrienne Rich, "Paula Becker to Clara Westhoff," 1975–76

When W. H. Auden, eager to make an impression at a Stravinsky dinner party, quipped that Rilke was "the greatest Lesbian poet since Sappho" (qtd. in Osborne 279), his words probably elicited more than mere chuckles of appreciation for a witty bon mot; they also evoked, no doubt, nods of knowing agreement. Rilke has long been considered a "feminine" poet on a number of counts: not only did he cultivate numerous close friendships with women both young and old, both destitute and wealthy (needless to say, he pursued the wealthy ones more avidly), many of whom would repay his attentions posthumously with grateful hagiographies, but he also sought to ally himself emotionally and creatively with women, in keeping with his belief that any true artist must possess such essentially "female" traits as receptivity and gestative patience. Rather than regarding women solely as patronesses to be milked financially or as muses to be sung and forgotten, he saw them, in a sense, as living prototypes of the kind of artist that he himself longed to become.

Writing in an era in which female artists were seldom recognized as the equals of their male counterparts and, in fact, were often denigrated on the basis of their gender, Rilke's self-identification with women rendered him vulnerable, predictably, not only to remarks like Auden's but also to allegations that the work of such a poet could only really appeal to women, whose tastes, presumably, would be less discriminating than those of their male contemporaries. "Et Rilke . . . Il y a peut-être encore des jeunes filles pour le lire," shrugged Carl Steinheim, coeditor of the Munich journal *Hyperion*, as early as 1925, a year before Rilke's death. "Mais il n'est pas, voyez vous, de notre époque" ("As for Rilke . . . Perhaps there are still some young girls left to read him. But he is not, you see, of our era").[1] Similarly, commenting nearly four decades later on the flourishing state of D. H. Lawrence scholarship in Germany, Armin Arnold noted offhandedly that "more women than men are usually attracted" both to Lawrence and to Rilke (42), probably due to both writers' tendency toward romantic sentimentality, lush description, and a thematics of love. In reality, of course, at least as many men as women have read and admired Rilke's work; as with Lawrence, in fact, male scholars and critics have hardly remained immune to precisely the kind of gushing enthusiasm most often ascribed to female fandom.

Nor was Rilke quite so simplistically feminine in his sensibilities as dismissals such as Auden's, Steinheim's, or Arnold's might imply. Rilke loved women, lauded women, emulated and even envied women, yet he also abandoned virtually all of the women he loved, justifying such emotional abdication as an act of creative necessity. If he often praised femininity, his poetry also contains its share of passages privileging a specifically masculine form of artistry and even linking the inseminating, phallic energies of stereotypical maleness—rather than, as elsewhere, so-called female receptivity—with the essential forces of creativity. Finally, even Rilke's most sincere and envious celebrations of the feminine are often troubling in their associations of women with self-sacrifice, loss, and death, the fertile void at the core of all meaning. "While women may find the privileged image flattering," notes Kathleen L. Komar, "—as, no doubt, Rilke's many patronesses did—it is disturbing that woman's position is defined by absence, deprivation or renunciation, and inescapable limitation" (129).

As Komar goes on to point out, however, "In order to understand Rilke's attitude toward women, we must understand the function of absence, renunciation and limitation in his poetics" (129); we must recognize, that is, the degree to which such concepts, though putatively negative, are generally rendered positive within Rilke's ideological schema, informing and enabling his poetics of inspiration. On the most obvious level the physical and spiritual receptivity that Rilke linked both to female sexuality and to the productive and reproductive capacities of the artist could be said to serve as necessary components of any poetics of prophecy; "L'inspiration . . . est puissante," as Maurice Blanchot explains in *L'Espace littéraire*, "mais à condition que celui qui l'accueille soit devenu très faible" ("Inspiration is powerful, but only on the condition that he who receives it become very weak" [191]). Artists desiring or laying claim to outside inspiration, in other words, must adopt a passive stance—what Rilke himself would call an "overwhelming obedience in the spirit"—vis-à-vis their sources of inspiration, renouncing their individuality and rendering themselves essentially absent in the face of such all-consuming presence. By his own example, then, Rilke demonstrates not only that absence and renunciation can serve as positive, necessary qualities for the artist but, indeed, that they provide the very means to his or her creative empowerment.

Women—particularly virgins, pregnant women, unrequited lovers, and those who have died young—would come to embody, for Rilke, this absence in its purest and most perfect form. Like the male artist who, in Anna Tavis's words, "always exists in anticipation of inspiration and thus becomes a messenger, a communicator between . . . two worlds" (110), such female figures serve as mediatory images both of expectation and of imminent fulfillment, inhabiting what eventually becomes, especially in his *Sonnets to Orpheus*, the privileged locus of Rilke's poetics, that site or moment of transformation between one condition or realm and its opposite: between pure presence and pure absence, motion and stasis, life and death. As mediators between the male poet and his sources of revelation, at least in the sense that the poet can open himself to inspiration only by emulating them, women thus serve as tremendously potent figures throughout much of Rilke's work; at times, in fact, they function not only as conduits of inspiration but also as sources in their own right, whose power, like that of any inspirational Other, Rilke seems to have feared as much as desired. In his later poetry, however, women's role eventually weakens, as Rilke usurps the female's mediatory function for himself, consigning women more firmly than ever to a realm of absence, mystery, and death to which he, in his guise as the male poet Orpheus, possesses easy access but from which "Eurydice's sisters" are allowed no egress.

Rilke can be classified neither, as H.D. often is, as a protofeminist (although he was strikingly progressive both in his political support of women's suffrage and in his encouragement of female artists) nor, like Lawrence, as a sometime misogynist (although his treatment of some of the women closest to him, particularly his own wife and daughter, certainly left much to be desired). Perhaps for this very reason, or perhaps because Rilke scholarship is currently somewhat out of fashion among young academics, or perhaps simply because feminist criticism has until recently had relatively little impact on German literary studies, no major critical work has yet sought to examine Rilke's poetry from a strongly gender-conscious point of view. Yet the intricacies both of Rilke's attitude toward women and of his literary responses to issues of gender difference, besides being fascinating in their own right, also reveal much about his poetic praxis and, particularly, about his poetics of inspiration. Unlike most twentieth-century poets who have drawn on prophetic discourse as a literary trope, Rilke genuinely believed in and apparently experienced firsthand what Frederick Prescott has called "primary inspiration," or visionary revelations resulting directly in poetic production. Certainly, his own descriptions of the three weeks in February 1922 during which he completed his masterful *Duino Elegies* and composed the fifty-five *Sonnets to Orpheus*—not to mention dozens of ecstatic letters to his friends and patrons describing the unexpected reversal of his poetic fortunes—leave little doubt, unless we are to believe that he perpetrated a sustained and elaborate hoax, that poetic inspiration was for Rilke a real phenomenon rather than a mere rhetorical construct. Yet his stance toward inspiration, like his attitude toward women, was ambivalent, paradoxical, and ultimately self-contradictory, perhaps in part because he so closely associated each with the other. Receptivity requires both strength and humility; inspiration entails both power and loss; prophecy is both a gift and a burden. Femininity, then, remained ever a mixed blessing for Rilke, both a state of grace toward which he would continually strive and a condition of weakness that he sought, albeit unconsciously, to avoid.

God, Women, and Rilke: *Das Stunden-Buch*

In some respects Rilke's representations of women have much in common with his representations of God: both are addressed as powerful beings whose mediation enables the poet's creativity, yet both are ultimately revealed as constructions rather than creators of the inspired poet himself. Particularly in the three otherwise distinct volumes, composed between 1899 and 1903, that together constitute *Das Stunden-Buch* (*The Book of Hours*), Rilke, taking on the persona of a Russian

monk, explores both his own relationship to God and God's relation-
ship to the world in terms that are heavily gendered. Like John Keats,
who once declared in a letter to Shelley that "My Imagination is a
Monastry and I am its Monk,"[2] Rilke asserts his own imagination as the
true locus of creativity, even while apparently humbling himself before
a higher being. God can only shape the poet, he implies, after the poet
has given shape to God. "Meine Seele ist ein Weib vor Dir" ("My soul is
a woman before you" [SW 1:313]), declares Rilke's monk to God in one
particularly abject moment—yet what is on the one hand presented as
a poetics of female receptivity ultimately reveals itself as a poetics of
self-assurance instead, linked by Rilke himself, especially at the end of
the volume, with a specifically male mode of creativity.

Already in the opening stanzas of its first book, "The Book of
Monastic Life," Das Stunden-Buch reveals itself as a work in which the
poet-monk's relationship both to his sources of inspiration and to the
material world he inhabits are constantly in flux, as passive reception
gives way, virtually from one line to the next, to images of active fash-
ioning:

> Da neigt sich die Stunde und rührt mich an
> mit klarem, metallenem Schlag:
> mir zittern die Sinne. Ich fühle: ich kann—
> und ich fasse den plastischen Tag.
>
> Nichts war noch vollendet, eh ich es erschaut,
> ein jedes Werden stand still.
> Meine Blicke sind reif, und wie eine Braut
> kommt jedem das Ding, das er will.
>
> (SW 1:253)

> [The hour bends down and touches me
> with a clear, metallic stroke:
> my senses tremble. I feel: I can—
> and I grasp the plastic day.
>
> Nothing was perfect till I looked upon it,
> each act of becoming stood still.
> My gazes are ripe, and to every man comes,
> like a bride, the Thing he desires.][3]

The poem begins with a moment of humble receptivity: the hour leans over toward the waiting poet-monk, like Michelangelo's God toward a languid Adam, and jolts him sharply into life. Shuddering shock leads to sensibility, sensibility to a sudden awareness of power; having been zapped into consciousness by time's "metallic" thunderbolt, the poet swiftly realizes his own materiality by reversing the proceedings and grasping—physically, conceptually, spiritually—the "plastic [tactile] day." Thus, he literally takes time, the very force that first set him in motion, into his own hands. In the second stanza of the poem the monk's self-sufficiency increases; although he initially relied on time, "the hour," to animate him, he now declares that it is he who will motivate and bring into being the rest of the world with his "ripe gazes": "Nothing was perfected until I looked upon it." Finally, he further demonstrates his control over the material Things he has "perfected" by figuring them as submissive brides who will obey his commands, the bidding of the poet-bridegroom: "and to every man comes, like a bride, the Thing he desires."

Since God, as we will learn a few pages later, not only lives "in allen diesen Dingen" ("in all these Things") but in fact is himself the ultimate "Ding der Dinge," or "Thing of Things" (*SW* 1:265–66), it follows that the poet, by feminizing and rendering submissive the Things he describes, is in effect feminizing God, even though it was God (in the guise of "the hour," or Father Time) who first brought about his own poetic empowerment. If, in the second part of the *Stunden-Buch*, the poet-monk's soul will become "a woman" before God, it is clear from the very beginning of the volume that God, conversely, is essentially a woman before the poet: he is the bride-Thing that obeys the poet's words, fulfills his desires, and assists in the production of his poetic progeny. And yet, although the poet, early in the volume, defines God by actively circumscribing him—"Ich kreise um Gott, um den uralten Turm" ("I circle about God, the ancient tower" [1:253])—this passive, immobile deity remains at the same time undeniably male, towering and phallic.

Two stanzas later Rilke once again reverses the gendering of his theological metaphor:

> *Mein* Gott ist dunkel und wie ein Gewebe
> von hundert Wurzeln, welche schweigsam trinken.

Nur, daß ich mich aus *seiner* Wärme hebe,
mehr weiß ich nicht.

(SW 1:254)

[*My* God is dark and like a web
of a hundred roots that silently drink.
I know only that I raise myself from *his* warmth,
nothing more.]

Here the poet-monk's personal, self-created God—"*my* God"—
becomes inward turned and stereotypically female, a silent being of
roots and darkness (exactly as Rilke will later portray Eurydice to be), a
maternal creature from whose womblike warmth the poet emerges into
the world. Already in the first few pages of "The Book of Monastic
Life," then, Rilke's God is revealed as a hermaphroditic, multivalent
being, male-female, active-passive, both creator and creature of the
poet-monk, who could not exist without God and indeed is dwarfed in
relation to him—"Du bist so groß, daß ich schon nicht mehr bin" ("You
are so big, that I am already nothing" [1:269])—yet without whom,
paradoxically, God could not exist either:

Was wirst du tun, Gott, wenn ich sterbe?
Ich bin dein Krug (wenn ich zerscherbe?)
Ich bin dein Trank (wenn ich verderbe?)
Bin dein Gewand und dein Gewerbe,
mit mir verlierst du deinen Sinn.

(1:275)

[What will you do, God, when I die?
I am your pitcher (if I should shatter?)
I am your drink (if I should spoil?)
I am your garment and your trade,
in losing me you lose your sense.]

Rilke's God is, in fact, a God of paradoxes: "Du bist der Wald der
Widersprüche" ("You are the forest of contradictions"). He is powerful
precisely because he is also weak—because, that is, he embraces oppo-
sites, inhabiting every object, emotion, and intangible in the universe

rather than merely those that signify only strength or virtue. Yet God holds no monopoly on paradox: Rilke's poet-monk, too, is simultaneously (or alternately) potent and passive, both arrogant and humble, both self-fashioning and self-effacing, both masculine ("to every man comes, like a bride, the Thing he desires") and feminine ("and my soul is a woman before you"). Such empowerment through paradox would remain a central trope of Rilke's poetics, despite various evolutions and permutations, until his death. The greatest poet, for Rilke, is the one who, at once receptive and self-assertive, can transcend opposites by negotiating a way between them, locating himself at the very point at which distinctions between male and female, human and divine, life and death, finally vanish.

Rilke's stereotypical female remains for the most part firmly on one side of this dialectical divide, guarding the threshold of the darkness, absence, and renunciatory virtue that she most clearly represents. In certain respects, however, she is every bit as paradoxical and thus as all-embracing a figure as Rilke's God or his poet. This is particularly true in the *Stunden-Buch*, in which she represents both the purity for which the poet strives and the worldly corruption in which he is nonetheless implicated. Thus, on the one hand, woman is the Virgin Mary, whose "dienendes Marien-Leben . . . königlich und wunderbar" ("obedient Mary-Life . . . regal and wonderful" [*SW* 1:272]) serves as a model of humility for the poet. On the other hand, however, Goethe's "eternal feminine" can also take on more sinister manifestations, as when Rilke's poet-monk describes himself and his fellow men not as women before God but, far more self-deprecatingly, as whores before Time:

> Sind wir nur Geschlecht
> und Schooß von Frauen, welche viel gewähren?
> Wir haben mit der Ewigkeit gehurt,
> und wenn das Kreißbett da ist, so gebären
> wir unsres Todes tote Fehlgeburt;
> den krummen, kummervollen Embryo,
> der sich (als ob ihn Schreckliches erschreckte)
> die Augenkeime mit den Händen deckte
> und dem schon auf der ausgebauten Stirne
> die Angst von allem steht, was er nicht litt,—

und alle schließen so wie eine Dirne
in Kindbettkrämpfen und am Kaiserschnitt.

                                           (1:348–49)

            [Are we merely the sex
and wombs of available women?
We have whored with eternity,
and when we lie on the labor bed, we bear
our own death's dead miscarriage,
the twisted, grievous embryo that
(as if frightened by frightfulness)
covered its eyes with its hands
and upon whose well-developed brow
stands fear of everything it's not endured,—
and we close up like a prostitute
in birth contractions and caesarean section.]

Anthony Stephens reads the section of the *Stunden-Buch* in which this passage occurs in terms of Rilke's ongoing attempt to reconcile his notion of sacred (i.e., personal, epiphanic) time with profane (unrepeatable, clock-driven) time. Stephens acknowledges that, after 1905, Rilke would generally depict women and femininity only in idealized terms; in the years during which the *Stunden-Buch* was composed, however, "In der Tat nehmen die Darstellungen der profane Weltgeschichte . . . immer wieder Embleme weiblicher Sexualität an" ("In fact [Rilke's] portrayals of profane world history . . . continually make use of emblems of female sexuality"). Stephens goes on to quote a 1903 passage in which Rilke condemns the great events of history (i.e., profane time) for performing "the naked belly-dance and the veil-dance of fate," calls fate itself a whore and a "Lustmädchen," and refers disparagingly to the deceptive "makeup" under which history has hidden its true nature.[4]

    Rilke's association of female sexuality with prostitution, miscarriage, and the most terrifying aspects of childbirth allows him to launch, immediately following his description in the *Stunden-Buch* of death as the aborted fetus of mankind's imagination, straight into a compensatory celebration of male sexuality, which the poet represents in terms of a heroic advancement of chivalric troops:

Mach Einen herrlich, Herr, mach Einen groß,
bau seinem Leben einen schönen Schooß,
und seine Scham errichte wie ein Tor
in einem blonden Wald von jungen Haaren,
und ziehe durch das Glied des Unsagbaren
den Reisigen, den weißen Heeresscharen,
den tausend Samen, die sich sammeln, vor.

(*SW* 1:349)

[Make that one glorious, Lord, make him great,
build for his life a beautiful womb
and erect his sex like a gate
in a blond forest of young hair,
and advance through the member of the unutterable
the rider, the armies of white troops,
the thousand seeds that congregate.][5]

Both the "whoring with eternity" passage and the phallic affirmation that follows occur in the third section of the *Stunden-Buch*, "The Book of Poverty and Death," which begins with a meditation on the latter and ends with the apotheosis of the former. Poverty and death clearly serve here as aspects or manifestations of the absence that Rilke privileges throughout his poetry. But, rather than linking them, as he does elsewhere, with the most positive aspects of femininity, Rilke now appropriates both conditions as essentially male realms of empowerment. Begging God to "gieb uns jetzt . . . des Menschen ernste Mutterschaft" ("give us now . . . mankind's serious motherhood" [1:350]), the poet-monk invokes not Mary, the "Gottgebärerin" ("the woman who bore God"), but, rather, the "Tod-Gebärer," a male savior who will give birth to a sacred death independent of time, utterly different from the profane, miscarried death borne, a few pages earlier in the poem, by mankind in the guise of Time's whore. With the image of this "death bearer," Rilke offers us a Christlike male figure, neither wholly divine nor wholly human, who reconciles us to death by appropriating female reproductive power and taking on, paradoxically, the essentially female function of giving birth.

Later in "The Book of Poverty and Death" Rilke shifts his focus from death to poverty, which he regards, similarly, as a redemptive state of purity and absence rather than as a burden: "Denn Armut ist ein großer Glanz aus Innen" ("For poverty is a great glow from inside"). God himself is the ultimate pauper: "Du bist der Arme, du der Mittellose" ("You are the poor one, the one without means"). Once again Rilke's descriptions rely largely on paradox; where he earlier characterized death in terms of childbirth, here, even more oddly, he likens poverty to a young woman's pregnancy:

Du bist so arm wie eines Keimes Kraft
in einem Mädchen, das es gern verbürge
und sich die Lenden preßt, daß sie erwürge
das erste Atmen ihrer Schwangerschaft.

(*SW* 1:356)

[You are as poor as the strength of a seed
in a girl who would gladly hide it
and presses her thighs together as if
to choke the first breath of her pregnancy.]

Much as he did with his descriptions of death and a male death bearer, Rilke begins by associating poverty with female gestation (although it is important to note that the seed, not the girl, is depicted as "poor" and therefore exalted) but then moves on to appropriate such a privileged condition of absence as a male prerogative and even as a manifestation of male sexuality. The pauper counterpart of Rilke's death bearer—his "poverty bearer," if you will—makes his appearance in the final pages of the *Stunden-Buch* in the figure of Saint Francis of Assisi, who upon renouncing worldly riches is compensated not with the female capacity to give birth but, rather, with the specifically male ability to inseminate.

Following a disconcerting moment of silence, broken only by the screaming hearts of nuns, "die er berührte wie ein Bräutigam" ("whom he touched like a bridegroom" [*SW* 1:365]), Saint Francis opens his mouth and fertilizes the whole world with "seines Liedes Pollen," the pollen of his song:

Und sie empfingen ihn, den Makellosen,
in ihrem Leib, der ihre Seele war.
Und ihre Augen schlossen sich wie Rosen,
und voller Liebesnächte war ihr Haar.

Und ihn empfing das Große und Geringe.
Zu vielen Tieren kamen Cherubim
zu sagen, daß ihr Weibchen Früchte bringen,—

und waren wunderschöne Schmetterlinge:
denn ihn erkannten alle Dinge
und hatten Fruchtbarkeit aus ihm.

(1:365–66)

[And they received him, the immaculate one,
in their bodies, which were also their souls.
And their eyes closed themselves like roses,
and their hair was full of nights of love.

And the great and the small received him.
Cherubim came to many creatures
to tell them that their females would bear fruit,—

and they were beautiful butterflies:
for all Things knew and recognized him
and had fertility from him.]

Thus, the Things of the world—women, plants, flowers, and even the male creatures, which receive fertility from the saint just as their mates do—are depicted, as they were in the opening stanza of the *Stunden-Buch*, as the feminized, receptive entities that Rilke elsewhere claims every poet should be; meanwhile, it is the vigorous, actively inseminating, stereotypically male Saint Francis, before whom every Thing is essentially a woman, who achieves the poetic power that Rilke himself clearly covets. Saint Francis is, in fact, a precursor of Rilke's Orpheus, the ultimate poet-priest, who can charm trees and stones with his song and whose severed head will continue to sing even after his death:

Und als er starb, so leicht wie ohne Namen,
da war er ausgeteilt: sein Samen rann
in Bächen, in den Bäumen sang sein Samen
und sah ihn ruhig aus den Blumen an.

(1:366)

[And when he died, as light as though unnamed,
he was distributed: his semen ran

in streams, and in the trees his semen sang
and watched him quietly from the flowers.]

Saint Francis's final dissolution into the fertilizing semen that
flows through the streams of nature is only made possible through his
commitment to poverty and, eventually, through his death—through
various acts, in other words, of renunciation and absence. Thus, the
Stunden-Buch ends on the same note of paradox with which it began:
just as the poet-monk of the opening "Book of Monastic Life" had to be
awakened by Time, "the hour," before he could summon the Things of
the world to him like obedient brides and create his own self-contra-
dictory, powerful-passive God, so Saint Francis, in the closing "Book of
Poverty and Death," must surrender himself to God and the elements
before he can rise up and sing them into life. Read in gendered terms,
the initial passivity that makes possible such empowerment could be
seen as the adoption or appropriation of a stereotypically feminine
stance. Yet the images of masculinity and male creative power scattered
throughout the *Stunden-Buch* ultimately belie Rilke's own stated belief
that poetic inspiration requires and depends on the feminization of the
poet.

More on God, Women, and Rilke

The mixed feelings toward women and femininity expressed by Rilke
in the *Stunden-Buch* had deep and complex roots in his own emotional
life, and particularly in his brief but intensive love affair with Lou
Andreas-Salomé, who was his lover, mother-substitute, confessor, and
mentor from 1897 to 1900 and who would remain, if intermittently, one
of his closest friends and confidantes until his death in 1926. An attrac-
tive "older woman" of considerable intelligence and accomplishment,
Andreas-Salomé had, by the time Rilke met her in Munich in 1897,
already acquired a formidable reputation not only as an author and
essayist but also as the woman who had supposedly driven Nietzsche
to madness. Taking it upon herself to turn her callow young lover into
the successful poet he longed to become, she provided the paradigm
for the type of brilliant, self-confidently artistic woman that Rilke
would admire for the rest of his life. Yet, if she served as a model for
femininity of the most powerful and productive kind, it is a measure of
Rilke's ambivalent relationship both to her and to his entire conception

of womanhood that one of her first transformative acts upon him involved convincing him, the poet who was forever longing to be more like a woman, to masculinize his own image; *René*, she insisted, was too effeminate, so he changed his name to the harsher, more Germanic *Rainer* (although he did retain the feminine *Maria* as his middle name).

It was largely through Andreas-Salomé's powerful example that Rilke developed the extraordinary awe of women that would lead him to write about women and God in often identical terms. Like the self-contradictory deity addressed by his poet-monk in the *Stunden-Buch*, Andreas-Salomé herself is frequently represented by Rilke as a source of inspiration so intense that her influence threatens to overwhelm him—a situation that he would continually try, both in his poetry and in his correspondence with her, to reverse. Whether or not Rilke ever actually succeeded in achieving the kind of emotional and artistic mastery over Andreas-Salomé that he attained over the *Stunden-Buch*'s God remains questionable. That he at least desired to do so, however, is made clear in a passage from his 1898 Florentine diary (assigned as a writing exercise by Andreas-Salomé) addressed to his intimidating lover:

> Ich haßte Dich wie etwas zu Großes. Ich wollte diesmal der Reiche, der Schenkende sein, der Ladende, der Herr, und Du solltest kommen, und, von meiner Sorgfalt und Liebe gelenkt, Dich ergeben in meiner Gastlichkeit. (*Tagebücher* 135)

> [I hated you like something too great. This time I wanted to be the wealthy one, the gift giver, the host, the master, so that you should come and, guided by my care and my love, surrender yourself to my hospitality.]

Humbly, the lover surrenders himself to his powerful, generous beloved, yet he cannot help wishing that, just for once, he could play the role of the beneficent, inspiring lover-deity, so that she instead might submit to him.

Rilke's implicit God/Lou association becomes even more apparent in the *Stunden-Buch* itself, particularly in a passage ostensibly addressed by the monk to God but actually first written as a love poem from Rilke to Andreas-Salomé in 1897:[6]

Lösch mir die Augen aus: ich kann dich sehn,
wirf mir die Ohren zu: ich kann dich hören,
und ohne Füße kann ich zu dir gehn,
und ohne Mund noch kann ich dich beschwören.
Brich mir die Arme ab, ich fasse dich
mit meinem Herzen wie mit einer Hand,
halt mir das Herz zu, und mein Hirn wird schlagen,
und wirfst du in mein Hirn den Brand,
so werd ich dich auf meinem Blute tragen.

                                                    (SW 1:313)

[Extinguish my eyes: I can see you,
slam my ears shut: I can hear you,
and without feet I can walk to you,
and without a mouth I can still beseech you.
Break off my arms, and I will grasp you
with my heart as though with a hand;
hold my heart closed, and my brain will beat;
throw fire into my brain,
and still I will carry you upon my blood.]

This passionate if rather gruesome declaration of love is immediately followed by Rilke's famous "Und meine Seele ist ein Weib vor dir" line ("And my soul is a woman before you"), an acknowledgment, it would seem, both of the monk's humility before God and of Rilke's humility before his lover, in whose all-consuming presence stereotypical gender roles are reversed. Yet, with its catalog of God's/Lou's silencing maneuvers and its defiant, poetry-affirming conclusion, the passage at the same time suggests an opposite trajectory of power: no matter what sacrifices his God or his lover may demand of him, the poet insists, he will still "carry you upon his blood"—that is, he will continue to convert his unquenchable passion into some form of creative articulation. In fact, like the hymn to Saint Francis with which the *Stunden-Buch* concludes, Rilke's bizarre love poem anticipates the poet's own later identification with Orpheus, the mythical poet-lover whose song will echo on even after his death and dismemberment—a fate enacted, in Rilke's love poem as in the Greek myth, by a dangerous, destructive force specifically defined as female.

In later poems Rilke comes to praise women's love—particularly the self-effacing, unrequited passion of historical figures such as Gaspara Stampa and Marianna Alcoforado—as a visionary, essential force far superior to men's distracted sexuality and ardor. Such love, Rilke even indicates in a passage from *The Notebooks of Malte Laurids Brigge* about Goethe and his lover, Bettina von Arnim, should be heeded and obeyed like a divine revelation:

> Solche Liebe bedarf keiner Erwiderung, sie hat Lockruf und Antwort in sich; sie erhört sich selbst. Aber demütigen hätte er sich müssen vor ihr in seinem ganzen Staat und schreiben was sie diktiert, mit beiden Händen, wie Johannes auf Patmos, knieend. (*SW* 6:898)

> [Such love requires no response, itself containing both the call and the reply; it answers its own prayers. But he should have humbled himself before her in all his splendor and written what she dictated, with both hands, like John on Patmos, kneeling.]

With passages such as this one, the gender dynamics of Rilke's poetics of inspiration become almost hopelessly complex. The poet envies and even fears women for their creative and inspirational power, which in some respects resembles even the dictates of God, yet at the same time he insists that such power depends on the kind of renunciation, self-denial, and visionary agony that one associates less with inspiration's sources than with its vessels. In his love poem to Andreas-Salomé, protesting that he will continue to sing her praises even if she rejects or destroys him, Rilke even expresses—although such abjection remains for him a relatively uncharacteristic stance—something akin to the kind of self-annihilating passion that he elsewhere praises as the province of women alone.

If Andreas-Salomé taught Rilke to fear and envy women, she also played an important role in leading him to admire and respect them. In fact, it was largely through her—along with such other female friends as Frieda von Bülow and the Swedish psychologist Ellen Key—that Rilke acquired the feminist sympathies that would lead to his lifelong support, in word if not always in deed, for women's political, economic, and creative equality with men. Andreas-Salomé was herself the author of a number of feminist tracts, including an article, published in 1899 during the period of her closest friendship with Rilke, entitled "Der Mensch als Weib" ("The Human Being as Woman").[7] Noting that assertions regarding men's supposedly "active" creativity, as opposed to women's essential "passivity," often rely on the example of male versus female reproductive processes, Andreas-Salomé argues in her essay that the female egg possesses as powerful a "bewegliche Element" ("mobile element") as does the male's sperm and that women, furthermore, make an additional "schöpferischen Beitrag" ("creative contribution") in bringing an embryo to term: "Das Bild vom Zeugen des Mannes und Empfangen des Weibes fällt daneben zu Boden" ("The image of the man engendering and the woman receiving thus cannot be sustained" [227]). In fact, Andreas-Salomé states, artistic creativity bears a far greater similarity to female gestation than to male sexuality:

> Jedoch sicher ist dies, daß der männliche Künstler als solcher dem Weibe außerordentlich nah steht und es daher sehr gut versteht, und zwar gerade durch seine schöpferische Veranlagung. Denn diese nimmt ihm viel vom scharf accentuirt Bewußten, vom Sachlichen und Handelnden des Mannesgeschlechtes, sie läßt ihn einheitlicher, organischer, mit dem verschmolzen erscheinen, was er schafft, gerade wie das Weib es ist, und erhält ihn gewissermaßen in einem Glück geistiger Schwangerschaft. . . . Nicht zufällig ist es, daß man Künstlern so oft weibliche Eigenschaften anmerkt, oder daß sie den Vorwurf der Unmännlichkeit hören müssen. (232)

> [Yet this much is certain: that the male artist stands extraordinarily close to woman and therefore understands her very well, precisely because of his creative disposition. For this disposition takes from him much of the sharply accentuated consciousness, the practical and active aspects, of the male sex; it leaves him to seem more unified, more organic, fused with that which he creates, just as the woman is, and preserves him, in a sense, in the joy of spiritual pregnancy. . . . It is no coincidence that one often notices feminine characteristics in male artists, or that they must so often hear the accusation of unmanliness.]

What is perhaps most startling about Andreas-Salomé's essay is not her questioning of traditional sexual stereotypes but her refusal, despite her assertion that male artists draw much of their creative

impetus from their kinship with women, to grant reciprocal empower-
ment to the female artist; women, she argues, should not compete with
or expect to equal men's "Geistesbefähigung" ("intellectual empower-
ment"), for the energies and desires that men sublimate into art are
internalized by women, who are intrinsically more fulfilled than men
and thus need not seek satisfaction elsewhere. Women may indeed pro-
duce creative works, just as a tree bears fruit, but the issue of any such
productive response "ist doch nur Fallobst, mühelos abgeworfen, und
soll nicht mehr als das bedeuten werden" ("is only fallen fruit, cast
down without effort, and shall come to signify nothing more than that"
[233]). From the mouth of a woman, then, we hear echoes of a gender
ideology both limited and limiting: men must emulate women in order
to create, Andreas-Salomé stresses, yet women's own creative success,
whether as mothers, lovers, or artists, depends in the end upon pre-
cisely those passive, receptive traits that the author at first set out to
demystify. Trees, with which Lou Andreas-Salomé equates women,
surely look beautiful, provide shade for the weary, and bear the fruit
that sustains (or, in the Old Testament, corrupts) mankind, but they
cannot walk or speak; like any pedestal, the one on which Andreas-
Salomé places herself and her sex allows little room for free movement.
Ultimately, "der Mensch als Weib" ("the human being as woman") nei-
ther equals nor guarantees "das Weib als Mensch" ("the woman as
human being").

Several years after Andreas-Salomé's essay appeared, Rilke, in the
series of 1903–8 letters to Franz Xaver Kappus known as his *Letters to a
Young Poet*, would express his own notions regarding creativity and
gender in terms strikingly similar to those employed by his former
lover in 1899. Like her, for instance, he emphasizes the activity of the
female egg as well as that of the male sperm when he links artistic cre-
ativity with "[dem] Gesetz, mit dem ein widerstandsfähiger kräftiger
Samen sich durchdrängt zu der Eizelle, die ihm offen entgegenzieht"
("the law whereby a resistant, powerful seed forces its way to the egg
cell, which moves receptively in its direction" [*Briefe*, 1:54]). Moreover,
Rilke also preaches the ideal of "de[m] weibliche[n] Mensch" ("the
feminine human being" [1:80]) and compares male creativity to female
reproduction:

> Und auch im Mann ist Mutterschaft, scheint mir, leibliche und
> geistige; sein Zeugen ist auch eine Art Gebären, und Gebären ist
> es, wenn er schafft aus innerster Fülle. (1:55)

[And it seems to me that in man, too, is motherhood, both physical and spiritual; his act of engendering is also a kind of childbearing, for he gives birth when he creates from his innermost fullness.]

Rilke proves, if anything, more progressive than Andreas-Salomé in his belief both in women's potential as artists (he would write to Julie Weimann in 1902 that "a woman-artist," at least once she has "completed" herself by having a child, "is capable in just the same way as a mature man of reaching all the summits of art")[8] and in their essential equality with men:

> Und vielleicht sind die Geschlechter verwandter, als man meint, und die große Erneuerung der Welt wird vielleicht darin bestehn, daß Mann und Mädchen sich, befreit von allen Irrgefühlen und Unlüsten, nicht als Gegensätze suchen werden, sondern als Geschwistern und Nachbarn und sich zusammentun werden als *Menschen*. (16 July 1903; *Brief* 1:54–55)

[And perhaps the sexes are more closely akin than one thinks, and perhaps the great renewal of the world will occur when man and girl, freed from all false feelings and aversions, will seek each other out not as opposites but rather as siblings and neighbors, and will come together as *human beings*.]

Like Andreas-Salomé, however, Rilke goes on to warn that women should not try to become *like* men; that is, they should not become "Nachahmer männlicher Unart und Art und Wiederholer männlicher Berufe" ("imitators of male incivility and manners and repeaters of male professions"):

> Die Frauen, in denen unmittelbarer, fruchtbarer und vertrauensvoller das Leben verweilt und wohnt, müssen ja im Grunde reifere Menschen geworden sein, menschlichere Menschen als der leichte, durch die Schwere keiner leiblichen Frucht unter die Oberfläche des Lebens herabgezogene Mann, der, dünkelhaft und hartig, unterschätzt, was er zu lieben meint. Dieses in Schmerzen und Erniedrigungen ausgetragen Menschentum der Frau wird dann, wenn sie die Konventionen der Nur-Weiblichkeit in den Verwandlungen ihres äußeren Standes abgestreift haben wird, zutage treten, und die Männer, die es heute noch nicht kom-

men fühlen, werden davon überrascht und geschlagen werden. Eines Tages . . . wird das Mädchen da sein und die Frau, deren Name nicht mehr nur einen Gegensatz zum Männlichen bedeuten wird, sondern etwas für sich, etwas, wobei man an keine Ergänzung und Grenze gedenkt, nur an Leben und Dasein. (14 May 1904; 1:79–80)

[Women, in whom life lingers and lives more immediately, fruitfully, and trustfully, must in effect become riper humans, more human humans than the superficial male, who, never having been dragged beneath the surface of life by the weight of a bodily fruit, conceitedly and harshly underestimates that which he thinks he loves. Woman's humanity, borne in pain and humiliation, will only become manifest when she has cast off the conventions of mere femininity in the transformations of her outer state, and men, who today do not yet sense this change coming, will be startled and shaken. One day . . . the girl and the woman will exist whose name will no longer signify merely the opposite of masculinity, but rather something in itself, something thought of in terms not of completion and limitation, but rather of life and existence.]

In the utopian society that Rilke envisions, women will be recognized and celebrated as women, rather than marginalized as poor imitations of men, yet he also hints that they will remain, much as Andreas-Salomé insists they should, self-fulfilled, self-sacrificing, and fruitlike beings, in keeping with Robert Graves's succinct aphorism "Man Does, Woman Is."[9]

While it is impossible to know for certain whose ideas influenced whom—did Rilke absorb his notions of creativity as an essentially feminine act from Andreas-Salomé, or was she first convinced by Rilke's own example to develop her theory that creative men often have "unmanly" characteristics?—the similarities between her arguments in "Der Mensch als Weib" and many of his own statements from the same period ("The deepest act of creativity is feminine," etc.) are striking. It may also have been through his relationship with her that Rilke developed his belief in sex as an important, perhaps essential, element of creative productivity. "In einem Schöpfergedanken leben tausend vergessene Liebesnächte auf," he wrote to Kappus in 1903, "und erfüllen ihn mit Hoheit und Höhe" ("In a creator's every thought a thousand nights of love are revived and fill him with nobility and grandeur"). In the fertile crucible of a poet's mind, he added, such memories of past love experiences take on a creative, even prophetic, power of their own:

> Und die in den Nächten zusammenkommen und verflochten sind in wiegender Wollust, tun eine ernste Arbeit und sammeln Süssigkeiten an, Tiefe und Kraft für das Lied irgendeines kommenden Dichters, der aufstehn wird, um unsägliche Wonnen zu sagen. Und rufen die Zukunft herbei. (*Briefe* 1:54)

> [And, gathered and intertwined at night in a swaying voluptuousness, they perform a serious work and gather sweetness, depth and power for the song of some future poet, who will arise to speak unutterable delights. And they will summon the future.]

These lines affirming the connection between inspiration and sex were written, to be sure, several years after Lou Andreas-Salomé had scrawled her famous imperative "Rainer must go" in her diary and cast her young lover from her life. By 1903, in fact, Rilke's relationship with Andreas-Salomé, although they would remain close friends until Rilke's death, had been irrevocably transformed: in April 1901 he had married the sculptor Clara Westhoff, who gave birth the following winter to their daughter, Ruth. This second major love affair of Rilke's life, however, was fraught with little or none of the anxiety, dependency, and ambivalence that had marked his liaison with Andreas-Salomé; indeed, his marriage would set the pattern for the emotional distancing and artistic self-absorption that would characterize virtually all of his future relationships. In 1899, linking divine inspiration with individuality and seclusion, Rilke had been careful to include close love relationships in his definition of solitude: "Wenn Gott ein Gesetz gegeben hat, so lautet es: Sei einsam von Zeit zu Zeit. Denn er kann nur zu einem kommen oder zu zweien, die er nicht mehr unterscheiden kann" ("If there is any God-given law, it is this: Be solitary from time to time. For he can only come to one person, or to two between whom he can no longer distinguish" (*Tagebücher* 203). By 1902, however, less than a year after his marriage to Clara Westhoff, Rilke was writing to their mutual friend Paula Becker-Modersohn a new, more restrictive definition of marriage's "höchste Aufgabe" ("highest purpose"): "daß einer dem andern seine Einsamkeit bewache" ("that each [partner] should guard the other's solitude."[10] Though often quoted as evidence of his enlightened view of marriage—and it is true that he was exceptional in insisting on the importance of his wife's artistic career as well as his own—Rilke's prescription for a happy marriage both anticipates and attempts to justify the evasive action that he would take shortly thereafter: by August 1902 he had essentially abandoned his family, leaving his wife to make arrangements for the baby (she left it in her parents' care), organize most of her own financial support, and follow him to Paris and beyond only if she agreed to live and work separately from him.

Several years later Rilke would admit to his wife that his behavior had been less than exemplary, yet he continued to justify it in the name of art:

> Durch jedes vorzeitige Eingehen auf das, was als "Pflicht" mich überwältigen und brauchbar machen will, schlösse ich wohl einige Unsicherheiten und den Anschein jenes beständigen Ausweichenwollens aus meinem Leben aus, aber ich fühle, daß damit auch die großen wunderbaren Hilfen, die in fast rhythmischer Folge in mich eingreifen, ausgeschlossen würden.[11]

> [If I were to grant premature attention to that which, as "duty," seeks to overcome me and make me useful, I might well shut out from my life some uncertainties and this appearance of constant evasion; but I feel that by doing so I would also shut out the great and wonderful powers that take hold of me in almost rhythmic succession.]

Divine inspiration, which Rilke earlier associated with female influence and elsewhere links to sex, here becomes wholly dependent upon the poet's solitude and his withdrawal not from "the female" or from sex per se but, rather, from the responsibilities accompanying marriage, fatherhood, and indeed any kind of emotional attachment. Tillie Olsen has noted, echoing Virginia Woolf's observations in *A Room of One's Own*, that the life of creative solitude so carefully cultivated by Rilke—a life "without duties, almost without external communication" in which vision, he boasted, would have "no limit" (Olsen 12)—has seldom been an option for women, who "are traditionally trained to place others' needs first, to feel these needs as their own" (16). Despite his genuine belief in women's creative potential, in other words, Rilke was not practicing "feminine" renunciation and self-sacrifice so much as exercising an almost exclusively male prerogative (shared only by a few remarkable women, such as Lou Andreas-Salomé herself, who had an independent income, no children, and a husband notorious for having abdicated all claims on her freedom) when he renounced what he acknowledged as his familial "duty" and abandoned himself fully to his art.

God, Women, and Things: *Neue Gedichte*

Rilke was by no means exaggerating when he wrote to his wife in 1906 of "the great and wonderful powers that take hold of me in almost rhythmic succession"; the years from 1904 to early 1910 were to prove among the most productive of his life, for they saw the creation both of *The Notebooks of Malte Laurids Brigge*, his novel of modernist angst set in Paris, and of *New Poems*, a fat double volume of remarkable verses that would remain unsurpassed in Rilke's oeuvre until he completed his *Duino Elegies* nearly a decade and a half later. Already in his *Buch der Bilder* (*The Picture-Book*), which serves as a sort of secular companion piece to *The Book of Hours*, he had honed his lyrical and observational skills, exploring many of the themes and figures that take on even greater significance in his later work: childhood, young brides, angels, saints, Christ, religion, loneliness, the city, autumn, beggars, blind men, paupers. Only with the *New Poems*, however, does his poetry clearly move in a new direction, illustrating what would become known as Rilke's theory of the "*Dinggedicht*," or "Thing-poem."

Ironically enough, it was Clara Rilke who first set her husband on the creative path that he would later invoke to justify his abandonment of her, for it was she who introduced him to her teacher, the French sculptor Auguste Rodin, who in turn became Rilke's idol, mentor, and creative prototype. Although Rodin, who read no German, remained rather nonplussed by the adulation that Rilke showered upon him, he apparently had some sense of his young admirer's talent and promise, for, in addition to encouraging Rilke to visit him (Rilke first came to Paris to write a book about the great sculptor), converse with him, and study his sculptural technique by the hour, he eventually engaged him as his secretary, a position that allowed Rilke ample free time for his writing even while affording him nearly constant proximity to "the Master." By the time Rodin, presumably wearied of Rilke's intense devotion and obsequiousness, used a rather minor dissatisfaction as a pretext for releasing him from his employ in May 1906, Rilke had not only gathered extensive material and impetus for his own poetry but had also generously returned the favor by promoting Rodin's reputation all over Europe, publishing a small but well-received monograph in 1903 and undertaking extensive lecture tours in 1905 and early 1906.

From Rodin, Rilke learned to cultivate the curious mixture of humility and poetic authority—the seeds of which are already evident in the *Stunden-Buch*—that would inform his poetry for the rest of his life. He also absorbed a second, even more valuable lesson: stimulated by the sculptor's example, he began to conceive of creative inspiration not as a divine gift bestowed randomly upon the artist but, rather, as a privilege of which he had constantly to prove himself worthy. As Rilke's biographer E. M. Butler explains, Rilke's entire creative ideology changed when he adopted for himself Rodin's famous edict that "il faut travailler, rien que travailler":

> The idea that hard, patient, laborious toil could take over the function and hasten the appearance of inspiration was an entirely new notion to Rilke, who had hitherto never dared to write unless the mood was on him. (146)

The paradox inherent in such a notion is obvious: if inspiration can result only from hard work, then even passive receptivity becomes dependent, first and foremost, upon self-conscious activity. Although Rilke had never really denied this—his belabored self-fashioning of his own poetic image testifies that he had always believed in self-creation as much as in chance revelation—it was not until he encountered Rodin that he began explicitly to believe that, in Maurice Blanchot's words, the true artist must struggle to "faire de l'oeuvre une voie vers l'inspiration" ("make work into a path toward inspiration") rather than vice versa (195).

Rodin's work-as-inspiration ethic would become more paradoxical than ever when translated, as Rilke was bound to do, into gendered terms. With its emphasis on constant effort and self-conscious discipline, Rodin's model seemingly leaves little room for Rilke's conception of female creativity, which, like Lou Andreas-Salomé's comparison of women's art to the ripened fruit that falls from a tree or Keats's famous declaration that "if Poetry comes not as naturally as the leaves to a tree it had better not come at all,"[12] regarded inspiration as an arboreal process of natural, unforced organicism. Rilke's great challenge, then, both in the *New Poems* and elsewhere, was to preserve a sense of Rodin's active, frenetic, "masculine" creative principle without sacrificing his own feminine ideal. He would accomplish this not only by reiterating his female identification—in his "Self-Portrait from the Year 1906," for instance, he notes that his own physiognomy, despite its aristocratic traits,[13] reflects the humility "of one who serves, and of a woman" (*SW* 1:522)—but also by feminizing the Master himself. Thus, even while comparing Rodin's appearance to such emphatically male figures as a river god and a prophet, Rilke is careful to delineate, in an adulatory essay of 1907, the great man's womanly qualities as well:

[Seine] Männlichkeit ist bei aller Hartnäckigkeit ohne Härte, so daß sogar ein Freund Rodin's, den er manchmal gegen Abend besuchte, schreiben konnte: "Es bleibt, wenn er geht, in der Dämmerung des Zimmers etwas Mildes zurück, als wäre eine Frau dagewesen." (*SW* 5:224)

[(His) masculinity, despite its obstinance, is without hardness, so that even a friend of Rodin's, whom he sometimes visited toward evening, could write: "When he departs, something mild remains behind in the half-light of the room, as though a woman had been there."]

Rilke's paradoxical stance regarding the nature and sources of inspiration—does it depend upon willful effort or unwilling reception? upon masculine "doing" or feminine "being"?—becomes especially apparent in his attitude toward "Things," the objects and creatures depicted in his justly acclaimed and often-anthologized *Dinggedichte* (Thing-poems), which are scattered throughout *Neue Gedichte*. Just as in the *Stunden-Buch*, in which they are on the one hand depicted as passive objects that obey the poet's commands yet on the other hand serve as active manifestations of God, the Things that make up Rilke's universe alternate between submitting abjectly to the poet's piercing gaze and exercising a reciprocal control over their observer. "Und nun will ich mich weiterstreiten mit meinen Dingen," complains Rilke in a 1907 letter to his wife; "einige sind auf meiner Seite und liegen brav da, wie Vorzugschüler in Benehmen, aber die meisten sind unerzogen und belustigen sich hinter mir." ("And now I must go on struggling with my Things; some of them are on my side and lie there obediently, behaving like model pupils, but most of them are naughty and are having fun behind my back.")[14] If Rilke indicates the tenuousness of his control over Things by figuring them as rambunctious "pupils," he at the same time emphasizes the importance of his own role by depicting himself as their instructor.

The central ideology of the Thing-poem, however, despite Rilke's Rodin-influenced emphasis on hard work, eschews any notion of really mastering Things at all; the true Thing-poet engenders poetry, Rilke implies, not by forcing himself upon his subject matter but, rather, by submitting humbly to the objects of his contemplation, allowing them to penetrate him with their mystical essence. This revelatory process is perhaps most vividly enacted in Rilke's 1908 poem "Archaïscher Torso Apollos" ("Archaic Torso of Apollo"), in which the poet's carefully constructed, objective description of an ancient statue unexpectedly leads to an abrupt reversal of scopic roles: "denn da ist keine Stelle, / die dich nicht sieht" ("for here is no place / that does not see you"). The statue, which has submitted through most of the poem to being a passive object of the poet's gaze, suddenly takes on, instead, the active role of viewing the viewer; indeed, in the poem's final sentence the headless Apollo usurps the poet's very voice, delivering, in stentorian tones that smack of prophetic revelation, its famous imperative: "Du mußt dein Leben ändern" ("You must change your life" [*SW* 1:557]). A similar creative process is described in "Der Berg" ("The Mountain"), in which a painter, having attempted "sechsunddreissig Mal und hundert Mal" ("thirty-six times and a hundred times") to capture on paper the essence of a certain landscape, finds that he must patiently wait until the "teilnahmslos" ("unparticipating") mountain that he has contemplated for so long at last reveals itself to him in full visionary relief: "um auf einmal wissend, wie Erscheinung, / sich zu heben hinter jedem Spalt" ("all of a sudden, knowingly, like a vision, / rising up behind every crevice" [1:638–39]). In both poems the poet's eventual success in describing the Thing he observes depends not only upon his own tenaciousness and skill—not only, that is, on each object's openness to his perceptual acuity—but also and above all on *his* openness to their essential being.

In a Thing-poem called "Die Laute ("The Lute"), Rilke specifically associates the poet's passive absorption of a Thing's mystical essence with the receptive capacities of women. Taking on the voice of the instrument he describes, Rilke in effect recites the secrets of his own poetic craft:

> Ich bin die Laute. Willst du meinen Leib
> beschreiben, seine schön gewölbten Streifen:
> sprich so, als sprächest du von einer reifen
> gewölbten Feige. Übertreib
>
> das Dunkel, das du in mir siehst. Es war
> Tullias Dunkelheit. In ihrer Scham
> war nicht so viel, und ihr erhelltes Haar
> war wie ein heller Saal. Zuweilen nahm
>
> sie etwas Klang von meiner Oberfläche
> in ihr Gesicht und sang zu mir.
> Dann spannte ich mich gegen ihre Schwäche,
> und endlich war mein Inneres in ihr.
>
> (SW 1:611–12)

> [I am the lute. If you wish to describe
> my body, its beautifully vaulted stripes,
> speak as you would of a ripe
> vaulted fig. Overemphasize
>
> the darkness that you see in me. It was
> Tullia's darkness. In her private parts
> there was not so much, and her illumined hair
> was like a bright hall. Sometimes she took
>
> a little sound from my surface
> into her face and sang to me.
> Then I strained myself against her weakness
> and at last my inner self was in her.]

Here the artist is explicitly a woman (the reference is probably to Tullia d'Aragona, a sixteenth-century courtesan), and her ability to sing with and about the lute—and, in the end, to internalize its very essence—is clearly dependent upon her female sexuality: Tullia's dark "Scham" denotes not only her shame or shyness but also her genitalia, the physical locus of her sexuality, and the poem's final line describes her stereotypically feminine submission to the "male" lute's penetrations. One reading, then, would find the poem's primary message in the advice given in the first stanza: if you would be a successful Thing-poet, the lute intimates, you must passively allow objects to enter you just as I entered Tullia. The sexual and creative ideology of the poem, however, turns out to be somewhat more complex than that. The lute itself, with its rounded body and figlike shape, is a feminized object (the fig, as Rilke may well have known, serves in Italian as a not-very-subtle metaphor for the female genitalia), while Tullia, far from being merely a female figure of "darkness" and "weakness," is also a successful artist on whom the lute depends for some of its own essential qualities. Finally, it is Rilke, elsewhere such a vocal advocate of the male poet's feminization, who actually accomplishes the poem's most ambitious "penetration" when he takes on the lute's voice in the first place.

As poems like "The Lute" make evident, Rilke's enthusiastic rhetoric of receptivity, employed throughout *Neue Gedichte* and elsewhere, belies an equally powerful desire for autonomous poetic authority. Even such famous Thing-poems as "The Panther," "The Unicorn," and "The Gazelle," although they undoubtedly bespeak long hours of observation and a genuine effort on the poet's part to open himself to the objects of his contemplation, actively probe, prod, and measure with a very human yardstick the secrets of animal life. Thus, Rilke's *Dinggedichte*—and the same is true of such later works in the Thing-poem tradition as D. H. Lawrence's 1923 *Birds, Beasts and Flowers* and Francis Ponge's 1942 *Le Parti pris des choses*—function successfully as poems not so much because they illuminate animal or object existence as because they speak so eloquently to human desire and human experience. Furthermore, the fact that so many of these poems, including "Archaic Torso of Apollo," "The Mountain," and "The Lute," take as their theme art and the artist suggests a deliberate self-reflexivity on Rilke's part; in providing an explicit commentary on the poet's practice, these Thing-poems serve, in a sense, as instructional treatises by the artist on art.

Even if one accepts the sincerity of Rilke's rhetoric of passive receptivity, a number of poems in *Neue Gedichte* betray the poet's obvious anxieties toward such feminization and, indeed, toward any form of visionary experience. In particular, six poems written in 1907—"The Comforting of Elijah," "Saul among the Prophets," "Samuel's Appearance before Saul," "A Prophet," "Jeremiah," and "A Sibyl"—explore the revelatory dilemmas of various biblical and mythical figures who, although their prophetic powers afford them a certain priestly stature, have come to dread the agony of relinquishing their bodies to God and speaking in a voice not their own (*SW* 1:563–68). One after another the figures in this sobering group of poems curse or lament their prophetic vocation: Elijah begs God, "gebrauche / mich länger nicht. Ich bin entzwei" ("use me no longer. I am torn in two"); Saul, spilling words from his mouth as a gutter spills overflowing rainwater, feels himself reduced to "nichts als [einen] Haufen / umgestürzter Würden, Last auf Last" ("nothing but [a] pile / of overturned dignities, burden upon burden"); the unnamed seer of "A Prophet" must take hard, unyielding words not his own—"Eisenstücke, Steine" ("pieces of iron, stones")—and melt them as a volcano would, finally hurling them out "in dem Ausbruch seines Mundes" ("in the eruption of his mouth"); and the ancient sibyl finds herself overtaken every evening by words "die sich unbewacht / wider ihren Willen in ihr mehrten" ("that, unheeded, / multiplied themselves within her against her will"). In "Jeremiah" Rilke renders such visionary agony even more vivid by speaking in the first person; "Einmal war ich weich wie früher Weizen" ("Once I was soft like early wheat"), the prophet laments, but now his mouth has become a wound: "nun blutet von ihm Unglücksjahr um Unglücksjahr" ("now one disastrous year after the next bleeds from it").

In all of these poems prophecy is clearly a torturous act, a burden, an invasion. Although only two of the figures depicted here—the sibyl and the medium of Endor, who conjures up Samuel's ghost in "Samuel's Appearance before Saul"—are female, the seven prophecy poems contain abundant imagery linking inspiration with specifically female receptive and reproductive capacities. Yet these very traits, elsewhere considered so positive and desirable by Rilke, are portrayed here in almost entirely negative terms. Words multiply like fetal cells in the fecund depths of the aged sibyl's body; blood flows at regular, painful intervals from Jeremiah's woundlike orifice; even the image of the prophet as a stone-melting volcano depicts prophecy as a laborious process of unwilling reception, painful gestation, and birthlike expulsion, a sequence highly reminiscent of the experience of a female rape victim.[15]

Even some of the more positive, powerful female figures that Rilke depicts elsewhere in *Neue Gedichte* are problematic in their association not with violation or suffering but, instead, with a perfection and self-fulfillment achieved only through a negative process of self-sacrifice and death. For instance, in "Orpheus. Eurydike. Hermes" (which I will discuss more substantially in chap. 4) Orpheus's dead wife is portrayed as a far more potent and self-possessed being than her uncertain, distracted husband. In "Alkestis," similarly, the young bride of the title, learning at her own marriage feast that her husband must die, offers herself in his place with these chilling words linking female sexuality with death:

> Ersatz kann keiner für ihn sein. Ich *bins*.
> Ich bin Ersatz. Denn keiner ist zu Ende
> wie ich es bin. Was bleibt mir denn von dem
> was ich hier war? Das *ists* ja, daß ich sterbe.
> Hat sie dirs nicht gesagt, da sie dirs auftrug,
> daß jenes Lager, das da drinnen wartet,
> zur Unterwelt gehört? Ich nahm ja Abschied.
> Abschied über Abschied.
> Kein Sterbender nimmt mehr davon. Ich ging ja,
> damit das Alles, unter Dem begraben
> der jetzt mein Gatte ist, zergeht, sich auflöst — .
> So führ mich hin: ich sterbe ja für ihn.
>
> (SW 1:548)

> [No one can be his replacement. I *am* it.
> I'm the replacement. For no one is finished
> as I am. What remains for me of that
> which I once was here? That's *it:* my dying.
> Did she [Persephone] not tell you, when she sent you here,
> that the bed waiting for me inside
> belongs to the Underworld? I've taken leave.
> Leave upon leave.
> No dying man takes more than that. I left
> so everything buried beneath the man
> who is now my spouse might fade, dissolve — .
> So lead me away; for I am dying for him.]

Like Orpheus, Alcestis's husband, Admet, finds himself reduced to relative insignificance and impotence by his wife's sacrificial gesture and by her eerie fulfillment in death. Power here is clearly a female commodity, yet it is a power that resides in and depends on self-denial and absence—traits that Rilke would continually profess to admire but that he would prove singularly unwilling to take on for himself.

Voices from Beyond: Poems and Experiments, 1911–15

Despite Rodin's assertion, quoted approvingly by Rilke in one of his essays on the sculptor, that for the successful artist there is "keine Inspiration sondern nur Arbeit" ("no inspiration, but rather only work" [*SW* 5:226]), Rilke would remain constantly on the lookout for outside inspiration, which he soon proved unable to summon through continuous effort alone. The nearly twelve years following the completion of *New Poems* and *The Notebooks of Malte Laurids Brigge* would remain for the most part strikingly barren ones when viewed within the context of his oeuvre as a whole, even though he was almost constantly reading, writing, and translating. Only the production, between 1912 and 1915, of the first four Duino Elegies would interrupt what is often referred to as his long *Schaffenskrise* (creative crisis). During the rest of this period Rilke was continuously seeking new paths to the inspiration for which he longed, a quest that would lead him beyond his imitations of Rodin's observational techniques and his occasional identification with receptive women—approaches that until then had served him rather well—to experiment with other means of communicating with the unknown.

The first of these means, one that Rilke seriously contemplated but did not ever employ, was psychoanalysis, or communication with the unknown in the form of the hidden self. Lou Andreas-Salomé, who would eventually become a fervent disciple of Freud, had in the past often encouraged her friend to undergo psychoanalysis; as early as 1901, in fact, she was already employing the vocabulary of the discipline in her correspondence with Rilke, describing the dangers of "[dem] was Du und ich den 'Andern' in Dir nannten,—diesen bald deprimierten, bald excitierten, einst Allzufurchtsamen, dann Allzugerissenen" ("That which you and I used to call the 'Other' in you,—this now depressed, now excited, first too-timid, then too-passionate being").[16] A decade later, in late 1911, a frustrated and creatively blocked Rilke reported to Andreas-Salomé that he had been seriously considering psychoanalysis but had tentatively decided against it: "Die Psychoanalyse ist eine zu gründliche Hülfe für mich, sie hilft ein für alle Mal, sie räumt auf, und mich aufgeräumt au finden eines Tages, wäre vielleicht noch aussichtsloser als diese Unordnung" ("Psychoanalysis is too thorough a solution for me, it helps once and for all, it tidies things up, and to find myself tidied up one day would be even more hopeless than this chaos").[17] By late January 1912 he had strengthened his resolve: "Etwas wie eine desinfizierte Seele kommt dabei heraus, ein Unding, ein lebendiges, rot korrigiert, wie die Seite in einem Schulheft" ("Something like a disinfected soul results from it, a living monstrosity, full of red correction marks, like a page in an exercise book").[18] Four days later he was explaining to Dr. von Gebsattel, a psychoanalyst who had been urging him to undergo treatment, "daß ich mir den Ausweg der Analyse nicht erlauben darf" ("that I must not allow myself the escape route of analysis"), citing his fear that, "wenn man mir meine Teufel austriebe, auch meinen Engeln ein . . . Schrecken geschähe" ("if one were to drive out my devils, my angels might receive a fright as well").[19]

Unlike H.D., then, who would eventually use her psychoanalytic sessions with Freud as a means to creative self-empowerment, Rilke remained wary of any attempts to harness the "Unordnung" ("disorderliness") within him. Not only did he believe that the angels of creative Otherness might accidentally be exorcised alongside the devils, but he may well have felt, with D. H. Lawrence, that his imaginative demons in fact played their own essential role in his artistic productivity. Although he clearly was eager to tap into the unknown energies of his own subconscious mind, he resisted doing so by any such institutionalized, rationalistic means as psychoanalysis. Freud's writings, he reported to Andreas-Salomé, were "unsympathisch und stellenweise haarsträubend" ("unsympathetic and in places hair-raising") to him, and he felt that his own poetry already functioned as "eine Art Selbstbehandlung" ("a kind of self-treatment") more effective in curing his mental and physical ills than any doctor's proposed therapy could be.[20]

If Rilke required any justification for his antipsychoanalytic bias, he received it during that month of January 1912, when he made his final decision—ultimately supported by Andreas-Salomé herself, who may well have feared that Rilke would reveal secrets about her to their mutual friend Dr. Gebsattel—to reject analysis. For, although his letters to Andreas-Salomé of 20 and 24 January make no mention of the fact, he had just experienced a rush of creative inspiration so powerful and productive that any recourse to medical treatment must suddenly have seemed to him both unnecessary and potentially harmful. Rilke was passing a solitary winter at the Princess Marie von Thurn und Taxis's castle at Duino, on the Adriatic coast. Having spent the morning occupied with a tedious business letter (probably concerning either Rilke's ever-perilous financial conditions or his frustrated attempts to grant his wife, Clara, a divorce), he wandered out, lost in thought, for a stroll along the wind-blown ramparts of the castle. The Princess Marie recounts in her memoirs the event as Rilke afterward described it to her:

> Da, auf einmal, mitten in seinem Grübeln, blieb er stehen, plötz-lich, denn es war ihm, als ob im Brausen des Sturmes eine Stimme ihm zugerufen hätte:
> "Wer, wenn ich schriee, hörte mich denn aus der Engel Ord-nungen?" . . .
> Lauschend blieb er stehen. "Was ist das?" flüsterte er halblaut . . .
> "was ist es, was kommt?" [. . .]
> Wer kam? . . . Er wußte es jetzt: der Gott . . .[21]

> [Then, all at once, in the midst of his brooding, he suddenly stood still, for it seemed to him as though, through the raging of the storm, a voice had called out to him:
> "Who, if I cried out, would hear me among the angelic orders?" . . .
> Listening, he stood still. "What is that?" he asked in an undertone . . .
> "What is it that is coming?" [. . .]
> Who was coming? . . . He knew now: the god . . .]

By that evening, having first dutifully responded to the business letter, Rilke had transcribed the First Elegy in its entirety; shortly thereafter he produced the Second Elegy and the opening lines of what would eventually become the Third and Tenth Elegies. "Dann aber," as the Princess Marie reports, "verstummte der Gott" ("But then the god fell silent" [49]). Not until ten years later, in a whirlwind of productivity that makes the Duino episode seem almost insignificant in comparison, would Rilke be granted a similar influx of poetic inspiration.

If I write here, as the Princess Marie does, of inspiration as something "granted" to Rilke by an unknown, external, presumably divine power, it is because Rilke himself so consistently described his revelatory experiences in such terms. "Ich schreibe wie eine Verrückter," he reported to the princess on 12 January 1912; "Die Stimme, die sich meiner da bedient, ist mehr als ich—, ich rausche nur wie der Busch, in den der Wind gefahren ist, und muß mirs geschehen lassen" ("I am writing like a madman. . . . The voice that now makes use of mine is greater than I; I only rustle like a bush through which the wind has passed, and must simply let it happen.")[22] Four days later, in an even more vivid description, he compared himself to John of Patmos, the visionary author of the Book of Revelation:

> Ich zögere unendlich, liebe Fürstin, nach dem Diktat von neulich, das mir hier auf diesem Pathmos so stürmisch eingerufen wurde, daß ich, wenn ich daran denke, meine, . . . mit beiden Händen geschrieben zu haben, nach rechts und links, um nur alles Eingegebene aufzufangen.[23]

> [I hesitate endlessly, dear Princess, after the recent dictation that was so stormily shouted to me here upon this Patmos, so that, when I think back on it, it seems . . . I must have written with both hands, both to the left and to the right, in order to catch every word granted to me.]

Later that same month, in a letter to Rudolf Kassner, he would liken the "Entschluß und Leistung" ("resolution and productivity") of an artist to that both of a prophet and a saint (Schnack 394).

Despite his earlier emphasis, then, on the hard work that made the *New Poems* and *Malte Laurids Brigge* possible, nowhere does Rilke attempt to suggest that the *Duino Elegies* or, later, the *Sonnets to Orpheus* were anything other than a divine gift—one, to be sure, that he had constantly labored to prove himself worthy of, yet over which he ultimately had no real control. Not since Coleridge, in fact, who claimed that "Kubla Khan" was the product of a drug-induced dream, has any Western poet of such stature insisted more on the visionary origins of his own work and less on the skill and craft involved in giving it form. Yet, whereas Coleridge, recounting that his poem had formed in his mind "without any sensation or consciousness of effort," laments that he was interrupted in the process of transcribing it by "a person on business from Porlock" and that he afterward could not recall the rest (Perkins 431), Rilke emphasizes that such minor distractions were of no consequence to him. Not only did he refuse to allow a tedious business letter to impede his creative flow, but his account of events (at least as reported by the princess) even suggests that the letter's very banality played some role in unleashing, as a sort of defiant, compensatory gesture, the Elegies' profound cadences.

Although he does not say so explicitly, Rilke almost certainly believed that his emotional identification with women played an important role in making the Duino experience possible. His letters and poetry from that month of January 1912, including the first two Elegies themselves, show that he was deeply immersed at the time in contemplating the nature of female self-sacrifice and love. Sometime between 15 and 22 January he wrote the twelve poems that constitute *Das Marien-Leben* (*The Life of Mary*), a cycle of verses about perhaps the most ideally receptive and unselfishly loving woman in Western mythology. And, although he had complained to a friend in a letter of 12 January about the physical and emotional dangers of the creative life, concluding that he could no longer imagine a woman producing art "ohne ihrer Natur unrecht zu tun" ("without doing an injustice to her nature"),[24] by 22 January he was writing to Annette Kolb of women's intrinsic superiority over men, if not necessarily as writers or painters then as artists, so to speak, of the heart. Citing such women as the Italian love poet Gaspara Stampa, the French love poet Louise Labé, and "certain Venetian courtesans," he names as his most perfect example of a selfless lover the seventeenth-century Portuguese nun Marianna Alcoforado:

dieser Unvergleichlichen, in deren acht schweren Briefen zum ersten Mal die Liebe der Frau ausgezogen ist von Punkt zu Punkt, ohne Aufwand, ohne Übertreibung oder Erleichterung, wie von der Hand einer Sibylle.[25]

[this incomparable woman, in whose eight weighty letters woman's love is for the first time drawn out from one point to the next, without extravagance, without exaggeration or mitigation, as though by a sibyl's hand.]

A year later Rilke would undertake to translate Alcoforado's letters and some of Louise Labé's love poems into German (he had already, in 1907, translated several of Elizabeth Barrett Browning's *Sonnets from the Portuguese*). Translation—which he would describe years later to Paul Valéry as an act "de consentement, d'obéissance et d'activité parallèle" ("of consent, obedience, and parallel activity" [qtd. in Schnack 895])—seems to have functioned for him as a readily accessible and controllable form of inspiration, allowing him to absorb some of an admired poet's most essential qualities and, in the cases of Alcoforado, Labé, and Barrett Browning, to speak with a woman's voice.[26]

The presence of Marianna Alcoforado and other women like her can be felt throughout the first Duino Elegy, which opens with the poet's fear of angelic influence—"Ein jeder Engel ist schrecklich" ("Every angel is terrible")—but moves on to suggest that God can also find other, less obviously sinister mouthpieces for his word:

> Nicht, daß du *Gottes* ertrügest
> die Stimme, bei weitem. Aber das Wehende höre,
> die ununterbrochene Nachricht, die aus Stille sich bildet.
> Es rauscht jetzt von jenen jungen Toten zu dir.
>
> (*SW* 1:687)

> [Not that you could endure
> *God's* voice—far from it. But listen to the blowing wind,
> the uninterrupted message that forms itself from stillness.
> It murmurs to you now from those who have died young.]

Although he envies both the young dead and unrequited lovers—"Jene, du neidest sie fast, Verlassenen, die du / so viel liebender fandst als die Gestillten" ("those abandoned women, you almost envy them, whom you / found so much more capable of loving than those who were satisfied")—precisely because their renunciatory nature protects them from being penetrated by another's being, the poet himself has apparently been penetrated by *their* visionary influence, to the point of asking toward the end of the Elegy, "*könnten* wir sein ohne sie?" ("*could* we exist without them?").

The Second Elegy, written within a week or two of the first (but accompanied by no similar tale of divine voices in the wind), betrays an equally conflicted view of active inspiration versus passive receptivity.

In the First Elegy angels are terrifying and more-than-human entities, unmistakably male, while the poet himself is frightened and feminized: "Und gesetzt selbst," Rilke speculates, "es nähme / einer mich plötzlich ans Herz: ich verginge von seinem / stärkeren Dasein" ("And even if one held me suddenly to his heart: I would be consumed by his / more powerful existence"). Despite his fear of such emotional/spiritual ravishment, however, the poet clearly requires the angels' otherworldly inspiration in order to live and create. Thus, at the beginning of the Second Elegy he once again invokes the "fast tödliche Vögel der Seele" ("almost deadly birds of the soul"), though with a renewed warning of danger:

> Träte der Erzengel jetzt, der gefährliche, hinter den Sternen
> eines Schrittes nur nieder und herwärts: hochauf-
> schlagend erschlüg uns das eigene Herz.
>
> (SW 1:689)

> [But if now the archangel, the perilous one, behind the stars
> took just one step down toward us: then, beating up high,
> our own heart would beat us to death.]

Threatening to "beat [him] to death" if the angel should approach, the poet's own heart, rather than the angel's embrace, suddenly becomes the potential agent of destruction. Indeed, the archangel becomes more an "almost deadly" internal entity than a terrifying external one. Written just around the time that Rilke refused psychoanalysis on the grounds that it might rid him of both his angels and his demons, the Second Elegy suggests that the angel *is* the demon and that both are forces residing as much within the poet (the angels are, after all, described as "birds of the soul" rather than of the heavens) as somewhere far above the Duino ramparts.

Whether it initially came from an external angel or from an internal demon, by February 1912 the inspiration that made the first two Elegies possible had once again abandoned Rilke, who, although he would complete two further Elegies by 1915, would not again experience such an intense rush of creative energy for another ten years. At the time, it seems, he was more relieved than regretful; in fact, as I will argue in chapter 5, the Duino episode seems to have warned him that a poet's self-conscious feminization always carries with it the danger of violation, or a sort of mental/spiritual rape by the inspiring Other. By the following autumn, however, Rilke was again searching for new ways of communicating directly with the unknown, this time by means of spiritualist séances. In the company of the Princess Marie—an enthusiastic if initially skeptical member, as H.D. would be three decades later, of the London Society for Psychical Research (SPR)—he participated in late 1912 in a series of evening séances during which his own written questions were answered by means of a planchette, a device designed to aid in automatic writing.[27] Rilke was so excited by the transcribed responses to his queries, and particularly by his "conversation" with the spirit of someone identified only as "die Unbekannte" ("the unknown woman"), that he soon thereafter followed this spirit's advice and started out on a journey to Spain (one that, to be sure, he had already long contemplated making). The following summer he asked the princess where he could acquire a planchette of his own: "Mich drängts zur Unbekannten" ("I am drawn to the unknown").[28] Soon afterward, however, he reported to her that his latest attempts to contact "the spirits" had been unsuccessful—"les Esprits ne voulaient pas de moi évidemment" ("apparently the Spirits wanted nothing to do with me")—and that both an encounter with a medium in Munich and a single attempt to use the planchette had left him "dégouté" ("disgusted"). "Et pourtant," he added rather plaintively, "je voudrais bien que 'l'Inconnue' me parle" ("And yet, I do wish that 'the Unknown' would speak to me").[29]

Many years later Rilke would refer to the occult as merely "ein Geheimnis unter zahllosen Geheimnissen" ("one mystery among [the] innumerable mysteries") to which a poet might turn his attention. Even the so-called external spirit forces in which he had once believed are, he argues in a 1924 letter, dwarfed to insignificance in comparison with "der Tiefendimension unseres Inneren" ("the profound dimension within us"). Declaring himself without talent as far as séances are concerned, he nonetheless goes on to depict his own poetic profession in terms of spiritual mediumship:

Ich bin, zum Glück, medial vollkommen unbrauchbar, aber ich zweifle keinen Augenblick, daß ich mich auf meine Weise den Einflüssen jener oft heimatlosen Kräfte eröffnet halte und daß ich nie aufhöre, ihren Umgang zu genießen oder zu erleiden.[30]

[I am, fortunately, completely useless as a medium, yet I do not
doubt for an instant that, in my own way, I hold myself open to
those often homeless powers, never ceasing to enjoy or to suffer
their companionship.]

Of course, the creative self-confidence expressed in this letter, written
at a time when Rilke once again felt firmly in touch with his sources of
inspiration, is a far cry from the uncertainties of 1912–13, when the
notion of communicating with the unknown virtually on demand must
still have seemed to him a highly compelling possibility. Certainly, the
spiritualist model, although it carried with it some obvious dangers,
would have fit in well with Rilke's understanding of the poet as a
receptive, feminine being, ever open to influences from beyond.

By late 1913, at any rate, Rilke had abandoned his flirtations with
the occult, focusing his attentions on a new source of inspiration and
Otherness, namely his own body. In October 1913 he had spent a week
with Lou Andreas-Salomé, who, although she still seconded his opin-
ion that he should avoid psychoanalysis, undertook an amateur analy-
sis of her own when she spent most of a long train ride assigning
mostly sexual interpretations to his current and childhood dreams.
Returning to Paris the following week, Rilke wrote to thank her for her
efforts: "Liebe Lou, irgendwie hast Du mir ja unendlich geholfen, das
Andere ist nun für mich und für den Engel da, wenn wir nur zusam-
menhalten" ("Dear Lou, somehow you have been of infinite help to me,
the Other is now there for me and for the Angel, if only we stick
together").[31] Shortly thereafter he completed the third Duino Elegy,
one of his most explicitly sexual poems, which takes as its theme the
primitive, phallic forces that inhabit the male body:

Eines ist, die Geliebte zu singen. Ein anderes, wehe,
jenen verborgenen schuldigen Fluß-Gott des Blutes.
Den sie von weitem erkennt, ihren Jüngling, was weiß er
selbst von dem Herren der Lust, der aus dem Einsamen oft,
ehe das Mädchen noch linderte, oft auch als wäre sie nicht,
ach, von welchem Unkenntlichen triefend, das Gotthaupt
aufhob, aufrufend die Nacht zu unendlichem Aufruhr.
O des Blutes Neptun, o sein furchtbarer Dreizack.
O der dunkele Wind seiner Brust aus gewundener Muschel.

                                                    (SW 1:693)

[It is one thing to sing the beloved. Another, alas,
to invoke that hidden guilty river-god of the blood.
Her young man, whom she knows from afar, what does even he
know of the lord of desire, who often, out of his solitude,
before the girl could soothe him, and as though she didn't exist,
raised up his godly head, ah, dripping with what unknown thing,
summoning the night to an endless uproar.
O the Neptune of the blood, o his terrible trident.
O the dark wind of his breast out of the winding shell.]

The poem ends with a plea to the young man's beloved to protect him
from the primordial forces of his own sexuality (which she herself, of
course, has played a role in unleashing):

> O leise, leise,
> tu ein liebes vor ihm, ein verläßliches Tagwerk,—führ ihn
> nah an den Garten heran, gieb ihm der Nächte
> Übergewicht . . . . . .
>   Verhalt ihn . . . . . .
>
>   (*SW* 1:696)

> [Oh gently, gently,
> do something loving for him, a daily task he can rely on,—
> lead him close to the garden, give him the extra weight
> of nights . . . . . .
>   Restrain him . . . . . .]

The young girl in the poem, as Adrienne Rich has noted, is a typically
self-sacrificing healer, a mediator between the young man and his
"'monstrous' inner life" (*Of Woman Born* 190). The real focus of the
Third Elegy, meanwhile, is the terrifying yet compelling power of the
"hidden guilty river-god of the blood," Rilke's phallic deity. "The body
itself [had] become 'the other' for him," Lou Andreas-Salomé would
reportedly say of Rilke in reference to this time (Prater 229), but, unlike
the "now depressed, now excited, first too-timid, then too-passionate
being" that she had earlier feared might destroy him, this newly dis-
covered, sexually potent internal Other played an essential role in revi-
talizing him creatively, at least to the extent of spurring the completion
of the Third Elegy itself.

Rilke's New Year's wish that year, as he wrote to Marie von Thurn und Taxis in late December 1913, was for a quiet place and the favorable circumstances that would allow him to complete the Elegies:

> Wenn Gott Einsehen hat, so läßt er mich bald ein paar Räume auf dem Land finden, wo ich ganz nach meiner Art wüthen kann und wo die Elegieen aus mir den Mond anheulen dürfen. . . . Dazu gehört dann die Möglichkeit, weite einsame Wege zu machen und eben der Mensch, der schwesterliche!!! (ach ach) der dann das Haus besorgt und gar keine Liebe hat oder so viel, daß er nichts verlangt, als, wirkend und verhütend, an der Grenze des Unsichtbaren dazusein. Hier der Inbegriff meiner Wünsche für 1914, 15, 16, 17, u.s.f.[32]

> [If God has true understanding, he will soon let me find a few rooms in the countryside where I can rave in my own way and where the Elegies can howl out of me at the moon. . . . Add to that scene the possibility of taking long, solitary walks, and also the one person, the sisterly one!!! (alas, alas) who will take care of the house and who feels no love at all, or else so much that she demands nothing except to be there, active and protective, on the borders of the invisible. Here, in sum, are my wishes for 1914, 15, 16, 17, etc.]

Rilke's earlier ideal of two artists "guarding one another's solitude," as he had once hoped he and his wife could do, now expresses itself in terms of a far more traditional domestic scenario (though one that is deeply untraditional in its exclusion of sexuality and family life): the male artist lives and creates in blissful solitude, with his daily needs provided for by a silent, housekeeping mother/lover/sister—a "healer, helper, bringer of tenderness and security" (Rich, *Of Woman Born* 190)—who adores him so intensely that she is even willing to forgo being loved in return. Perhaps Rilke's recent discovery of the "phallic god" within him had decreased his sensitivity to women's own needs for artistic independence. In any event, despite his celebrations elsewhere of female self-sacrifice, he gives no indication here that he would himself be willing to take on the tediously domestic, traditionally female task of "protecting the borders" of someone else's solitary existence.

Rilke's New Year's wishes saw a certain fulfillment, for, if 1914 and 1915 did not bring him his longed-for workplace in the countryside, those years did at least witness the advent of two women who came close to fitting his requirements for a nurturing, "sisterly" companion. Magda von Hattingberg ("Benvenuta") and Loulou Albert-Lazard were not only intelligent, attractive, and artistic women (the former was an accomplished pianist, the latter a painter), but both also seem to have been willing, in their own ways, to provide Rilke with the kind of unconditional love and carefully protected privacy that he so ardently desired. Yet Rilke broke off or curtailed each of these liaisons after just a few months of intensive ardor.[33] Although he continued to celebrate the relationship of sexuality to creativity, he complained more and more frequently that artistic inspiration is invariably stifled by love. Indeed, several years later, immersed in yet another passionate affair (this time with Baladine Klossowska, known as "Merline"), he would write in a private document called *Das Testament* that love destroys creativity precisely because the two impulses are so closely akin:

> So erscheint das Liebeserlebnis als eine gleichsam verkümmerte, unfähige Nebenform der schöpferischen Erfahrung, als ihre Herabsetzung,—und bleibt ungekonnt, unbeherrscht und, an der höheren Ordnung jenes Gelingens gemessen, unerlaubt. (111)

> [Thus the love experience appears as it were as a stunted, unfit variant of the creative experience, as its debasement—and remains incompetent, unmastered, and, measured against the higher order of such success, impermissible.]

Soon after the break with Benvenuta in 1914, Rilke sent Lou Andreas-Salomé a new poem, "Wendung" ("Turning"), so called "weil's die Wendung darstellt, die wohl auch kommen muß, wenn ich leben soll" ("because it depicts the turning that must occur if I am to live"). Although concerned, like so many of Rilke's earlier Thing-poems, primarily with the force and limitations of the poet's external gaze, the poem ends by urging the poet to chart a new path to creativity, one based on contemplation of his inner self:

> Siehe, innerer Mann, dein inneres Mädchen,
> dieses errungene aus
> tausend Naturen, dieses

erst nur errungene, nie
noch geliebte Geschöpf.[34]

[Look, inner man, at your inner girl,
the one achieved from out of
a thousand natures, this
barely achieved, never
yet beloved creature.]

Searching, ever more intensely, for his own "inner girl," Rilke would never abandon his ideal of self-feminization. He would, however, almost systematically continue to reject real women—women whose Otherness he could or would not assimilate—as potential sources of inspiration, apparently fearing that any penetration by their "alien nature" might adversely affect and even annihilate his own.

Of the various other visionary strategies that Rilke employed during his long period of poetic fallowness one more deserves special comment here. In the late autumn of 1915, more than two years after Lou Andreas-Salomé's analysis of the sexual content of Rilke's dreams, Rilke wrote seven poems of such sexual and anatomical explicitness that the occasional erotic passages found in Rilke's earlier poetry seem almost subtle in comparison. For instance, in the first poem of this group, simply labeled "Seven Poems," a rose-plucking maiden reaches out to grasp "the full bud" of her lover's "vital member" ("die volle Knospe seines Lebensgliedes"); in the second the poet begs his beloved to let him plunge his "jähen Baum" ("irascible tree"), which has already grown upward in the direction of the sky, down into the "counter-heaven" of her vagina ("O stürz ihn, daß er, umgedreht / in deinen Schooß, den Gegen-Himmel kennt"); in the third the poet's member becomes a column erected in a forest thicket ("die Säule . . . in meinem Schamgehölze"); and in the fourth it is a tower from whose cupola he launches "womb-dazzling rockets" ("schooßblendend[e] Raketen"). Scattered in among all the vegetative and architectural imagery are several even more remarkable lines in which Rilke specifically depicts the phallus as a god: "Das ist mein Körper, welcher aufersteht" ("This is my body, risen from the grave"), he writes in one poem, anticipating by nearly fifteen years D. H. Lawrence's description in *The Escaped Cock* of a lusty Christ enlisting a compliant priestess of Isis to assist him in his fleshly "resurrection" (*SW* 2:435–39).

Unlike the Third Elegy's mythical, Neptune-like river-god, however, who seems to exist independently both of the young man and his beloved, the phallic god of the "Seven Poems" depends upon the female lover both to give him form—"Von dir gestiftet steht des Gottes Bild / am leisen Kreuzweg unter meinem Kleide" ("Erected by you, the god's image stands / at the delicate crossroads under my clothing")—and to assist in his ultimate salvation:

> Nun hilf ihm leise aus dem heißen Grabe
> in jenen Himmel, den ich in dir habe:
> daß kühn aus ihm das Überleben geht.
> Du junger Ort der tiefen Himmelfahrt.
> Du dunkle Luft voll sommerlicher Pollen.
> Wenn ihre tausend Geister in dir tollen,
> wird meine steife Leiche wieder zart.
>
> (*SW* 2:438)

> [Now help it gently out of the hot grave
> into the heaven that I have in you,
> so that new life can bravely leap from it.
> You, first site of the profound Ascension.
> You, dark air full of summer pollen.
> When its thousand spirits romp within you,
> my stiff corpse will once again grow soft.]

If the penis, for Rilke, is a tree, a column, a tower, a god, and even, bizarrely, a "stiff corpse" about to be revitalized through the ejaculation/exorcism of its "thousand spirits," his lover's vagina/womb is figured in terms that are even more visionary: her body, potent and all-encompassing, becomes in turn the sky, Heaven, the summer, the night, and a magical landscape, "wie sie Seherinnen / in Kugeln schauen" ("like those that fortune-telling women / see in crystal balls"). Yet Rilke's seven "phallic hymns," although they insist on the sexual interdependence of men and women, do so primarily by perpetuating gender stereotypes that, even while granting a certain symbolic importance to women, nonetheless privilege male sexuality as a creative paradigm. The power, such as it is, of the vagina/womb is dedicated almost entirely to bringing into being and nurturing the phallic god, so that the female lover contributes to but does not necessarily share in the inseminating energies of the male artist.

Here, as in the Third Elegy, the poet's godlike phallus is an unpredictable, potentially unruly Other, signifying the poet's sexual anxiety as much as his virility. All the same, Rilke's notion that inspiration can arrive on a wave of sexuality (as once, during his apprenticeship with Rodin, he believed it could be conjured up by work) seems to have been confirmed almost immediately following the production of his phallic hymns: within weeks he was enthusing to a friend, in terms that hardly seem accidental in their sexual overtones, that "gute starke strömende Arbeit" ("good strong gushing work") had been flowing from his pen,[35] and by 23 November 1915 he had gone on to compose what would become the fourth Duino Elegy. Tempering his erotic energies of just a few weeks earlier with a healthy dose of self-questioning, Rilke focuses now not on sexual harmony alone so much as on the disjunctions between internal and external, human and divine, physical and spiritual existence: "Wir kennen den Kontur / des Fühlens nicht: nur was ihn formt von außen" ("We do not know the contours / of our emotions: only what forms them from outside"). Unfortunately, however, where this line of thought might have led him—encompassing, as it does, the complexities both of childhood and of parenthood, of nature and of artifice, of angels (pure internality) and of dolls (pure facade)—must forever remain a matter of speculation. A day later his "gushing" creative flow was suddenly and drastically stanched, as Rilke received his orders to report for what would prove an uneventful but tedious and artistically sterile period of military service.

Orpheus in Muzot

Rilke's stint shuffling papers for the Austrian army was to last for only a few months; his influential friends eventually arranged for his demobilization, and by July 1916 he was back in Munich attempting to resume his literary life. Yet, although he continued, as always, to occupy himself with reading, translating, composing the occasional poem, and scribbling ream upon ream of letters, many of which certainly stand as works of art in their own right, both the steady productivity that had brought the *New Poems* into being in Paris and the inspirational voices that had sparked the first Duino Elegies would continue to elude him. Even when, in 1920, friends installed him in a luxurious Swiss country house, where his solitude was assured and his every material need was met with alacrity (including his earlier desire for an efficient but unobtrusive housekeeper), he was able to produce nothing more impressive than a series of rather conventional verses for which, perhaps wisely, he refused to take direct responsibility. Instead, he attributed them to a ghostly eighteenth-century figure called "Count C. W.": "Er dichtet manches, was ich nie gebilligt haben würde." ("He composes many poems that I myself would never have approved of.")[36]

In February 1922, however, the creative breakthrough for which he had been longing occurred at last. A few months earlier, newly ensconced in a rented thirteenth-century château at Muzot, Rilke had enthusiastically written to the Princess Marie that he was reading the poetry of Paul Valéry:

> Er hat etwa durch zwanzig Jahre geschwiegen und Mathematik getrieben, erst seit 1915 giebt es wieder Gedichte von ihm, *en récompense de "la longue attente de sa vie."* In seinem Gedicht "Palme" steht:
>> Patience, patience
>> patience dans l'azur,
>> chaque goutte de silence
>> est la chance d'un fruit mûr!
> (Könnt ich das auch für mein Schweigen erhoffen.)[37]

> [He remained silent for nearly twenty years and occupied himself with mathematics; only since 1915 have there once again been poems by him, *in compensation for "the long wait of his life."* In his poem "Palm" stands the line:
>> Patience, patience
>> patience in the blueness,
>> every drop of silence
>> is the chance for a ripe fruit!
> (If only I could have such a hope for my own silence.)]

Some years later Rilke is reported to have remarked, "J'étais seul, j'attendais, toute mon oeuvre attendait, un jour j'ai lu Valéry et j'ai su que mon attente était finie" ("I was alone, I waited, my whole work waited, then one day I read Valéry and I knew that my wait was over" [Saint-Hélier 21]).[38] While other factors obviously played important roles as well in ending his long poetic silence, it is easy to understand why Rilke would have found both Valéry's words and his example inspirational. In particular, the image in "Palme" of the poet developing slowly, like a fruit, to ripeness must have held a special appeal for Rilke, who had himself so often used the ripening fruit metaphor in his descriptions of creativity as a gestative, feminine process.

Rilke finally achieved his visionary breakthrough almost exactly ten years after his Duino experience. In the space of about three weeks he not only completed his ten *Duino Elegies* but also produced, as though by pure serendipity, the fifty-five free-form sonnets that make up the *Sonnets to Orpheus*.[39] As he had done a decade earlier, when describing his Duino "voices," Rilke afterward recounted the Muzot experience in almost exclusively visionary terms. Although ambivalent about whether the poems sprang from a subconscious internal source or were imposed by an outer one, he insists, in letter after letter, that his own role was merely that of a mouthpiece for or transcriber of what he calls, variously, "une dictée intérieure, toute spontanée" ("an inner dictation, completely spontaneous"); "ein namenloser Sturm, ein Orkan im Geist" ("a nameless storm, a hurricane in the spirit"); "cette tempête divine" ("that divine tempest"); and, in one particularly ecstatic missive to Lou Andreas-Salomé, simply "Wunder. Gnade" ("Miracle. Grace").[40] Moreover, in a letter to Nanny Wunderly-Volkart he quite specifically describes the poems as a divine gift and himself as their "vessel": "In was für eine Welt der Gnade leben wir doch! Welche Kräfte warten darauf, uns zu erfüllen, uns immer gerüttelte Gefäße" ("But what a world of grace we live in! What powers are waiting to fill us, forever vibrating vessels that we are").[41]

Rilke's accounts of the Muzot "dictation" call to mind his earlier designations of patience and passive obedience as essentially feminine traits; yet nowhere does Rilke employ specifically gendered terms to describe the experience. If anything, in fact, words like *tempest, hurricane,* and even *blessing* and *grace* invoke Old Testament (male) prophecy and priestly authority. Some of Rilke's more enthusiastic readers, however, have eagerly made the associative leap that the poet himself avoided, describing the Muzot incident as a sort of cosmic nativity scene in which Rilke figures not as the poems' inseminating father—although Michael Grant's description of the Sonnets as "an extraordinary, climactic lyrical spasm" suggests an image of male orgasm (323)—but, rather, as their proud but passive mother. Norbert Fuerst, for instance, proclaims that the "release," or "delivery," of the

Elegies "took place with the eager necessity, with the triumphant convulsions of a natural birth" (166). Fuerst goes on, to be sure, to blend his rhetoric of receptivity with images of male religious authority:

> The *Sonnets* are the other side of, the descent from, the Sinai of the *Elegies*. To one who has surrendered to the mysteries of the *Elegies*, who has been initiated, not by intellectual penetration (that is not necessary) but by consent and acceptance, the *Sonnets* are even more satisfying, more whole, more holy. (191)

Similarly, Stephen Mitchell, who as the poet's most sensitive and eloquent English translator has surely earned the right to appropriate Rilke's visionary vocabulary, alternates between birth imagery and the language of divine revelation in his assessment of the Sonnets:

> These poems were born perfect; hardly a single word needed to be changed. The whole experience seems to have taken place at an archaic level of consciousness, where the poet is literally the god's or Muse's scribe. (8)

If their genesis, at least as described by Rilke, required the poet himself to take on certain "feminine" receptive characteristics, the *Sonnets to Orpheus* were also in a very real sense inspired by a young woman, namely a family friend named Wera Ouckama Knoop, news of whose premature death had deeply affected the poet and whose ghostly presence, as Rilke told her mother while the Sonnets were still in progress, "beherrscht und bewegt" ("commands and impels") the cycle as a whole.[42] The central figure of the Sonnets, however, is not Wera, the girlish dancer who appears in a few scattered poems, but, rather, Orpheus, the paradigmatic male poet, whose power, as I will argue more fully in chapter 4, devolves above all from his capacity both to undergo and to mandate transformation. The Sonnets enact the Orphic poet's search for what, in Sonnet 2:12, Rilke calls "nichts wie den wendenden Punkt" ("nothing but the point of inflection" [*SW* 1:758]); their primary exhortation is "Wolle die Wandlung" ("Will transformation"). In contrast to T. S. Eliot, who in *The Four Quartets* attempts to transcend all contradiction by locating "the still point of the turning world," Rilke's quest is for that instant or place of metamorphosis (he had been reading Ovid's *Metamorphoses* the previous year) where stillness is always being converted into motion and motion, conversely, into stillness: where, to state the case both more clearly and more paradoxically, a condition of permanent transience is achieved. "Verwandlung ist nicht Lüge," Rilke would write a few years later (SW 2:266); the purpose of the Sonnets is to show that transformation not only "is no lie" but, in fact, represents truth of the deepest kind.

Perhaps the poem that most vividly illustrates the transformative process as Rilke understood it is Sonnet 2:18, which apostrophizes Wera, the young dancer whose death provided the immediate impetus for the Sonnets:

> Tänzerin: o du Verlegung
> alles Vergehens in Gang: wie brachtest du's dar.
> Und der Wirbel am Schluß, dieser Baum aus Bewegung,
> nahm er nicht ganz in Besitz das erschwungene Jahr?
>
> Blühte nicht, daß ihn dein Schwingen von vorhin umschwärme,
> plötzlich sein Wipfel von Stille? Und über ihr,
> war sie nicht Sonne, war sie nicht Sommer, die Wärme,
> diese unzählige Wärme aus dir?
>
> Aber er trug auch, er trug, dein Baum der Ekstase.
> Sind sie nicht seine ruhigen Früchte: der Krug,
> reifend gestreift, und die gereiftere Vase?
>
> Und in den Bildern: ist nicht die Zeichnung geblieben,
> die deiner Braue dunkler Zug
> rasch an die Wandung der eigenen Wendung geschrieben?
>
> (SW 1:763)

> [Dancer: oh you displacement
> of all transience into movement: how you offered it there.
> And the whirl at the end, this tree made of motion,
> did it not fully possess the accomplished year?
>
> Did not its top branches, so that your previous swirling might
>   swarm around them,
> suddenly bloom with stillness? And above them, too,
> was it not sunshine, was it not summer, the warmth,
> this immeasurable warmth out of you?

But it bore too, it bore, your tree of ecstasy.
Are not these its tranquil fruits: the pitcher,
streaked with ripeness, and the even more ripened vase?

And in the pictures: does not the drawing remain
that your eyebrow's dark stroke
swiftly inscribed on the surface of its own turning?]

Thematically, the poem celebrates the metamorphosis of ceaseless motion into a kind of frail but ecstatic substance: the swirling dancer produces a "tree made of motion," which in turn bears as its "fruit" a vase on which the dancer herself draws, with the stroke of her whirling eyebrow, a lasting picture of her own ephemeral movement.[43] Yet the poem also demonstrates Rilke's Orphic power as a worker of semantic transformations. Even while the poet describes a continual "displacement" of transience into permanence, the poem's very language undergoes precisely the kind of metamorphic process enacted by the dancer. For instance, many of the poem's most important nouns—*Verlegung, Vergehen, Gang, Bewegung, Zeichnung, Zug, Wandung, Wendung*—are actually substantivized verbs, having themselves undergone, on a syntactical level, a transformation that parallels the solidification of the dancer's gestures into a tree, vase, and picture. Through complex wordplay, too, the poem tropes on notions of physical and conceptual instability: for instance, *Wandung* and *Wendung*, identical nouns but for one vowel, stand for the opposing principles of solidity and motion (*Wandung* signifies the wall of a vase or other vessel, while *Wendung* means "turning"), so that their close juxtaposition in the poem serves to question oppositions between transience and permanence yet also confirms the poet's own agility in slipping from one condition to the other. The precariousness both of language and material substance, both of signifier and signified, is further underscored by the word *Wandung* itself, an unusual and unexpected noun that might easily be misread as the more familiar *Wandlung*, which means (needless to say?) transformation, or metamorphosis.

In Sonnet 1:15, a poem that serves as a sort of companion piece to Sonnet 2:18, it is not the dance that leads to the creation of a tree or fruit but, rather, the fruit that inspires the dance. "Tanzt die Orange!" the poem's dancing girls are exhorted; "tanzt den Geschmack der erfahrenen Frucht!" ("Dance the orange. . . . Dance the taste of the experienced fruit!" [*SW* 1:740]). Even more so than the other "Dancer" sonnet, this poem bears clear traces of the influence of Valéry, whose "Le Cimetière marin," a poem greatly admired by Rilke, similarly describes a transformative experience through the metaphor of a tasted fruit:

> Comme le fruit se fond en jouissance,
> Comme en délice il change son absence
> Dans une bouche où sa forme se meurt,
> Je hume ici ma future fumée.
>
> (Valéry, Poésies 101)

> [Just as a fruit melts into pleasure,
> Just as it renders its absence into delight
> In a mouth where its form expires,
> So I inhale here my future smoke.]

In an influential 1939 essay called "Poésie et pensée abstraite," Valéry explains that poetry itself enacts a continuous oscillation between "la forme et le fond" ("form and essence"), between sound and sense, voice and thought, presence and absence (*Oeuvres* 1332–33). In "Le Cimetière marin," accordingly, the poet attempts to capture in language that ephemeral moment when "the fruit"—language itself, perhaps—melts ("se fond") into essence ("le fond"), both transforming presence into absence by surrendering its material form and, conversely, rendering absence into presence by releasing into the "mouth where its form expires" the pure but substanceless pleasure of flavor. Rilke's sonnet describes a similar process of presence-absence, form-essence exchange, as the "warm" and "mute" girls, dancing "the taste of the experienced fruit," themselves become (i.e., render present) the orange's imminent essence:

> Tanzt die Orange. Wer kann sie vergessen,
> wie sie, ertrinkend in sich, sich wehrt
> wider ihr Süßsein. Ihr habt sie besessen.
> Sie hat sich köstlich zu euch bekehrt.
>
> (SW 1:740)

> [Dance the orange. Who can forget it,
> how, drowning in itself, it struggles

against its own sweetness? You have possessed it.
Deliciously, it has converted to you.]

For Rilke as for Valéry, then, poetic pleasure—several generations of French literary theorists, from Barthes to Derrida to Kristeva, have taught us all the possible connotations of Valéry's word *jouissance*—resides in that instant of delicious conversion when fruit and flavor, sweetness and girl, become indistinguishable: when, to paraphrase Yeats, we can no longer tell the dancer from the dance.

Although Orpheus is both the central figure of the Sonnets and, as singer, priest, and magician, the one with whom Rilke most closely identifies himself and his poetic project, the two dancer poems make it abundantly clear that men and demigods have, nonetheless, no monopoly on metamorphic power. Wera the dancer, having fulfilled the Rilkean ideal of dying young, has found, like Orpheus, "den wen-denden Punkt," the "point of inflection" where "transformation is no lie," where an orange can dissolve into a gesture and a gesture, in turn, into pure being. Yet, while Orpheus can return from the world of the dead to that of the living—"Ist er ein Hiesiger? Nein, aus beiden / Reichen erwuchs seine weite Natur" ("Is he from here? No, out of both / realms his wide nature grew" [*SW* 1:734])—Wera, strongly identified with his lost bride, can no longer cross that threshold: "Sei immer tot in Eurydike" ("Be forever dead in Eurydice" [1:759]), the poet exhorts her. For Stephen Mitchell she is Orpheus'

> complement . . . and the second focal point around which the Son-nets elliptically move. . . . She represents absolute receptivity. . . . Like the rose which Rilke later chose for his epitaph, this inner woman is pure Self, the delight of being nobody under so many eyelids. (9)

Charles Segal notes that, in contrast to Orpheus' self-sufficient bride in "Orpheus. Eurydike. Hermes," the Eurydice of the Sonnets "symbol-izes a part of Orpheus himself, . . . those deep springs of his knowledge that extend down into the realm of the dead in a mysterious unity with all being" (143). One might say, then, that Wera/Eurydice is the "inner girl" whom Rilke invoked in "Wendung," the 1914 poem that he had hoped would signal his poetic turning point; she both inhabits and embodies what, in his penultimate Sonnet, he calls "die unerhörte

Mitte" ("the unheard/unheard-of center"): the death at the core of every life, the feminine self at the core of the male poet's being (SW 1:770).

Forever longing for Orpheus to return to her at that "unheard center," the Eurydice of the Sonnets becomes as much a figure of anticipation as one of fulfillment, roused to complete attention—becoming "völlig hörend" ("totally hearing")—only when her powerful husband sings (SW 1:770). Orpheus, meanwhile, by now clearly a figure for Rilke himself, closes the cycle's final poem with an emphatic affirmation of the linguistic potency, identificative autonomy, and transformative possibility ultimately denied to his hell-bound bride: "Zu der stillen Erde sag: ich rinne. / Zu dem raschen Wasser sprich: Ich bin" ("To the silent earth, say: I'm flowing. / To the rushing water, say: I am" [Sonnet 2:29; SW 1:770]). Thus, even more so than in his earlier poetry, Rilke links his own male creative power with an all-encompassing poetic vision, while female existence, however important, still makes up only half the picture. That he generally figures Eurydice's feminine qualities in positive terms is not to be denied. All the same, renunciation, absence, and death are not necessarily the most desirable traits with which female readers—especially those who consider themselves to be self-affirming, present, and very much alive—might wish to be archetypally allied. Clearly, Rilke was less inclined than most male writers of his generation to regard "the female" as a dangerous, weak, or merely frivolous Other. Nevertheless, his poetry exhibits everywhere the self-contradictions of a man who, while avidly searching for inspiration from his "inner girl," often lost sight of the needs and desires of real-life outer women.

Chapter 2

D. H. Lawrence and the
Poetics of Contradiction

Every male comprises male and female in his being, the male always strug-
gling for predominance. A woman likewise consists in male and female, with
female predominant.
                    —D. H. Lawrence, *Study of Thomas Hardy*, 1914–15

A child is either male or female; in the whole of its psyche and physique is
either male or female, and will remain either male or female as long as life
last. And every single cell in every male child is male, and every cell in every
female child is female.
                    —D. H. Lawrence, *Fantasia of the Unconscious*, 1922

Conviction, with Lawrence, provides no sure measure of consistency;
the more he sounds like Moses thundering God's truth from the moun-
taintop, in fact, the greater seems the likelihood that he will just as fer-
vently espouse an opposite "truth" later on. Hence the confusingly
varied view of Lawrence with which both scholarship and popular
mythology confront us. Critics and biographers, like the devil, can
quote him to their own purposes and have thus managed to reveal him,
according to their biases, either as sensitive feminist or violent misogy-
nist, as profound prophet or petulant hysteric, as effeminate weakling
or macho brute. In fact, Lawrence betrayed the traits of all these per-
sonae, alternatingly and at times simultaneously. He has, accordingly,
inspired a rash of often oxymoronic epithets: Stuart P. Sherman called
him a "philosophic caveman," Paul Rosenfeld a "mystic realist" and
"realist mystic," T. S. Eliot both a "blind servant" and a "fatal leader,"
Witter Bynner "a bad baby masquerading as a good Mephistopheles,"
William Tindall a man with "the sensitivity of a cat" but "the impa-
tience of Donald Duck," and Norman Mailer "a Hitler in a teapot" who
was also, nonetheless, "the blessed breast of tender love."[1] Yet, if
Lawrence's personality was self-contradictory, the literature he pro-
duced was even more so; the intensity with which he lived, thought,
and wrote drove him to artistic extremes both of stunning brilliance

and, at times, of appalling awfulness. As John Middleton Murry, whose own love-hate relationship with Lawrence was marked by a pendulatory ambivalence, noted in a 1922 review: "Mr. Lawrence is like the little girl. When he is good, he is very, very good; and when he is bad, he is horrid."[2]

Edward Sackville-West stated the case even more colorfully: "When Mr. Lawrence is at his best, he is the equal of Blake in his finest prophetic mood; at his worst, we seem to hear a street-arab shrieking abuse at someone who has not given him a large enough tip."[3] Lawrence as prophet is a familiar figure, intense eyes blazing from the dustcovers of a shelf load of dramatically titled books: *D. H. Lawrence: Novelist, Poet, Prophet* (Spender); *The Utopian Vision of D. H. Lawrence* (Goodheart); *Oedipus in Nottingham* (Weiss); *Pilgrim of the Apocalypse* (Gregory); *The Savage Pilgrimage* (Carswell); *The Psychic Mariner* (Marshall); *"Not I, but the Wind . . ."* (Frieda Lawrence); *The Priest of Love* (Moore).[4] Yet the more balanced of these accounts—those without the purely adulatory or declamatory agendas that mar far too many studies of Lawrence—are careful to acknowledge the ridiculous side of Lawrence alongside the sublime. For, as E. M. Forster noted in 1930, even Lawrence's most bizarre or irritating conceits were no aberrations:

> We are inclined to say: "What a pity! What a pity to go on about the subconscious and the solar plexus and maleness and femaleness and African darkness and the cosmic beetle when you can write so touchingly about men and women, and so beautifully about flowers." But we must realize that, in his queer make-up, things were connected, and that if he did not preach and prophesy he could not see and feel.[5]

It is the furious energy of the "street-arab," in other words, that fuels the fervor of the prophet and the prophet's intense straining after vision that guarantees, in turn, the heightened perceptivity and imaginative insight that characterize Lawrence's finest work.

Graham Hough asserts that Lawrence, much though he may have longed to be a "teacher of wisdom," never really achieved the visionary status he sought; a true prophet, for Hough, "can only utter his mature message when his personal problems have been transcended, as Lawrence's never were" (230). Yet prophecy, as an inherently paradoxical mode of discourse, could be said not to require transcendence so much as tension—between passive receptivity and active utterance, between self and self-effacement, between pure emotion and the shaping forces of language. Lawrence himself was well aware of this. Like his Romantic predecessor Blake, he inhabited an intensely dualistic universe in which creativity and even prophecy were seen to spring not from harmony but, rather, from opposition. "Without Contraries is no progression," wrote Blake in *The Marriage of Heaven and Hell*, and Lawrence echoes him in his "Notes for *Birds, Beasts and Flowers*": "In the tension of opposites all things have their being."[6] Whether he envisions these opposed forces as ultimately merging or postulates their eventual transcendence into a third, mystically charged element (the "Holy Ghost") or holds them eternally "balanced in equilibrium" like Birkin's two marriage stars in *Women in Love*, it is on their creative interaction that Lawrence's emphasis invariably falls.[7]

At the heart of his dualistic schema is his theory of gender. As the two quotes opening this chapter demonstrate, Lawrence's views on sexual and psychic morphology changed radically between 1915 and 1922; whereas in the *Study of Thomas Hardy* he claims that "every male comprises male and female in his being" and that "a woman likewise consists in male and female," in *Fantasia of the Unconscious* he insists that "a child is either male or female; in the whole of its psyche and physique is either male or female, and will remain either male or female as long as life last." What links both statements, despite their disagreement about the gender composition of human individuals, is Lawrence's continuing belief in "maleness" and "femaleness" as universal principles that are fundamentally separate, invariable, and opposed. His conviction in *Study of Thomas Hardy* that "Everything that stirs in life, every single impulse, is either male or female" (55) is intensified rather than contradicted in *Fantasia of the Unconscious*, with its rigid insistence on "pure maleness in a man, pure femaleness in a woman" (185).

"Maleness," as defined in *Study of Thomas Hardy*, means movement, change, knowledge, action, light, abstraction, consciousness, spirit, utterance, the movement toward discovery, and the "will-to-motion"; while "femaleness" denotes stability, immutability, feeling, being, darkness, the senses, the body, instinct, the soul, the movement toward origin, and the "will-to-inertia."[8] H. M. Daleski has argued that Lawrence, "though believing intensely in himself as a male, was fundamentally identified with the female principle as he himself defined it in the essay on Hardy" (10), an identification that precipitated both emotional conflict and artistic inconsistency. Certainly, like Rilke, Lawrence at first enthusiastically welcomed, indeed encouraged, the intrusion of "the female principle" into his own life and art, affirming its importance to his creative vitality. Later, however, in his attempt to reject all that might be construed as "feminine" about himself and his writing, he came to formulate both writing and prophetic vision as exclusively male activities, although, in doing so, he was forced not only to find new names for some of his most fertile sources of inspiration but also to disclaim the tenderness, balance, and emotional complexity that constituted his own greatest strengths as a writer. Without the tension between opposed forces—between the maleness and femaleness that he so carefully set against each other in *Study of Thomas Hardy*, claiming both elements to be necessary to artistic creativity—Lawrence's work tended to collapse into a one-dimensional didacticism.

It is in part that didacticism, no doubt, that has earned him the epithet of prophet, yet Lawrence's lasting acclaim as a writer has depended not on the thundering conviction of his essays and misanthropic "leadership" novels but, instead, on a formal and ideological complexity that foregrounds rather than represses paradox and oppositional tension, including especially gender tension. His poems, to be sure, have been criticized ever since their publication precisely for their marked lack of self-restraint, their formal incoherence, and their frankly confessional tone. "Too much body and emotions" was H.D.'s pronouncement upon reading the manuscript of *Look! We Have Come Through!*,[9] and Bertrand Russell famously complained, "They may have come through, but I don't see why I should look" (qtd. in Moore 369). R. P. Blackmur continued the declamatory trend in 1935, when he labeled Lawrence's poetry "hysterical," insisting that the "demon" that Lawrence himself identified as the source of his poetic power was "exactly that outburst of personal feeling which needed the discipline of craft to become a poem" (255).[10] Yet critics since Blackmur have gradually come to acknowledge that Lawrence's poetry, though ranging, at its worst, from the rawly undisciplined to the embarrassingly sentimental, exhibits at its best a complexity of form and feeling that characterizes the finest efforts of literary modernism. Sandra Gilbert places Lawrence in the confessional tradition of Whitman, Meredith, Hardy,

Yeats, and, more recently, Lowell, Plath, and Sexton, suggesting that his poetry has been disregarded only because, as "a Romantic in modern dress," Lawrence cultivated an anti-ironic stance toward his subject matter more reminiscent of Wordsworth or Coleridge than, for instance, of Eliot or Stevens (Gilbert, *Acts* 13, 61). And Ross Murfin goes even further, defending Lawrence as a full-blown, double-visioned modernist whose anxiety of influence toward his Romantic and post-Romantic predecessors—Blake, Shelley, Swinburne, Hardy, and especially Whitman—results not in a "casual poetry for the present" but, rather, a sophisticated "new hybrid of past forms" (32). Lawrence's whole originality as poet, for Murfin, in fact resides not in any flight from self-reflective irony but in his conscious heightening of the paradoxes inherent to his own, and to his Romantic predecessors', visionary poetry (52).

A 1930 obituary in the *Manchester Guardian* called Lawrence, in a single breath, both "a magnificently equipped craftsman" and "a man possessed" (Draper 326). As craftsman alone, Lawrence could rely neither on the versification skills of a Rilke or Yeats nor on the finely attuned ear of an H.D.; his poetic power in fact depends largely on his prophetic mannerisms, or on what Yeats would have called his "passionate intensity," which is perhaps why his self-conscious early verse seems, for the most part, precious and strained. But, although his most powerful work, and particularly his best poetry, is that which achieves a fine balance between inspiration and craft—between what Lawrence called "pure passionate experience" and the shaping forces of language—his own discussions of poetry tend to focus on inspiration alone, with little mention of the "subtle inter-relatedness" that he was to name as a primary characteristic of the novel.[11] From his 1913 description of the "purely lyric poet" giving himself, "right down to his sex, to his mood, utterly and abandonedly, whirl[ing] himself round . . . till he spontaneously combusts into verse," to his 1919 assertion that free verse conveys "the instant, the quick; the very jetting source of all will-be and has-been," to his 1928 image of the poet making a slit in the umbrella of poetic convention and thus furnishing a glimpse of the "strange and forever surging chaos" in which we really live, Lawrence would consistently figure poetry as prophecy: a visionary awareness achieved and expressed through submission to a powerful, unknown force.[12]

Inspiration and Sex: The *Study of Thomas Hardy*

The inconsistencies in Lawrence's work appear only when he tries to give that creative force a name. In the preface to his 1928 *Collected Poems*, recalling the Sunday afternoon on which, at age nineteen, he "perpetrated" his first two poems, he calls it "my demon":

> Any young lady might have written them and been pleased with them; as I was pleased with them. But it was after that, when I was twenty, that my real demon would now and then get hold of me and shake more real poems out of me, making me uneasy. (*LCP* 27)

A few paragraphs later he adds:

> A young man is afraid of his demon and puts his hand over the demon's mouth sometimes and speaks for him. And the things the young man says are very rarely poetry. So I have tried to let the demon say his say, and to remove the passages where the young man intruded. (28)

The young man, or for that matter the young lady, is Lawrence as conventional poet; the demon, his creative or prophetic self, is the powerful Other whom he desired yet feared to let speak through him. That Other was in some sense, of course, a part of himself, the Id in Freud's psychic constellation. Yet the demon also seems to have represented something or someone external to Lawrence, a dangerous and at times terrifying force to which he nevertheless consciously tried to hold himself open and which he figured, when not as demon, as deity: "I often think one ought to be able to pray, before one works," he confessed in a 1913 letter to Ernst Collings; "I always feel as if I stood naked for the fire of Almighty God to go through me—and it's rather an awful feeling."[13]

Another name for the demon/deity was sex: contact with the Other in the form of a woman. Lawrence's boyhood friend William Hopkin made the association humorously when he recalled how Alice Dax, a married woman with whom the young Lawrence had had a brief affair, once admitted:

> "I gave Bert sex. I had to. He was over at our house, struggling with a poem he couldn't finish, so I took him upstairs and gave

him sex. Then he came downstairs and finished the poem." (qtd. in Moore 112)

Lawrence himself would no doubt have given the story a more mystical cast, injecting at the very least some of the "witty, *Yellow Book* eroticism" (Gilbert, *Acts* 30) that permeates "Mystery," an early poem about sex and inspiration whose fine Beardsley-drawing contours make it one of Lawrence's most polished pre-1912 efforts. It forms part of his "Helen" sequence, a group of poems, with titles such as "Tease," "Repulsed," and "Coldness in Love," concerned largely with the hot-blooded young writer's passion for an unyielding, intellectual woman. While many of the poems in the series strike an unsubtle tone of embittered male frustration ("Is there no hope / Between your thighs, far, far from your peering sight?" [*LCP* 119]), in "Mystery" the poet adopts what Lawrence himself could only have described as a feminine stance toward his beloved, figuring himself as a vessel of pure emotion:

> Now I am all
> One bowl of kisses,
> Such as the tall
> Slim votaresses
> Of Egypt filled
> For divine excesses.

> (96)

Waiting passively to be consumed by the "Most High"—the lover as deity—the poet places himself in the adulatory, servile role of the Egyptian votaresses he evokes. Yet it is not only abject self-annihilation that he desires when he begs his beloved to "drink me up"; for, in consuming him, she gives him back his male sexual role, as he literally fills her with himself. The result is a mingling, a merging, and, ultimately, a mystery:

> Ah, drink me up
> That I may be
> Within your cup
> Like a mystery,
> Like wine that is still
> In ecstasy.

Glimmering still
In ecstasy
Commingled wines
Of you and me
In one fulfil
The mystery.

(96–97)

The notion of sex as mystery, expressed here with measured play-fulness, was soon to become a major preoccupation for Lawrence, one that, especially with his 1914 *Study of Thomas Hardy* and the poems of *Look! We Have Come Through!,* he would come to take very seriously indeed. His theories linking sex and inspiration began to find their most explicit expression after 1912, the year in which, following a series of intellectually stimulating but sexually frustrating relationships with young women such as Jessie Chambers, Louie Burrows, and Helen Corke, Lawrence eloped to Germany with the older, married, and sex-ually savvy Frieda Weekley. By 1913, in rapturous letters home to friends in England, he was specifically linking sexual union with visionary experience, gushing to Henry Savage that "sex is the foun-tainhead, through which life bubbles up into the self from the unknown"[14] and declaring, in a much-quoted letter to Arthur McLeod, that gender relations represent the key to all creativity:

> I think the only re-sourcing of art, re-vivifying it, is to make it more the joint work of man and woman. I think *the* one thing to do, is for men to have courage to draw nearer to woman, expose themselves to them, and be altered by them: and for women to accept and admit men. . . . Because the source of all life and knowledge is in man and woman, and the source of all living is in the interchange and the meeting and mingling of these two: man-life and woman-life, man-knowledge and woman-knowledge, man-being and woman-being.[15]

Although critics have disagreed violently about whether Frieda Lawrence ultimately acted as a help or a hindrance to her husband's artistry,[16] her importance to his early work should not be understated. She probably introduced him, through her own close personal connec-tion with the writer and former Freudian disciple Otto Gross, to the ideas of what Martin Green has called the German "matriarchalist" movement: a school of thought, promoted by such Munich intellectuals as Alfred Schuler, Ludwig Klages, Karl Wolfskehl, and the poet Stefan George, "naming love [as] the supreme locus of the unconscious, the emotional, the spontaneous, the primitive, the original, the organic, and the fertile" and embodied, according to Green, in the "inarticulate flesh" of Frieda Weekley herself (368–69). Her most significant influence on Lawrence, both in the early years of their relationship and during Lawrence's later misogynist period, lay in her role as a sort of living archetype, as she helped first to confirm Lawrence's positive stereotypes concerning women and inspiration and later, when their marriage began to sour, to shape his most negative ones. Frieda also contributed to Lawrence's work in a very concrete way, serving as a model for several of his fictional characters, offering criticisms of his portrayals of women, and even penning, as Jessie Chambers did for *Sons and Lovers*, "little female bits" of text for inclusion in his novels (Simpson 150).

Although his wife undoubtedly provided the richest source, Lawrence was to solicit similar aid and inspiration from numerous women throughout his career. He virtually never sought literary advice from or undertook joint projects with men, for, as Hilary Simpson has noted in a discussion of Lawrence's literary "trespassings" into the realm of the female, "it seems to be the pervasive concept of femininity as 'raw material' and masculinity as 'shaping force' which underlies his use of women's writing" (147).[17] The *Study of Thomas Hardy*, with its insistence that "the male exists in doing, the female in being," confirms that he ultimately regarded literary production as the prerogative of men alone. Yet at the same time Lawrence willingly granted to certain women an actively prophetic role akin to his own vatic function. To be sure, he condemned the excessive spirituality of such fictional characters as Hardy's Tess Durbeyfield and Sue Bridehead, insisting that they belonged to "the old-woman type of witch or prophetess, which adhered to the male principle, and destroyed the female" (*Study* 109). But he regarded several real-life women, personal friends such as Ottoline Morrell and Hilda Aldington (H.D.), as powerful priestesses and prophetesses of female mystery, representing "a special type, a special race of women" who, "like Cassandra in Greece and some of the great woman saints," could serve as "the great *media* of truth, of the deepest truth."[18]

That "deepest truth," however, would turn out for Lawrence to reside not in a special female knowledge but, rather, in "the great male principle"—a principle that, as Lawrence speculates in *Study of Thomas Hardy*, is "only weakly evidenced in man during certain periods," so that at such times "the Bridegroom," "hidden away from woman, for a century or centuries," can appear to certain properly receptive females (the "great woman saints") only in the form of "the voice, or the Wind" of religious vision:

> So I think it was . . . during the medieval period; that the greatest women of the period knew that the Bridegroom did not exist for them in the body, but as the Christ, the Spirit. (*Study* 85–86)

As for Cassandra, Lawrence regards her as "a true prophetess" primarily because of her total submission to Apollo, the male god of poetry and prophecy:

> Cassandra submitted to Apollo, and gave him the Word of affiance, brought forth prophecy to him, not children. . . . He breathed His Grace upon her: and she conceived and brought forth a prophecy. It was . . . the marriage of the female spirit with the male spirit, bodiless. (109)

Lawrence's choice of Cassandra as the ideal female prophet is a problematic and tellingly paradoxical one, for he neglects to mention that, although she is remembered as an acute and grimly accurate seer, the great Homeric prophetess was doomed in her own lifetime never to be believed, a curse inflicted upon her by Apollo when she ultimately rejected his sexual advances. Cassandra in fact represents, if anything, the negative face of possession and prophecy, and particularly—given the myth's explicitly sexual dynamics of conquest, resistance, and revenge—of female prophecy.[19]

Despite the lip service, then, that Lawrence pays to female prophecy and prophetic power, the overarching argument of the *Study of Thomas Hardy* is that, since man represents activity and woman passivity, woman in the final count embodies little more than the dark and silent inspiration for man's virile creativity—a familiar and damning message. Yet in his system of gender classification, based though it is on a whole series of Western gender stereotypes,[20] Lawrence also offers several startling surprises. Under the rubric *female*, for instance, he includes not Love, which he labels a male principle, but, rather, its opposing force, Law—his reasoning being that women, as rearers of children and arbiters of household order, have a far greater stake than their wage-earning, financially independent husbands in upholding those societal standards dictating a man's legal responsibility to support his family. While this line of thought is not, perhaps, in itself unconventional, Lawrence's association of women with "the Law" leads him in turn to classify "God the Father," the ultimate lawgiver, as a female principle or entity. That Christ, the God-Made-Flesh of Christian mythology, should be considered a pure, abstract, "male" spirit, while God, Western civilization's most potent symbol of patriarchal authority, becomes allied with the "female" body, soul, and senses, represents only one of the more bizarre aspects of Lawrence's dualistic schema.

Feminists have, of course, long since pointed out the unavoidable contradictions produced by any system of gender classification as rigid as Lawrence's. Victorian society, for instance, on one level viewed women as spiritually refined beings whose role was to hold the raw, animal urges of their men in check yet at the same time perpetuated, whether through art, rhetoric, or political structure, the traditional association of man with culture and intellect and of woman with nature and emotion. Lawrence's attitude toward his own family in fact betrays just such a self-contradiction: his mother, as portrayed in letters, stories, and especially *Sons and Lovers*, exhibits many of the characteristics that Lawrence himself most strongly linked with maleness, such as excessive abstraction, spirituality, and intellectualism, while his coarse miner father embodies "female" physicality, sensuality, and, through his association with the mines, access to the forces of mystery and darkness. Lawrence fiercely sided with his mother against his father during his parents' lifetimes but then retrospectively reversed his alliance, an indication of his own confusion about where his own stronger allegiance lay.

The poetics of inspiration that Lawrence articulates in the *Study of Thomas Hardy* is, not surprisingly, laced with similar paradoxes. Lawrence points to poetry itself, for instance, as a specific example of the male and female impulses working in fruitful conjunction. Yet, rather than linking the female principle, as he does elsewhere, with the dark, uncontrolled, intuitively charged "raw material" of creativity, he suggests that the visionary, progressive impulse in poetry corresponds to the male will-to-motion, while the constraints of traditional form represent the female will-to-inertia:

> The very adherence to rhyme and regular rhythm is a concession to the Law, a concession to the body, to the being and requirements of the body. They are an admission of the living, positive inertia which is the other half of life, other than the pure will-to-motion. In this consummation, they are the resistance and response of the Bride in the arms of the Bridegroom. (91)

Elsewhere in the *Study*, listing creative men throughout history in order of their degree of "pure maleness"—from Shelley, Plato, and Raphael, men of excessive spirituality and hence of excessive maleness, down through more female-identified figures such as Michelangelo, Shakespeare, Tolstoy, and Saint Paul—Lawrence asserts that "it is only a disproportion, or a dissatisfaction, which makes the man struggle into articulation" (71), thus implying that the greatest artists are in fact not those androgynous types who "comprise male and female in [their] being" but, rather, those who, lacking the female element in themselves, must strive to achieve sexual unity in art; for, as Lawrence would write in a 1915 letter to Bertrand Russell, "the man embraces in the woman all that is not himself."[21] Despite such self-contradictions, the *Study of Thomas Hardy* does make one point consistently and adamantly: whatever maleness and femaleness may actually denote, and whether great male artists have a feminine side to themselves or must seek "the female" elsewhere, all creativity in any case requires, for Lawrence, the participation of both principles, for "no new thing has ever arisen, or can arise, save out of the impulse of the male upon the female, the female upon the male" (56). This interaction of male and female includes but is not limited to sexual union, for, if sex itself proves unsatisfactory and unfulfilling, then

> a man must seek elsewhere than in woman for the female to possess his soul, to fertilise him and make him big with increase. And the female exists in much more than his woman. And the finding of it for himself gives a man his vision, his God. (57)

What is particularly striking about this passage is Lawrence's own self-identification with traditionally female sexual passivity and with the female processes of gestation and birth. If on the one hand Lawrence's poetics of prophecy places women in the passive, receptive roles of Cassandra or the medieval mystics, on the other hand he stresses that man's search for "his vision, his God" cannot be accomplished through any macho overpowering of the female principle; rather, the man himself must be "possessed," "fertilised," and made "big with increase," much as the poet in "Mystery" can only be fulfilled by yielding himself completely to the sexual ministrations of his beloved. Lawrence's humbly receptive stance resembles that of Rilke's monk in the *Stunden-Buch*, who figures himself as a woman begging a powerful male God to come to him as a man comes in sex to his beloved. But, like Rilke, Lawrence further confuses the issue by linking his God not only with fertilizing maleness but also with the "Eternality, Infinity, Immutability" of the female principle (*Study* 58); "if you read David['s] psalms," he writes in a 1913 letter to Henry Savage, "you will see that God is to him like a great woman he adores."[22] Hence, "a man, when he lies with his woman, . . . may concurrently be with God, and so get increase of his soul" (57).

More on Inspiration and Sex: *Look! We Have Come Through!*

God Almighty, the demon, the female principle, the Other without or within: in *Study of Thomas Hardy* and works of the same period Lawrence associates all of these with creative inspiration and thus, in a sense, with one another. The poems of his 1917 volume *Look! We Have Come Through!* represent his most sustained attempt to open himself to these sources of vision and to draw poetic power from his new-found sexual identity without being overwhelmed by the very forces he invokes to inspire him. He readily enough abandons himself, with a quasireligious prophetic fervor still quite new to him, to the voice of creative inspiration ("Not I, not I, but the wind that blows through me!" [*LCP* 250]). Yet at the same time, in poems such as "Manifesto," he cautions against "mixing, merging" with the woman, "the terrible *other*" (267). Although eager to submit to the unknown in nature, to "the surpassing impulse which has our end in view beyond us,"[23] he remains unwilling to abandon himself in the same way to sexual ecstasy, "the unknown within the dark embrace of a wife" (*Study of Thomas Hardy* 105).

Lawrence himself readily acknowledged that his attitude toward women, and particularly toward his own wife, was highly self-contradictory. In the summarizing "Argument" that opens *Look! We Have Come Through!* he identifies emotional ambivalence as the volume's major theme:

> After much struggling and loss in love and in the world of man, the protagonist throws in his lot with a woman who is already married. Together they go into another country, she perforce leaving her children behind. The conflict of love and hate goes on between the man and the woman, and between these two and the world around them, till it reaches some sort of conclusion, they transcend into some condition of blessedness. (*LCP* 191)

In "The Reality of Peace," published in the same year as *Look! We Have Come Through!*, Lawrence calls "the conflict of love and hate" the key, ultimately, to peace and creative fulfillment—for "it is not of love that we are fulfilled, but of love in such intimate equipoise with hate that the transcendence takes place" (*Phoenix* 693). Eleven years later, however, in his 1928 *Collected Poems*, Lawrence would omit from *Look!*'s opening "Argument" the last seven words—"they transcend into some condition of blessedness"—perhaps because he had by then ceased to believe that any "condition of blessedness" was possible in a marriage or perhaps simply because he recognized that the poems in the volume enact the "conflict of love and hate" itself rather than promising a simple, harmonious conclusion to the battle of the sexes.

Lawrence's 1912 poem "Bei Hennef," which he would later identify as opening *Look!*'s "new cycle" of poems about his life as a married man (*LCP* 28), conveys the ambivalence with which, even in the salad days of his relationship with Frieda, he viewed his dream of fulfillment through knowledge of the female. Waiting for a train in the small German town of Hennef,[24] he invokes the banal yet slightly melancholy tranquillity of his surroundings—"The little river twittering in the twilight, / The wan, wondering look of the pale sky"—before declaring, "This is almost bliss." The unexpected qualification, "*almost* bliss," jars, casting a doubtful shadow upon the poet's epiphanic love declaration a few lines later: "And at last I know my love for you is here; / I can see it all, it is whole like the twilight." Heterosexual love, according to the dualistic cosmogony that Lawrence would schematize two years later in *Study of Thomas Hardy*, should result in utter fulfillment and satisfaction. Yet somehow, he suggests here, the union of complementary impulses does not alone guarantee happiness:

> You are the call and I am the answer,
> You are the wish, and I the fulfilment,
> You are the night, and I the day.
>
>> What else? it is perfect enough.
>> It is perfectly complete,
>> You and I,
>> What more—?
>
> Strange, how we suffer in spite of this!

                                                                    (203)

The poem's final sentence, with its assonental echo of "This is almost bliss," underlines the poet's sense of bafflement and lack, yet at the same time it hints at subtle self-critique. "You are the call and I am the answer" is the kind of Lawrentian aphorism that gets frequently quoted, and appropriately so, to illustrate the poet's rigidly dualistic but affectionately celebratory theory of gender difference.[25] Yet the poem itself, set in those murky twilit hours when darkness cannot be distinguished from light, belies Lawrence's own faith in any simple night-day paradigm of complementary calls and answers. Indeed, by inscribing failure in its own claim to success, the poem questions the validity of the very gender ideology it seems to espouse. "You are the call and I am the answer," a phrase perhaps intended more as wishful fiat than as declared truth, itself seems to represent a wistful "call" for the kind of emotional fulfillment to which the poet claims to be, but obviously is not, the "answer."

Another 1912 poem, "In the Dark," presents a similar self-critique in the form of an argument between a husband and wife, as the woman rebels against her husband's insistence labeling her a creature of darkness and night: "No, no, I dance in the sun, I'm a thing of life" (LCP 211–12). When the husband tries to soothe her back to sleep by linking her to the mystery of the natural world, the wife retorts, "But let me be myself, not a river or a tree"—words that H.D. may well have echoed five years later, when Lawrence cast her as the Tree of Life (and himself as "Gawd Almighty") in a Garden of Eden charade.[26] With the poem's dialogical structure Lawrence heeds, quite literally, his own recommendation that poetry should combine the voices of both male and female. Yet, with the wife's dogged resistance to her husband's attempts to define her, he also admits not only that his gender categories—"You are the night, and I the day"—may not be universally accepted but that they can be hurtful, even harmful, to women.

The wife's fear of losing her own identity in the face of her husband's defining power in fact mirrors Lawrence's own anxiety toward his sources of inspiration—especially toward "the *female*," which he defined in 1913 as "not necessarily woman but most obviously woman," and without which, he would assert a year later, "there is no getting of a vision."[27] In poems such as "Mutilation" and "Humiliation" the poet contemplates the possibility that his wife might leave him and arrives at last at the anguished realization that "she is *necessary*! / *Necessary*, and I have no choice! (*LCP* 215): a recognition, in Sandra Gilbert's gloss, that if "she—the other—left him, he would no longer, paradoxically, be himself" (Gilbert, *Acts* 101). At the same time, Lawrence's "Song of a Man Who Is Not Loved" vividly illustrates how the poet's fear of isolation, of being deserted by the fertilizing female, shades into an opposite, even contradictory, fear of being overwhelmed by inspiration, by the powerful creative force of the Other. "The space of the world is immense, . . . / If I turn quickly, I am terrified," he laments, suggesting that, as long as he remains "a man who is not loved," "isolated in the universe," he cannot harness, and even risks being annihilated by, the force of creative inspiration: the "big wind" that blows him "like a gadfly into the dusk" (*LCP* 223).

Later in *Look! We Have Come Through!* Lawrence seems to pass into a state of poetic grace wherein the previously frightening "big wind" of inspiration becomes a "fine, fine wind" "blowing the new direction of Time." Following on the heels of his rapturous "Song of a Man Who Is Loved"—"So at last I touch / All that I am-not in softness, sweet softness, for she is such"—is love's happy consequence, the "Song of a Man Who Has Come Through," with its joyously self-admonitory declaration of submission:

> Not I, not I, but the wind that blows through me!
> A fine wind is blowing the new direction of Time.
> If only I let it bear me, carry me, if only it carry me!
> If only I am sensitive, subtle, oh, delicate, a winged gift!

> If only, most lovely of all, I yield myself and am borrowed
> By the fine, fine wind that takes its course through the chaos of
>   the world
> Like a fine, an exquisite chisel, a wedge-blade inserted:
> If only I am keen and hard like the sheer tip of a wedge
> Driven by invisible blows,
> The rock will split, we shall come at the wonder, we shall find the
>   Hesperides.
>
> (LCP 250)

The unquestionably sexual imagery of these final lines—the hard, driving wedge tip, the climactic "we shall come"—suggests that "the wonder" itself represents that mystical sexual transcendence for which the poet of "Mystery" longed: knowledge of the unknown, that is, through fruitful contact with the Other. "Love," after all, as we recall from Lawrence's letters of this period, "is that I go to a woman, to know myself, and knowing myself to go further, to explore in to the unknown, and open my discovery to all humanity;[28]" and "Sex is the fountainhead, through which life bubbles up into the self from the unknown."[29]

Ecstatically optimistic through its first two stanzas, Lawrence's "Song" introduces in its third a momentary note of trouble:

> What is the knocking?
> What is the knocking at the door in the night?
> It is somebody wants to do us harm.
>
> No, no, it is the three strange angels.
> Admit them, admit them.
>
> (LCP 250)

Like the three angels who appear to Abraham in the Old Testament with news of Sarah's fertility,[30] the enigmatic figures banging on the poet's door seem to represent some kind of fertilizing force—perhaps demonic, perhaps godly, but in either case powerful and absolutely Other—that the poet must not only admit but also submit to if he is to be inspired creatively. In a slightly earlier poem called "Lady Wife," however, Lawrence explicitly associates the three angels who "came to Abraham" and "stayed / In his house awhile" not with a divine creative power but, rather, with the poet's own wife, a "bird-blithe, lovely / Angel in disguise" whom he peevishly commands to

> Rise up and go, I have no use for you
> > And your blithe, glad mien.
> No angels here, for me no goddesses,
> > Nor any Queen.

> > > > > (234)

The poem is one of Lawrence's not infrequent tirades against motherhood, a rebellion against the female Law that he elsewhere names as a necessary component of creativity. Unwilling here to allow women even their humble sphere of domestic influence, he forcefully evicts the "Angel in the House," that self-sacrificing Victorian ideal later critiqued by Virginia Woolf:[31]

> Queens, ladies, angels, women rare,
> > I have had enough.
> Put sackcloth on, be crowned with powdery ash,
> > Be common stuff.

> And serve now, woman, serve, as a woman should,
> > Implicitly.
> Since I must serve and struggle with the imminent
> > Mystery.

> > > > > (234)

That the poet's own "Lady Wife" might also serve as his "strange angel" of poetic inspiration is an admission that Lawrence does not seem willing to make here except intertextually. Yet the circularity of his logic is undeniable: although he commands woman to serve man, he also covertly implies that man must serve woman, since the "wonder" and the "Mystery" to which he willingly submits himself are so inextricably linked throughout *Look! We Have Come Through!* with the female principle or, at the very least, with the interaction of male and female impulses.

Lawrence's ambivalence toward the female as a source of inspiration is perhaps most vividly expressed in "Rabbit Snared in the Night," a poem that both recalls his early, haunting "Love on the Farm" and anticipates the fascination with brutality, victimization, and power that marks such later "leadership phase" prose works as "The Fox," "The Woman Who Rode Away," and *The Plumed Serpent*. Intimating that creativity is fueled by both love and hate and, moreover, that sexual desire and physical violence share a common impulse, Lawrence goes on to suggest, even more disturbingly, that violence is ultimately the fault of the victim because it is the victim—the rabbit, the woman—whose Otherness "sparks" a glaring "bale-fire" on "the tinder of my [the poet's] nerves." Thus, speaking to the terrified creature that lies on his lap "with a hot, plumb, live weight, / heavy as a stone, passive," the poet answers his own cold-bloodedly curious question, "Why should I want to throttle / you, bunny?" with a vehement self-conviction that seems to feed upon its own increasing fervor:

'Tis not me, bunny.
It was you that engendered it,
with that fine, demoniacal spark
you jetted off your eye at me.
I did not want it,
this furnace, this draught-maddened fire
which mounts up my arms
making them swell with turgid, ungovernable strength.

'Twas not *I* that wished it,
that my fingers should turn into these flames
avid and terrible
that they are at this moment.

It must have been *your* inbreathing, gaping desire
that drew this red gush in me;
I must be reciprocating *your* vacuous, hidden passion.

(*LCP* 241)

The implications of this argument in terms of Lawrence's gender ideology are at once convoluted and frighteningly clear. If, Lawrence suggests here, the apparently passive rabbit, a figure for the woman-as-Other, throws off a creative spark from the "unutterable darkness" (241) of her eye, then she should not be surprised when the poet subsequently turns, as he does in poems such as "She Looks Back" and

"Lady Wife," and uses against her the forces of the newfound demonic power to which she, paradoxically, first granted him access.

Not all the poems of *Look! We Have Come Through!* present such a grim view of gender relations; in fact, the volume ends with an attempt to resolve the love-hate conflict once and for all, not through the achievement of an unrealistic state of harmony but, rather, through an admission of mutual Otherness, accomplished through a submission by both parties to a

> balanced, eternal orbit
> wherein we circle on our fate
> in strange conjunction.
>
> ("Both Sides of the Medal," *LCP* 236)

Two of Lawrence's most sweepingly visionary long poems, "New Heaven and Earth" and "Manifesto," act as a sort of bridge between the autobiographical marriage diary of *Look! We Have Come Through!* and the new, very different thematic preoccupations of *Birds, Beasts and Flowers*, describing how a "new world" of visionary awareness, mystic knowledge, and sexual fulfillment can be entered only once the poet has passed through a terrifying but regenerating death experience: the epic descent to the underworld that Frank Kermode has identified as part of a persistent eschatological trope in Lawrence's major novels.[32] "New Heaven and Earth" opens with a description of the kind of self-annihilating universal harmony that Lawrence loathed; the poet recalls his sense of horror upon realizing that he, his creations, and even his sources of inspiration—his God, his woman—have all merged with one another, so that everything in the world has become "tainted with myself":

> I shall never forget the maniacal horror of it all in the end
> when everything was me, I knew it all already, I anticipated it all
>   in my soul
> because I was the author and the result
> I was the God and the creation at once;
> creator, I looked at my creation;
> created, I looked at myself, the creator:
> it was a maniacal horror in the end.
>
> I was a lover, I kissed the woman I loved,
> and God of horror, I was kissing also myself.
>
> (*LCP* 257)

"Manifesto" describes, in turn, a way out of the horror: the man and the woman must descend into the terrifying, deathlike realm of the unknown, so that, having dared contact with utter Otherness—"that which is not me in any sense"—they can both be reborn into "a surpassing singleness of mankind":

> When she has put her hand on my secret, darkest sources, the
> darkest outgoing,
> when it has struck home to her, like a death, "this is *him!*"
> she has no part in it, no part whatever,
> it is the terrible *other*,
> when she knows the fearful *other flesh*, ah, darkness unfathomable
> and fearful, contiguous and concrete,
> when she is slain against me, and lies in a heap like one outside
> the house,
> when she passes away as I have passed away,
> being pressed up against the *other*,
> then I shall be glad, I shall not be confused with her,
> I shall be cleared, distinct, single as if burnished in silver,
> having no adherence, no adhesion anywhere,
> one clear, burnished, isolated being, unique,
> and she also, pure, isolated, complete,
> two of us, unutterably distinguished, and in unutterable conjunc-
> tion.
>
> Then we shall be free, freer than angels, ah, perfect.
>
> (267)

One need not join the long and rather obsessive critical debate on anal sex and anal caresses in Lawrence's work to acknowledge that "Manifesto"'s regenerating contact with the "fearful *other flesh*" seems to entail something besides "ordinary" (i.e. heterosexual, penile/vaginal) sexuality.[33] Most striking about this contact is its reciprocity; the woman touches the man, his "secret, darkest sources," in the same way that he touches her. Doing away, at least temporarily, with his usual hard-soft, day-night, active-passive distinctions, Lawrence indicates, instead, that Otherness works both ways. "Manifesto" is not one of his best poems, perhaps precisely because it lacks the tension between opposing forces, and between Lawrence's own conflicting beliefs and desires, that lends even to some of his most didactic works an underlying sense of complexity. Written at a time when Lawrence was trying to articulate an optimistic theory of marriage in *Women in Love*, and when he felt that he and Frieda had finally achieved "equilibrium" in their own relationship, it is, however, one of his most egalitarian and optimistic ones.

It is also one of his most explicitly visionary poems, suggesting, as did his early "Mystery," that sex—the fruitful, mutually fertilizing interaction of man and woman—can lead to prophetic illumination, an influx of mystic knowledge. But, whereas in "Mystery" Lawrence eulogized the fulfillment achieved in the "Commingled wines / Of you and me," in "Manifesto" he urges against any such "mixing, merging" into oneness, into a unified personality, or even, it seems, into a unified opinion (although Lawrence's own didacticism often belies his theoretical commitment to diversity of thought). In the "new world" that both "Manifesto" and "New Heaven and Earth" herald, the poet's aim, he suggests, is not to end the battle of the sexes so much as to acknowledge and celebrate it as a source of inspiration and thus, ultimately, of poetic and prophetic power:

> we shall love, we shall hate,
> but it will be like music, sheer utterance,
> issuing straight out of the unknown,
> the lightning and the rainbow appearing in us unbidden,
>   unchecked,
> like ambassadors.
>
> We shall not look before and after.
> We shall *be, now*.
> We shall know in full.
> We, the mystic NOW.

> (*LCP* 268)

The Poetics of Machismo

In "Poetry of the Present," a 1919 essay that "should have come as a preface to *Look! We Have Come Through!*," Lawrence explicitly attempts to formulate a poetics of "the mystic NOW," by which he means not only, as in "Manifesto," a form of visionary fulfillment but also, more concretely, a new form of poetry that will present a "direct utterance from the instant, whole man." Insisting that he wants to write poetry that exhibits "no plasmic finality, nothing crystal, permanent," he tries instead to communicate "the insurgent naked throb of the instant moment" in "the seething poetry of the incarnate Now" (*LCP* 181–86):

> This is the unrestful, ungraspable poetry of the sheer present, poetry whose very permanency lies in its wind-like transit. Whitman's is the best poetry of this kind. Without beginning and without end, without any base and pediment, it sweeps past forever, like a wind that is forever in passage, and unchainable. (183)

In formal terms what he really seems to mean by all this is free verse:

> The most superb mystery we have hardly recognised: the immediate, instant self. The quick of all the universe, of all creation, is the incarnate, carnal self. Poetry gave us the clue: free verse: Whitman. Now we know. (185)

"Wind-like transit," "superb mystery," "the quick of all the universe": this is the vocabulary of prophecy, for, although "Poetry of the Present" contains no explicit reference to divinity, a conviction that the "direct utterance from the instant whole man" actually comes from somewhere outside the man, or from some inaccessible, untapped source deep within, shapes the essay's rhetoric. "We can be in ourselves spontaneous and flexible as flame, we can see that utterance rushes out without artificial foam or artificial smoothness," writes Lawrence. "But we cannot positively prescribe any motion, any rhythm" (184). Thus, the poet of the "incarnate Now" positions himself squarely at the center of the prophetic paradox: he must, Lawrence suggests, actively cultivate a passive attitude toward his source of inspiration, consciously willing himself, in other words, to be unconscious and unwillful.

Yet although he acknowledges the essential passivity of his own receptive stance, a passivity that corresponds to traditionally feminine behavior, Lawrence's "poetry of the present" sounds, according to his own gender definitions in *Study of Thomas Hardy*, like the poetry of pure maleness. "Give me nothing fixed, set, static," he urges. "Don't give me the infinite or the eternal: nothing of infinity, nothing of eternity" (*LCP* 182–83). Gone is the "adherence to rhyme and regular rhythm" that constitutes, in *Study of Thomas Hardy*, a "concession to the Law" of the female, an "admission of the living, positive inertia which is the other half of life, other than the pure will-to-motion" (*Study* 91). Gone too is the notion of poetry as a consummation between male and female principles, "the Bride in the arms of the Bridegroom," for "in the immediate present there is no perfection, no consummation" (*LCP* 182). Even the "concession to the body" (*Study* 91), formerly a female principle, is appropriated by the male poet: "Free verse is, or should be, direct utterance from the instant, whole man. It is the soul and the mind and body surging at once, nothing left out" (*LCP* 184).

Lawrence had been reading Whitman, whose influence can be felt not only in the rich, rolling, free verse cadences of "New Heaven and Earth" and "Manifesto" but also in Lawrence's newfound sense of prophetic authority and, above all, in his turn from an ostensibly female-inspired poetics to a poetics of machismo. For "Poetry of the Present," though claiming to be a gloss on *Look! We Have Come Through!*, actually speaks of an entirely different kind of inspirational force than that invoked in poems such as "Manifesto": a "mystic NOW" that depends less upon sexual union and fulfillment than upon submission to a specifically male creative power. Biographical cause and artistic effect are difficult to separate here, but it is certainly worth noting that Lawrence's optimism about marriage, so marked between 1912 and 1914, had begun to fade by the time his "male comradeship" phase set in and had hit rock bottom about the time he wrote "Poetry of the Present" in 1919; although he would remain essentially faithful to his wife and to the concept of monogamy for the rest of his life, never again would he write so glowingly about female inspiration as during those rapturous prewar years. Lawrence scholars have put forward a number of other possible reasons for Lawrence's ideological change of heart. Hilary Simpson, for instance, attributes it to an increasing sense of futility in the face of the Great War's ravages, noting that his growing misogyny reflected "a whole society's inability to come to terms with the massive change in sexual ideology which the war had engendered" (15), while Cornelia Nixon, who argues that Lawrence's metamorphosis from "an optimistic socialist revolutionary" into "a paranoid antidemocratic misanthrope" took place as early as 1915, attributes the radical shift in Lawrence's outlook above all to some "private disaster"—probably, she suggests, a guilty brush with homosexuality (10).

Much has already been written about Lawrence's flirtations with homosexuality;[34] too many of these accounts, unfortunately, reveal more about the drawbacks of psychoanalytical criticism than about Lawrence's own literary, social, or psychosexual motivations. His frequently expressed attraction to other men has been used to explain, or has been glibly explained by, his physical fragility and tendency to illness; his abnormally close relationship to his mother; his preference, as a child, for girls rather than boys as playmates; his ability to write convincingly about women's thoughts and emotions; his close friendships with women; his close friendships with men; his literary allusions to (albeit heterosexual) anal intercourse; and even his legendary penchant for housework. That neither a weak constitution nor a liking for cooking necessarily indicates, even by the most conventional definitions, a "feminine" temperament, and that in any case "effeminacy" (a word notable for its derogatory connotations) does not automatically indicate homosexuality, any more than does a thematization of anality, would seem to me obvious points enough.[35] Given especially that the extent to which Lawrence put whatever homosexual desires he may have had into practice remains largely a matter of conjecture, one fact alone is indisputable: if his attitudes toward women and heterosexual love as keys to creative inspiration were ambivalent, his feelings about "the love that dare not speak its name" were even more so.[36]

As early as 1913, Lawrence, in a letter with a confused but decidedly confessional tone, not only admitted to a certain bias toward homosexuality but also explicitly associated male homosexuality with artistic power:

> I should like to know why nearly every man that approaches greatness tends to homosexuality, whether he admits it or not: so that he love[s] the *body* of a man better than the body of a woman— as I believe the Greeks did, sculptors and all, by far. . . . He can always get satisfaction from a man, but it is the hardest thing in life to get one's soul and body satisfied from a woman, so that one is free from oneself. And one is kept by all tradition and instinct from loving men, or a man.[37]

In 1915, when Lawrence came, perhaps for the first time, into close contact with a group of openly homosexual men, it was tradition in the guise of instinct that dictated his emotional response; he found himself gripped by feelings of pure, unadulterated revulsion, as he reported to his young friend David Garnett, whose "set" at Cambridge he had recently visited:

> It is foolish of you to say that it doesn't matter either way—the men loving men. . . . I never knew what it meant until I saw [Maynard] K[eynes], till I saw him at Cambridge. . . . [S]uddenly a door opened and K. was there, blinking from sleep, standing in his pyjamas. And as he stood there a knowledge passed into me, which has been like a little madness to me ever since. And it was carried along with the most dreadful sense of repulsiveness—something like carrion—a vulture gives me the same feeling. . . . It makes me dream of beetles. . . . Somehow, I can't bear it. It is wrong beyond all the bounds of wrongness.[38]

Yet the Lawrence who dreamed of beetles was at the same time so powerfully attracted to other men, both physically and emotionally, that even so staid and careful a biographer as Harry T. Moore has admitted that "today we might use the term bisexual" to describe Lawrence's sexual proclivities (88). The literary products and the philosophical utterances of the war years show us Lawrence at an ideological and emotional crossroads, trying desperately to evolve a sexual and social *weltanschauung* that might allow him not only to desire men and women both but also to combine in his own works the "male" and "female" elements that he had defined in his 1914 Hardy essay and, thus, in some sense to break free altogether from such socially determined gender norms. The contradictory impulses toward definition and transcendence of gender roles, the mixed feelings of desire for other men and aversion to homosexuality, all come together in *Women in Love*, completed in 1916 and widely considered Lawrence's greatest novel, precisely because it foregrounds the emotional complexity that Lawrence would later, especially in such works as *Aaron's Rod* and *Fantasia of the Unconscious*, seek to repress.

Emile Delavenay has linked Lawrence's fascination with homosexuality to the writings of the controversial sexologist Edward Carpenter, whose books Lawrence may or may not have read—Delavenay provides no particularly convincing evidence—but whose theories linking male comradeship to revelatory power closely resemble Lawrence's own. Delavenay sees *Women in Love*'s Birkin, in particular, as a member of what Carpenter calls "the Intermediate Sex": men of feminine temperament, privy, like Tiresias, to "a certain freemasonry of the secrets of both sexes," whose roles as the priests, artists, and seers of countless primitive cultures Carpenter uses to advance his claim that so-called feminine men have attained a further degree of evolution than their more macho cohorts.[39] Yet, in calling Birkin the "prototype" of Carpenter's "Future Man," Delavenay neglects an essential point: Lawrence's protrayals of Birkin and other similar brains-over-brawn characters (Lilly in *Aaron's Rod*, Richard in *Kangaroo*) are heavily spiked with irony and self-censure, and these characters' prophetic pretensions, like Lawrence's own, are as often the issue of a reedy, self-conscious spirituality as of a hermaphroditic vigor. In any case, by the time he wrote his 1922 *Fantasia of the Unconscious*, in which he argues for "pure maleness in a man and pure femaleness in a woman," Lawrence's condemnation of concepts such as Carpenter's "Intermediate Sex" and what he contemptuously calls "the hermaphroditic fallacy" (97) had become as explicit as it is emphatic: "A child is either male or female. . . . The talk about a third sex, or about the indeterminate sex, is just to pervert the issue" (93).

Lawrence's ambivalence toward homosexuality, male comradeship, and maleness as a source of poetic inspiration mirrors an equally complex attitude toward what I have already called a "poetics of machismo": a commitment, that is, to a set of formal, philosophical, and thematic principles that Lawrence himself defined, though his definitions were seldom stable and often self-contradictory, as "male." In the same letter of 2 June 1914 in which he asserted that "the only re-sourcing of art, revivifying it, is to make it more the joint work of man and woman," Lawrence praised the poetry of the Italian futurists "because it is the applying to emotions of the purging of the old forms and sentimentalities, . . . the weary sickness of pedantry and tradition and inertness." At the same time, however, he warned of the dangers of such "purely male" poetry:

> They will progress down the purely male or intellectual or scientific line. They will even use their intuition for intellectual and scientific purposes. The one thing about their art is that it *isn't* art, but ultra scientific attempts to make diagrams of certain physic or mental states.[40]

During the war Lawrence scathingly condemned the military's "terrible glamour of camaraderie," labeling it "a decadence, a degradation, . . . a merging in a sticky male mess."[41] Yet by 1920, writing to Godwin Baynes about Whitman's "Calamus" and "Comrades," he was proclaiming enthusiastically that "I believe in what [Whitman] calls 'manly love,' the real implicit reliance of one man on another: as sacred a unison as marriage."[42] In another essay Lawrence goes so far as to praise Whitman as a kind of superman whose creative and prophetic power is fueled by his glorification of the man-as-warrior and his reduction of "the woman" to "a submissive function":

> Acting from the last and profoundest centres, man acts womanless. It is no longer a question of race continuance. It is a question of sheer ultimate being, the perfection of life, nearest to death. Acting from these centres, man is an extreme being, the unthinkable warrior, creator, mover, and maker.[43]

But in a revised version of this same essay, published four years later, Lawrence once more turns against Whitman, for much the same reasons that he had rejected the Italian futurists ten years earlier: "Walt was really too superhuman," and "the danger of the Superman is that he is mechanical" (167).

Lawrence's fascination with Whitman thus remains tempered by the suspicion that a purely male art risks "mechanical" sterility; "If I'd been one of his women," he even asserts, in what is perhaps as much a self-critique as a condemnation of Whitman's misogynist bias, "I'd have given him Female, with a flea in his ear" (*Studies* 167). The problem was that Lawrence's Female—that archetypal being, both a dark Other and an even darker part of himself, to whom he had earlier looked for mystery and inspiration—had, he felt, failed him by succumbing to the mechanical impulses of postwar society. Martin Green, reflecting on the "seeming paradox that so many of the major figures of [what Green calls] the erotic movement were not personally very erotic—or if they were, . . . were not lovers of women," explains that the call of men such as Otto Weininger, Edward Carpenter, and Havelock Ellis for a "feminization" of experience represented above all a movement "*against* something, against patriarchal authority, industrialism, militarism, and the like," so that their turn to "a matriarchal mode of being" served more as a means to a rebellious end than as a demonstration of any particularly deep-seated empathy with women them-selves (74). Similarly, Lawrence's prewar belief that men should open themselves to the female in themselves was strongly motivated by antipatriarchal and anti-industrial sentiments; certainly, as Hilary Simpson notes, he had never argued "that women should enter the masculine world of industry and technology which he hated" (66), as, to Lawrence's dismay and eventual disgust, they did in ever-increasing numbers during and after the war.

Natural Misogyny: *Birds, Beasts and Flowers*

Whether he was impelled primarily by personal or by historical devel-opments, by 1919 Lawrence had radically shifted both the thematic content of his poetry and prose and the focus of his poetics of inspira-tion. Whereas *Look! We Have Come Through!* (originally slated to be called *Man and Woman* or *Poems of a Married Man*)⁴⁴ focuses, as do his novels *The Rainbow* and *Women in Love*, on "the conflict of love and hate" between a man and a woman, the primary emphasis of Lawrence's three "leadership" novels (*Aaron's Rod, Kangaroo,* and *The Plumed Serpent*) is on the relationship between a man and a man. Women are, to be sure, present in all three novels—Kate, in fact, is the central character of *The Plumed Serpent*—but their role is no longer a mystically generative one; instead, it depends upon their enthralled submission to the dark power of the male:

> As [Cipriano] sat in silence, casting the old, twilit, Pan-power over her, [Kate] felt herself submitting, succumbing. He was once more the old dominant male . . . the Pan male. And she was swooned prone beneath, perfect in her proneness.
>
> It was the ancient phallic mystery, the ancient god-devil of the male Pan. . . . Ah! and what a mystery of prone submission, on her part, this huge erection would imply! Submission absolute. (*Plumed Serpent* 347)

It is not only of women, however, that Lawrence requires "submission absolute" to "the phallic mystery" of the dominant male; men, too, as he repeatedly urges in his novels and essays of the late 1910s and early 1920s, must "choose their leaders, and obey them to the death" (*Fanta-sia* 179)—a startling assertion coming from a man who had recently witnessed so many young countrymen (though few were granted the luxury of "choosing") do exactly that. The leadership novels document mindless subservience rather than a balanced equilibrium of opposites; thus, although Lawrence, who was given more to pseudophilosophical ranting than to sustained conviction or active political engagement, might well have been as appalled as anyone had he lived long enough to witness the rise and consequences of European fascism, his authoritarian ideology during the early 1920s cannot but appear sinister and even deadly when viewed through the grim filter of World War II.

Lawrence's leadership novels, although they occasionally achieve that blend of imagistic subtlety and mystical power that marks Lawrence's best writing, are generally long on the latter quality and short on the former—hence their failure, if not as dogmatic treatises, then certainly as effective works of art. Surprisingly, however, even while he was writing some of his most unfortunate prose, Lawrence was also composing *Birds, Beasts and Flowers*, which contains much of his finest poetry. Sandra Gilbert explains this seeming paradox by noting that, although the static fixedness of the leader-follower relation allows for little of the "subtle inter-relatedness" that Lawrence himself proclaimed as an essential characteristic of the novel, the "concept of power" promoted in the leadership novels "is an idea that has always been compatible with the writing of poetry, particularly the sort of anti-ironic, visionary poetry Lawrence wrote best" (*Acts* 127). Graham Hough advances a somewhat different theory, arguing that Lawrence's postwar verse in fact breaks with the post-Romantic tradition of "passive appreciation":

> Instead it makes an energetic and intuitive attempt to penetrate into the being of natural objects, to show what they are in themselves, not how they can sustain our moral nature. (201)

Although Hough's description of Lawrence's poetics may seem very much at odds with Gilbert's, the two arguments are not entirely contradictory; in fact, they illustrate how opposing principles—what Gilbert calls the "visionary," which she classifies as a passive, submissive mode of perception, versus what Hough calls the "intuitive," which he characterizes as penetratingly "energetic"—are simultaneously at work in Lawrence's poetry, and particularly in the poems of *Birds, Beasts and Flowers*. For, even when he is most explicitly articulating his leader-follower paradigm, it is seldom possible to say whether Lawrence himself, either in his private or in his literary life, was more inclined to play the role of leader or of follower. *Birds, Beasts and Flowers*, published in 1923, is not as boomingly prophetic in tone as *Look! We Have Come Through!*, with the latter's apostrophes to the "fine, fine wind" of inspiration, its jubilant discovery of a "New Heaven and Earth," and its triumphant invocation of "the mystic NOW." Here as before, however, Lawrence lays claim to a visionary mode of perception that balances submissive receptivity and artistic autonomy, drawing its creative energy both from the poet's personal dynamism and from his identification, acknowledgment, and occasional admission into the self of a creatively potent Other.

Yet, whereas for the Lawrence of *Look!* that Other, whether god or demon, was almost always associated with the female, women play a relatively minor role in *Birds, Beasts and Flowers*. Indeed, as the title suggests, Lawrence's search for inspiration depends now on the Otherness of nature: of birds, beasts, trees, fruit, and flowers, or, as Rilke would put it, of Things. As in most of Rilke's Thing-poems, however, virtually all of Lawrence's meditations on nature somehow turn out to be comments, often only thinly disguised, on human nature as well—including, as often as not, human sexual conflict. And, also as with Rilke, Lawrence's claim, implicit or explicit, of submission to the objects of his observation belies an opposite trajectory of power: the poet, who selects those objects and the way in which he writes about them, in a sense forces the objects to submit to him.

The most successful poems of *Birds, Beasts and Flowers* are those in which Lawrence keeps his dogmatic theories and authoritative energies at bay, recognizing and admitting the often baffling Otherness of flora and fauna rather than using plants and animals to illustrate what he takes to be the ills of humanity. He comes closest to doing this in poems that focus on animal life, such as "Snake," in which the poet presents himself as a baffled "second comer" in relation to the peaceful, strangely beautiful serpent that comes to drink at his water trough (*LCP* 349–51); "Man and Bat," in which he decides not to kill an intrusive bat because "death . . . [is] no solution" and "bats must be bats" (342–47); "Hummingbird," in which he endeavors to cast an imaginative glance down "the long telescope of Time" and picture "this little bit chipped off in brilliance" as a "jabbing, terrifying" primeval monster (372); and "Fish," in which he admits, with a sudden and rather poignant shock, that

I am not the measure of creation.
This is beyond me, this fish.
His God stands outside my God.

(334–40)

In "The Revolutionary," a poem rather incongruously situated in the "Fruits" section of *Birds, Beasts and Flowers*, Lawrence figures himself as a blind Samson, "sightless among all your visuality," pulling down the bland, pale-faced caryatids of Western literary and philosophical tradition so that he himself might emerge as a dark ruler over the anarchy he has caused:

See if I don't move under a dark and nude, vast heaven
When your world is in ruins, under your fallen skies.
Caryatids, pale-faces.
See if I am not Lord of the dark and moving hosts
Before I die.

(*LCP* 287–89)

This is Lawrence the would-be leader, commanding the world to conform to his perceptions (born, he admits himself, of blindness) and to worship, in the end, at his feet. In poems such as "Snake" and "Fish," however, taking on the obedient stance of the follower, Lawrence gazes open-eyed and humbly at the world around him, figuring the visionary poet not as a raging iconoclast but, rather, as a receptive, attentive witness: "the servant," as he puts it in his 1919 essay "Education of the People," "of the inscrutable, unfathomable soul" that lies deep within man and nature (*Phoenix* 608).

Elsewhere he demands complete obedience from the objects of his attention, a submission that takes on its most obvious sexual cast in "Fruits," the first section of *Birds, Beasts and Flowers*. Lawrence opens this section by explicitly associating the fruits he examines with femaleness—particularly with "the fissure," the female genitalia—and then goes on to assert his control over these fruits in the most literal and destructive way possible: by dissecting, consuming, and discarding them. "For fruits are all of them female, in them lies the seed," Lawrence declares in his brief prose introduction to the section. "And so when they break and show the seed, then we look into the womb and see its secrets" (*LCP* 277). His desire to discover these secrets at first seems innocent enough, even rather tender, as in "Pomegranate":

Do you mean to tell me there should be no fissure? . . .
For my part, I prefer my heart to be broken.
It is so lovely, dawn-kaleidoscopic within the crack.

(279)

In poems such as "Figs," however, the poet moves from longing to brutality, introducing a dismissive didacticism completely lacking in emotional ambivalence.

Lawrence begins "Figs" by contrasting "the proper way to eat a fig, in society"—whereby one carefully splits it in four parts, like a flower—with the "vulgar" way: "[You] put your mouth to the crack, and take out the flesh in one bite." His own presentation (or consumption) of his subject matter undeniably favors the latter approach, for, rather than allowing the fig/woman metaphor to unfold gently and poetically, he takes, so to speak, "the flesh" of the simile "in one bite":

The Italians vulgarly say, [the fig] stands for the female part; the
    fig-fruit:
The fissure, the yoni,
The wonderful moist conductivity towards the centre.

Involved,
Inturned,
The flowering all inward and womb-fibrilled;
And but one orifice.

(*LCP* 282)

Although he opens the poem by comparing methods of eating, or exposing, the fig—dissection versus raw suction—he goes on to argue that "the female should always be secret, . . . [f]olded upon itself, enclosed like any Mohammedan woman," with only "one small way of access": through, that is, "the fissure," the vulva, or what Lawrence, later in the poem, will derisively call "the purple slit." The male poet, who knows how to "put [his] mouth to the crack, and take out the flesh in one bite," is authorized, it seems, to explain the "unutterable" secret of the female, to examine and expose that which is otherwise meant to remain "inturned" and "enclosed." Yet Lawrence hotly condemns modern women for desiring to do the same thing: to take control of their own lives and secrets, to "burst into affirmation" like ripe figs. For, he warns,

That's how the fig dies, showing her crimson through the purple
  slit
Like a wound, the exposure of her secret, on the open day.
Like a prostitute, the bursten fig, making a show of her secret.

That's how women die too.

(285)

The misogynistic fervor of Lawrence's postwar ideology, particu-
larly poisonous in "Figs," takes many different forms throughout *Birds,
Beasts and Flowers,* a volume that was, after all, conceived and com-
posed over a period of several years in locations as diverse as Italy,
Ceylon, Australia, and New Mexico. "Purple Anemones," for instance,
reaches into the distant world of Greek and Roman mythology, expli-
cating Persephone's cyclical return from the underworld in terms of a
domestic drama of pursuit and capture; Pluto, "Proserpine's master,"
allows his "enfranchised" wife to escape from hell once a year only so
that he might have the pleasure of hunting his "white victim" down
again: "Poor Persephone and her rights for women" (*LCP* 307–9). In
"Bibbles," addressing subject matter closer to home, Lawrence attacks
the promiscuous and undiscerning love of his small black dog, calling
her a "democratic little bull-bitch, dirt-eating little swine," a "high-bred
little love-bitch," a "nigger" (though Lawrence felt a certain fascination
for the dark-skinned natives of Mexico and New Mexico, one senses
that he did not intend this epithet as a compliment), and even, curi-
ously enough, a "little Walt-Whitmanesque bitch"—a criticism not,
obviously, of the mechanical maleness that Lawrence earlier attributed
to Whitman but, rather, of Bibbles's overly democratic tendency to love
everyone. Reminding Bibbles that "the great ranch-dogs are all after
you"—in other words that she, a bitch in heat, is about to get what she
deserves—the poet decides in the end that he will protect her from
them but only upon one condition: she must sacrifice her emotional
generosity to his leader-follower demands and "learn loyalty rather
than loving" (394–400).

In poems like these we see Lawrence's poetics of machismo in full
force, enacted not only stylistically, in the poems' untempered, unsub-
tle rhetoric, but thematically as well, in the poet's penetration of the fig,
his gleeful glorification of divine domestic violence, and his incessant
verbal kicking of the little tail-wagging dog. "Ripe figs won't keep,"

declares Lawrence darkly at the end of "Figs"; "What then, when women the world over have all bursten into self-assertion? / And bursten figs won't keep?" (*LCP* 284). The poet, one can hardly help thinking, would have done well here to direct his criticisms of modern womanhood toward his own poetics; a poem such as "Figs," itself bursting into unchecked self-assertion, would surely have been more powerful and convincing had Lawrence not permitted the rot of his didactic fervor to set in among the lush ripeness of his language and imagery. To borrow from Graham Hough an even more aptly Lawrentian metaphor, Lawrence as poet all too often permits "too lax an outflow from too wide an orifice" (205).

In poems such as "Figs," "Bibbles," and "Purple Anemones," in fact, we see Lawrence's idealistic longing to write the "Poetry of the Present"—to grasp the "insurgent, naked throb of the instant moment" in the unshackled language of free verse—fail most miserably, as his prophetic fervor crumbles into the rather pathetic rantings of a man who cannot control a small pet. Lawrence's tone in these poems is bitterly sarcastic, but one cannot even argue on his behalf that it is ironic; the violence of Pluto's "purple husband-tyranny" and of Lawrence's dog beating is all too accurately mirrored rhetorically in the poet's one-sided verbal attacks on females of all species. Somewhat more ambivalent in their ideology are poems such as "He-Goat," "She-Goat," and the "tortoise" series, particularly "Lui et elle," "Tortoise Gallantry," and "Tortoise Shout," which focus not on the dominance of male over female but, if anything, on the reverse: on the Mona Lisa–like imperturbability of the large, placid female while the male of the species, striving painfully for orgasm, finds himself "crucified into sex" (*LCP* 364). Where the she-goat looks, true to Lawrence's association of the female with law and patriarchal religion, like "some hairy horrid God the Father in a William Blake imagination" (385), the he-goat, "poor domesticated beast," fails miserably as the "black procreant male of the selfish will and libidinous desire" that Lawrence would like to see him become (383). And, while the female tortoise remains "earthily apathetic" to her mate's libidinous sexuality, the ridiculous little male runs "beside her like a dog, . . . / Nipping her ankles" until he is able to catch and rather awkwardly mount her:

> Doomed, in the long crucifixion of desire, to seek his
>   consummation beyond himself.

Divided into passionate duality,
He, so finished and immune, now broken into desirous
    fragmentariness,
Doomed to make an intolerable fool of himself
In his effort toward completion again.

                            (358–62)

"In the tension of opposites all things have their being," Lawrence reminds us in his prose introduction to the "Reptiles" section of *Birds, Beasts and Flowers* (LCP 348). But, whereas in *Look! We Have Come Through!* the tension between male and female fed the poet's creative vitality, here the tiny tortoise's pursuit of the large, lumbering female threatens to reduce sexual libido from a mystically generative force to a merely embarrassing one. *Look!*, however conflict-laden, presented sex as an act of mutual desire and mutual struggle; the goat and tortoise poems, in contrast, comment only on the sexual needs of the male, with the female considered not so much as an inscrutable source of mystery and power (although her lack of interest in the proceedings, at least, does lend her a certain secretive air) but, rather, as a clumsy but necessary medium for male orgasm. Nonetheless, Lawrence seems determined to salvage from his observation of the tortoises some possibility for mystical transcendence, if not for the female tortoise then at least for the desperate male. "Tortoise Shout" ends with a passage that might easily have been set among the ringing injunctions of "Manifesto" or "New Heaven and Earth":

Sex, which breaks us into voice, sets us calling across the deeps,
    calling, calling for the complement,
Singing, and calling, and singing again, being answered, having
    found.
Torn, to become whole again, after long seeking for what is lost,
The same cry from the tortoise as from Christ, the Osiris-cry of
    abandonment,
That which is whole, torn asunder,
That which is in part, finding its whole again throughout the
    universe.

                            (366–67)

Although Graham Hough considers Lawrence's tortoise series to be "probably the most sustained attempt in literature to penetrate the mysterious life of a remote part of the brute creation" (204), a poem such as "Tortoise Shout" clearly has an anthropomorphic agenda: the poet's own account of human sexuality is projected onto the reptiles' clumsy and excruciating copulation. Yet, if *Birds, Beasts and Flowers* is supposed to communicate to us some clear-cut gender ideology, the volume as a whole fails; Lawrence's poetics of contradiction is revealed more acutely here than ever before. Many of the poems batter the reader with misogynist rhetoric, yet several admit to the male poet's vulnerability and doubt. And, while some continue to probe for the Otherness of the female, others assert that such a creatively generative force can only be found in nature—or, as in "Medlars and Sorb-Apples" (which will be discussed in detail in chap. 4), in the egoistic depths of the male poet himself.

Lawrence and the Phallic God

Less ambivalent about gender relations than *Birds, Beasts and Flowers* (although published in the same year) are the pseudopsychological deliberations of Lawrence's 1923 essay *Fantasia of the Unconscious.* Lamenting here that modern man "has assumed the gentle, all-sympathetic role" of the female, while "woman has become the energetic party, with the authority in her hands" (94), Lawrence emphatically rejects his earlier celebrations of male-female interaction, instead dismissing female artistic achievement as the imitative mouthings of a purely receptive sex:

> Man, acting in the passive or feminine polarity, is still man, and he doesn't have one single unmanly feeling. And women, when they speak and write, utter not one single word that men have not taught them. (99)

Elaborating on some of his most outrageous notions from his 1919 essays "Education of the People" and *Psychoanalysis and the Unconscious,* he goes on to encourage a complete separation of the sexes during childhood. For when boys and girls become "pals," he asserts,

> they lose their own male and female integrity. And they lose the treasure of the future, the vital sex polarity, the dynamic magic of life. For the magic and the dynamism rests on *otherness.* (100)

As for adulthood, Lawrence urges not quarantined separation but out-and-out battle:

> And so, men, drive your wives, beat them out of their self-consciousness and their soft smarminess and good, lovely idea of themselves. . . . But fight for your life, men. Fight your wife out of it till she's stunned. Drive her back into her own true mode. (188)

This passage, with its bitter glorification of violence against women, pushes to a ferocious extreme the misogynist agenda of such *Birds, Beasts and Flowers* poems as "Figs" and "Purple Anemones." Lawrence now explicitly espouses a poetics not of receptivity but of conquest, as female Otherness, once a mysterious source of inspiration and power for the male poet, becomes, instead, a justification for sexual apartheid and for the political and domestic oppression of women.

Fantasia of the Unconscious documents, to be sure, Lawrence's "male leadership" phase in its most immoderate and virulent manifestation. But, even when Lawrence softens his ideology, many of his essays throughout the 1920s remain virtually unreadable, or at best difficult to take seriously, due to their one-sidedness of tone, vision, and doctrine. In a series of essays written in New Mexico about his black cow Susan, for instance, Lawrence couches his awed obeisance to the mysteries of nature in the language of visionary rapture:

> But when I see her suddenly emerging, jet-black, sliding through the gate of her little corral into the open sun, does not my heart stand still, and cry out, in some long-forgotten tongue, salutation to the fearsome one?[45]

In a wittingly scathing, if one-sided, attack on Lawrence called *D. H. Lawrence and Susan His Cow*, William Tindall takes Susan to be an emblem of all that is wrong with Lawrence: his misplaced mysticism, his mindless enthusiasm, his privileging of the primitive to the point of a dangerous fondness for cults of the blood. The cow may well be the sacred beast of the Hindus, a representative of the Egyptian goddess Isis, and even an embodiment of the Eternal Feminine, but somehow Lawrence's depictions of Susan's "queer cowy mystery" and "changeless cowy desirableness" fall short of such weighty associations.[46]

Lawrence's failure here is one not only of vision but also of

rhetoric. His untempered prose style, whether angrily ranting or senti-
mentally gushing, could perhaps be called "prophetic" in the sense that
it calls upon a number of traditionally prophetic tropes: intensity, con-
viction, charisma. But, if an effective visionary mode also requires
humility and sensitivity—the clarity of insight that comes from recog-
nizing and embracing contradiction—then Lawrence as essayist is all
too often a failed prophet. Works such as *Fantasia of the Unconscious* and
the Susan passages suffer less from what Joyce Carol Oates calls the
mystic's traditional dilemma of having to "use ordinary language . . . to
express an extraordinary event" (28)[47] than from Lawrence's own
chronic inability to distinguish the extraordinary from the ordinary,
prophecy from fanaticism, mysticism from mere silliness.

A similar failure haunts much of his late poetry. Lawrence himself
insisted that his *Pansies*—the flower metaphor belies the poems'
acidity—stemmed "as much from the heart and the genitals as from the
head" (*LCP* 417). Richard Aldington attributed them to an even less
cerebral source:

> It seems to me that nearly all these Pansies and Nettles came out of
> Lawrence's nerves, not out of his real self. They are one long ham-
> mer, hammer, hammer of exasperation. Sometimes they are like
> the utterances of a little Whitman, but without Walt's calm
> *sostenuto* quality; and sometimes they are like a little Blake raving,
> but without the fiery vision. (595)

Certainly, all too many of Lawrence's "pansies" read not like the pro-
found *pensées* of one of our century's great writers but, as Virginia
Woolf tartly noted, "like the sayings that small boys scribble upon stiles
to make housemaids jump and titter."[48] Throughout all four volumes
of his late poetry—*Pansies* (1929), *Nettles* (1930), and the posthumously
published *More Pansies* and *Last Poems* (1932)—Lawrence offers a
lengthy catalog of his discontents with the modern world: instead of
the dark, energizing forces of erotic love, he complains, we now are left
only with "sex in the head"; where we should be attending and sub-
mitting to the natural world, we worship and emulate the machine. The
problem with so many of these poems, which certainly voice some
legitimate social gripes, is that the uncrafted, untempered, prosaic lan-
guage that Lawrence uses to lament humankind's fall from mystery
itself all too accurately reflects that fall. Some of the poems are witty,

clever, even aphoristic; but for the most part they spark no visionary flame, set no vibrations swinging, and allow the reader no imaginative space for speculation, play, or wonder.

There are, to be sure, notable exceptions among the hundreds of verses that make up these four volumes: poems that recover the mystery and vitality of Lawrence's earlier work by exploring paradoxes, by casting doubts, by evoking conflicting images rather than baldly stating opinions. In *Last Poems* Lawrence replaces his earlier metaphors of contradiction and conflict—"In the tension of opposites all things have their being"—with *strife*, a word that denotes both violent dissension and, in a less common usage, earnest endeavor or striving:

> When strife is a thing of two
> each knows the other in struggle
> and the conflict is a communion
> a twoness.
>
> But when strife is a thing of one
> a single ego striving for its own ends
> and beating down resistances
> then strife is evil, because it is not strife.
>
> ("Strife," LCP 714)

These two stanzas summarize Lawrence's own shift, in much of his late poetry, from a poetics of fruitful opposition—"a communion / a twoness"—to a poetics of stridency, "a single ego striving for its own ends." Unfortunately, the poem also enacts the consequences of that shift, for it offers precisely the kind of blunt, unnuanced argument that "beat[s] down resistances" and allows for little or no contradiction from within. Lawrence achieves a more successful expression of the same principle, however, in "Death Is Not Evil, Evil Is Mechanical":

> Know thyself, and that thou art mortal
> . . . .
> a thing of kisses and strife
> a lit-up shaft of rain
> a calling column of blood
> a rose tree bronzey with thorns
> a mixture of yea and nay

a rainbow of love and hate
a wind that blows back and forth
a creature of beautiful peace, like a river
and a creature of conflict, like a cataract.

(*LCP* 714)

Here Lawrence uses evocative images rather than sermonistic state-ments to make his argument about the dual nature of humankind. He embraces contradiction, "strife," in deed as well as in word, portraying man as "a creature of conflict" by employing oppositional metaphors that themselves invite dualistic interpretations: the "lit-up shaft of rain," for instance, suggests both phallic elevation and gentle descent, both destruction (the shaft of an arrow) and the life-giving energies of nature, both hollowness and plenitude, both sun and storm.

In other late poems, too, Lawrence takes his search for inspiration back to the realm of contradiction and dualistic conflict, exploring the Otherness of the natural world ("The Elephant Is Slow to Mate"), of sci-ence ("Give Us Gods"), even of his own imminent death ("Ship of Death"). Images of violence, blood, and male leadership are compli-cated or undercut by admissions of anxiety toward the forces of uni-versal mystery, which appear in a variety of guises: as swans and geese ("Swan," "Leda," "Won't It Be Strange"), as heroes and gods ("For the Heroes Are Dipped in Scarlet," "Spiral Flame"). And in *Last Poems* especially, titles such as "Female Coercion," "Volcanic Venus," and "What Does She Want?" (all from *Pansies*) give way to a renewed emphasis on female beauty ("The Man of Tyre"), female mystery ("Invocation to the Moon"), and heterosexual union ("Whales Weep Not," "Bavarian Gentians").

A similar shift in emphasis and ideology occurs in Lawrence's late fiction as well, especially in his novels *Lady Chatterley's Lover* and *The Man Who Died*, both of which invoke the universal mystery of life as it is manifested in the complex interactions of men and women. A num-ber of critics have hailed this focus on heterosexual desire as the prodi-gal's return to the feminist fold. Hilary Simpson points out, however, that Lawrence does not so much reaffirm femininity as subvert it when, in works such as *Lady Chatterley's Lover*, he transforms the phallus, the ultimate signifier of male presence and female lack, into a symbol embodying tenderness and fragility as well as strength and power (129). The debate has stirred many passions: Kate Millett's attack on

Lady Chatterley's Lover, which she denounces as "a celebration of the penis of Oliver Mellors, gamekeeper and social prophet" (238), is justly famous, and Norman Mailer's self-righteous response is hardly less so:

> Dominance over women was not tyranny to [Lawrence] but equality, for dominance was the indispensable elevator which would raise his phallus to that height from which it might seek transcendence. (135)[49]

Mailer neglects to mention that Lawrence never really succeeded in "dominating over" any of the most important women in his life, from his mother and Jessie Chambers to Frieda Lawrence and Mabel Dodge Luhan. Yet he is not so far off the mark in his assessment of Lawrence's phallic quest, for Lawrence did eventually come to regard the ithyphallus—the erect penis represented symbolically—as the key to the universal insight and mystical transcendence that he had for so long been seeking.

It is in *John Thomas and Lady Jane*, a recently published early draft of *Lady Chatterley's Lover*, that Lawrence explicates his phallic cosmogony most directly:

> To most men, the penis was merely a member, at the disposal of the personality. . . . But in a true man, the penis has a life of its own [and] the personality must yield before the priority and the mysterious root-knowledge of the penis, or the phallus. For this is the difference between the two: the penis is a mere member of the physiological body. But the phallus, in the old sense, has roots, the deepest roots of all, in the soul and the greater consciousness of man, and it is through the phallic roots that inspiration enters the soul. (233)

If, earlier in his life, Lawrence professed that mystic knowledge could only be attained through contact with the female, here he argues precisely the opposite, subversively using a woman's voice (Connie Chatterley's) to make his androcentric, phallocentric claim:

> "I *know* it is the penis which connects us with the stars and the sea and everything. It is the penis which touches the planets, and makes us feel their special light." (307)

John Thomas and Lady Jane is by no means Lawrence's only organ, so to speak, for such claims. For instance, where in *Study of Thomas Hardy* he associated "God the Father" with the female principle, in his 1925 essay "Aristocracy" he describes God's emblem as the ithyphallus instead, which he sees figured everywhere in nature:

> Behold! Look at the strong, fertile silence of the thrusting tree! God is in the bush like a clenched dark fist, or a thrust phallus. (*Phoenix II* 480)

And in his 1929 novel, *The Man Who Died*, the phallus evolves into an even more potent religious symbol, an anatomical manifestation of Christ's resurrection: "I am risen!" exclaims the novel's Christ/Osiris figure as he contemplates his own erect member, just before his regenerative sexual encounter with the worshipful priestess of Isis in whose temple he has taken refuge (*Escaped Cock* 57).[50]

Throughout his poetic career Lawrence would oscillate continually in his speculations about where poetic inspiration comes from: from outside or from inside the self, from woman or from man, from God or from an inner demon. In claiming the phallus, an organ of both tenderness and strength, as the source of all inspiration, power, and even religious fulfillment, he in some sense resolves these conflicts, absorbing the outer universe within the human body, the female within the male, even the spiritually divine within the sexually demonic. Yet Lawrence's energizing, complicating poetics of contradiction still finds its way even into his seemingly single-minded phallic discourse. *The Man Who Died*, for instance, which focuses on Christ's wanderings in Egypt following what his disciples have interpreted as his death and resurrection, was originally published as *The Escaped Cock*, and the discrepancy between the two titles—the latter emphasizes Christ's vitality, sexuality, and kinship with the animal world, the former his humanity and supposed death—provides some hint of how the novel's phallic celebration is nonetheless tempered by a strong sexual anxiety and by Lawrence's growing awareness of his own mortality.

Written at a time when Lawrence himself, whose health had been steadily deteriorating for some time, was almost certainly sexually impotent, *The Man Who Died* glorifies Christ's erotic self-discovery but also, more covertly, laments the author's own loss of connection with the "phallic roots" through which "inspiration enters the soul" (*John*

Thomas 233). The "escaped cock" of the original title refers both to the rooster that, at the beginning of the novel, eludes its human imprisoners and to Osiris/Christ's liberation from the sexual restrictions imposed by his supposed godliness. But the title also highlights the disconcerting independence of Lawrence's own phallic god, which possesses a life independent of its author's body and thus alienates him from the very sources of inspiration and prophetic power to which it grants access. Like the "hidden guilty river-god of the blood" that represents Rilke's sexual consciousness, Lawrence's escaped cock thus denotes both poetic power and creative anxiety, symbolizing not only libido liberated but also potency lost.

As a writer, Lawrence is often strongest when he is weakest; his most striking and memorable works are those that hold themselves open to contradiction and doubt, acknowledging the disconcerting Otherness of women, of the natural world, or even, as in *The Man Who Died*, of the phallic self.[51] Rigidities either of ideology or of expressive form, on the other hand (or, worse yet, of both at once), seem almost invariably to have propelled his prophetic intensity, elsewhere such an energizing force, into aesthetic disaster. His theory of gender dualism, for instance, whether figured in the fruitful interaction of men and women or in the conjunction of timeless male and female "principles," at first provided Lawrence with a ready-made oppositional model of tremendous symbolic force, social significance, and personal relevance. Yet, when his formerly fluid and celebratory conceptions of gender difference solidified into dogma, Lawrence's "tension of opposites" all too quickly collapsed into the tedium of cant. This is not to argue that maleness and femaleness, whatever those terms may be taken to mean, must be mutually present and interactive in every viable creative work. If Lawrence had found a way to give creative voice to his ambivalences regarding homosexuality, for instance, rather than so swiftly channeling his fears of sexual indeterminacy into the ideological austerities of misogyny and male leadership, he might perhaps have discovered a new oppositional model to replace the traditional male-female one; indeed, he might have done away with such dualistic models altogether, as H.D. would at least briefly attempt to do. For the most part, however, an aesthetics of heterosexuality does seem to have provided Lawrence's most consistently constructive creative paradigm. His finest work celebrates the kind of essential, eternal, life-giving "strife" that he believed gender difference both to symbolize and to enact.[52]

Chapter 3

H.D. and the Poetics
of Possession

Should we be able to think with the womb and feel with the brain? . . . The
love-brain and the over-brain are both capable of thought. This thought is
vision.
> —H.D., "Notes on Thought and Vision," 1919

I keep dreaming of literary men, Shaw, Cunninghame Graham, now Noel
Coward and Lawrence himself, over and over. It is important as book means
penis evidently and as a "writer," only, am I an equal in the uc-n [uncon-
scious], in the right way, with men. Most odd.
> —H.D., letter to Bryher, 1933

but I went on, I had to go on,
the writing was the un-born,
the conception.
> —H.D., *Hermetic Definition*, 1960–61

"She herself is the writing," declares H.D. in *Helen in Egypt* (22), her revi-
sionary epic about perhaps the most self-identified of her many mytho-
logical alter egos, Helen of Troy. Yet even in this late work, composed
when H.D. was nearly seventy years old, such parthenogenetic self-
confidence is a relatively rare commodity; much of *Helen in Egypt*
focuses not only on Helen's search for creative and emotional auton-
omy but also on her problematic relationships with such powerful male
figures as Theseus, Paris, and Achilles. Sharing with her contempo-
raries Rilke and Lawrence a conception of poetic inspiration as a pow-
erful force that works upon the self, whether from outside or from deep
within the self, in a way that is as often terrifying as fertilizing, H.D.
spent most of her literary career grappling with the authoritative
dilemma that any prophetic enterprise entails. But, if her poetic devel-
opment—from stereotyped Imagiste to mystical Eleusinian initiate to
historical witness to epic seer—reflects the evolution of her self-confi-
dence as visionary writer and thinker, it also bears witness to the many
difficulties she had to overcome in attaining such a role.

119

Where Rilke and Lawrence sought to tap into female power without sacrificing their own identities as authoritative males, H.D. faced a similar yet opposite predicament: how could she, in Sandra Gilbert's words, "assimilate the wisdom of western culture without acquiescing to its misogyny"? ("H.D." 506). Male prophetic poets, even when making unconventional visionary claims, can draw upon established prophetic traditions for authority and justification, whether by echoing biblical cadences, by employing images associated with classical prophecy, or simply by introducing a thematics of privilege. Female poets, however, are likely to regard tradition and authority more as dangerous adversaries than as appropriable allies. If a female writer relies, like her male counterparts, primarily on strong male biblical and classical prophets as stylistic models, she implicitly denies the very possibility of a female-centered poetics of prophecy. Yet, if she chooses instead to imitate female seers such as Cassandra, the Delphic Pythia, and minor Old Testament prophetesses—women seldom granted the stature and authority of such great male prophets as Jeremiah, Samuel, or John of Patmos—she covertly suggests that her own visionary capacities depend less on an active penetration of male power structures than on traditionally feminine traits of receptivity and passivity.

H.D. eventually overcame this prophetic dilemma, but not until she had learned to marshal every expressive weapon at her command. Whereas her early poetry frequently depicts divine inspiration as a debilitating form of possession, in *Trilogy*, a three-part visionary poem written in London during World War II, she at last acknowledges prophecy as a potent means to self-expression. She accomplishes this through a process of identification that is itself, like the poem, tripartite: first, by appropriating the voices of male seers such as Isaiah and John of Patmos; second, by identifying herself with a variety of strong female figures; and, finally, when traditional models of prophecy prove inadequate, by drawing upon alternative sources of authority and authenticity as well, replacing classical and Judeo-Christian visionary hierarchies with a heterodox framework of her own.

In the course of the extended visionary quest that her writing both describes and enacts, H.D. would posit many different models for inspiration. For instance, she figures her own visionary capacity through a remarkable array of metaphors: a womb (see epigraph), a jellyfish, a radio, a telegraph receiving station, an Aeolian harp, a switchboard, a battery, an opera glass, a film projector, a magic lantern, a kaleidoscope. She identifies the products of her inspired creativity—"the book," "the writing"—at times with a strong female self, at times with a compensatory male phallus, and, eventually, in her 1961 *Hermetic Definition*, with a genderless child/grandchild called Espérance. Finally, she variously depicts the source of her poetic inspiration as a female goddess/muse, a male brother/lover/initiator, a stalking Spirit, and a frightening inner "Daemon."[1] This extraordinary multiplicity of creative metaphors occasionally leads her, to be sure, into the kind of self-contradiction so typical, for instance, of Lawrence. Yet it also vividly demonstrates the imaginative lengths to which H.D. was willing to go in her struggle to construct a poetics of inspiration that was not also necessarily a poetics of self-effacement.

Even so grudging an admirer as Hugh Kenner, who barely accorded her standing room in his *Pound Era* pantheon of modernist heroes, has acknowledged that to remember H.D. solely as an Imagist is "as though five of the shortest pieces in *Harmonium* were to stand for the life's work of Wallace Stevens."[2] Nonetheless, H.D. was carelessly dismissed for many years by the (mostly male) custodians of literary modernism as a writer of limited talent and scope, "the poet of a few gems . . . which gleam perhaps the more for the mediocrity of their setting" (Engel 522). Recently, however, her literary reputation has been resuscitated by feminist scholars eager to carve a place for her in the modernist canon. Arguing against critical assessments that would label "Eliot deeply religious, Pound profound, Crane prophetic, Williams archetypal, and Yeats visionary while the same phenomenon in H.D. is 'escapist'" (Friedman, "Who Buried H.D.?" 808), H.D.'s defenders have sought both to convey the remarkable range of her imaginative work and, more specifically, to document her difficult evolution into the self-confident visionary of *Trilogy*. Susan Stanford Friedman, for instance, demonstrates how H.D. transformed the potentially crippling doctrines of classical Freudian analysis into a feminist ideology confirming her own role as artist; Mary K. DeShazer traces her inventions and invocations of a potent female mother/goddess/muse; and Rachel Blau DuPlessis shows how even her "romantic thralldom" to a heterosexist vision of binary gender opposition contributed, in the end, to her artistic self-empowerment.[3]

The task of these critics, and of much feminist scholarship in general, has been not only to establish a place for female writers such as H.D. in a previously male-dominated literary canon but also, where necessary, to rewrite the criteria for induction. Such a revisionist agenda carries, of course, certain risks; for instance, the weaknesses in a female poet's work can all too easily be celebrated as "subversive" or excused as a consequence of male oppression. The best studies of H.D. are those that avoid facile veneration, casting a cold eye on H.D.'s real and potential artistic failings as well as on her strategies for success. Like Rilke and Lawrence, H.D. drew much of her poetic power from her willingness to confront paradoxical emotions, yet contradictions of impulse and expression frequently imperiled as much as they impelled her visionary poetics.

Unsheltered Gardens

The poems of H.D.'s "Imagist" period, although they frequently thematize divine inspiration, seldom claim to partake of it; throughout most of the three decades preceding World War II, in fact, H.D. would portray visionary experience more often as a curse than as a source of power. Nonetheless, even her earliest poetry betrays a deep-seated fascination with the tropes of inspiration and prophecy. Indeed, as in so much of Lawrence's poetry, H.D.'s apparent terror of being overwhelmed by a frightening Other is frequently matched by a simultaneous desire for contact with some powerful external source of knowledge and vision. These contradictory emotions of fear and longing dovetail, in turn, with questions of sexuality and sexual identity not unlike those voiced by Lawrence. Particularly in the poems of the late 1910s and early 1920s, composed during a period of deep personal and emotional turmoil, H.D. continually conflates divine possession and sexual possession, associating both with a loss of self that she finds at times frightening but at times deeply consoling.

Even the poems of her early *Sea Garden* (1916), although they can be called "prophetic" neither in voice, vision, nor thematics, squarely confront the poet-prophet's recurrent fear of being overwhelmed by the very inspiration that she requires in order to write. William York Tindall almost certainly had H.D. in mind when, in a polemic directed primarily at Lawrence, he castigated the Imagist poets for their "girlish enthusiasm" and accused them of "swooning at the fall of a fruit or over the color of a tile" (56). Certainly, one or two of H.D.'s early poems, such as "Orchard" (*CP* 28) and "Pear Tree" (39), might be said vaguely to fit Tindall's description, yet *swooning* and *girlish* (words that condemn merely by feminizing) nonetheless seem singularly inappropriate appellations for H.D.'s stark and often anguished verses. Nor, however, do her poems constitute the crystalline, temporally static, emotionally controlled linguistic constructs that the adjectives most frequently applied to them—stereotypically masculine words such as *hard*, *spare*, and *direct*—would imply. Although they do exhibit the kind of precision and economy of language for which Ezra Pound repeatedly called in his Imagist manifestos, the thematic territory of these poems is not a site of purity but, rather, what Louis L. Martz calls a "seething junction of opposite forces" that meet and clash in a violent yet exhilarating union (*CP* ix).

Throughout *Sea Garden* and *The God* the liminal space at that junction of forces—a physical and psychological zone both of confrontation and retreat that H.D. herself would later term "borderline"[4]—is represented by the narrow strip of shoreline where the sea meets the land. Patron and protector of this space is Hermes, who in H.D.'s poem "Hermes of the Ways" faces "three ways": not only out to sea and back toward the shore but also sideways along the littoral, the band of shoreline between high and low tide that constitutes neither sand nor surf alone.[5] As mercurial messenger god, Hermes serves as an even more powerful mediatory figure than Rilke's Orpheus, for, in addition to traversing two opposing worlds, he also serves as a protector and guide to the inhabitants of both. In later works H.D. links "the winged messenger, Hermes of the Greeks, Mercury of the Romans" first with J. J. van der Leeuw, the "Flying Dutchman" whose death in a 1934 plane crash had had an inexplicably shattering effect on her (*Tribute* 4–8), and then with the seven male "initiators" (Ezra Pound, Richard Aldington, John Cournos, D. H. Lawrence, Cecil Gray, Kenneth Macpherson, and Walter Schmideberg) who had, she declared, most profoundly affected her artistic self-definition: "*Hermes of the Ways.* Hermes, actor, charlatan, magician. Ezra was the first of these initiators" (*Compassionate Friendship* 24). Eventually, H.D. even comes to identify herself with the messenger god: "H.D.—Hermes—Hermeticism and all the rest of it" (*End to Torment* 40). Certainly, in titles such as *Hermetic Definition* and *HERmione* (like the Greek Hermione, H.D. had a mother named Helen, and, like Shakespeare's Hermione, she had a daughter named Perdita), she deliberately encodes Hermes' name in connection with her own.

Beyond merely acting as the poet's guide and helper, then, H.D.'s

Hermes, like Rilke's Orpheus, stands in for the visionary poet herself, bridging, mediating between, and perhaps even transcending the opposing realms of life and death, turbulence and calm, darkness and light, human and divine, male and female. In "Hermes of the Ways" the messenger god straddles the elements of earth and water. While sea and shore do not fit any more neatly than did Lawrence's concepts of "Love" and "Law" within a rigid system of binary gender oppositions (do we posit a fluid "female" sea and a rigid "male" land? a passive "female" shore and an active "male" sea?), it is nonetheless striking how closely Hermes' three "ways"—sea, shore, and the tidal strip that divides them—correspond to H.D.'s triple visionary strategy in later works such as *Trilogy*, in which she acknowledges both male and female prophetic traditions yet also charts a third path, narrow but liberating, between them. For the most part, however, the Hermes of H.D.'s early poems remains more a mentor and protector than an alter ego to the poet, who, although she tries in poems such as "Oread" to effect a merging of sea and land by means of an impassioned fiat (*CP* 55), has not yet fully realized her own potential as poetic go-between.

Indeed, if H.D., in *Sea Garden*, could be said to identify very closely with anyone or anything, it would be not with any human figure or god but with the fragile yet defiant sea flowers that give the volume its name. H.D. herself always "enjoy[ed] the harsher aspects of nature" (Swann 15); her walk with William Carlos Williams during their college days in Pennsylvania, when she refused to take shelter from a raging thunderstorm and instead opened her arms to the downpour and cried, "Beautiful rain, welcome" (Williams 69), has by now become legendary. Yet poems such as "Sheltered Garden," in which she begs the wind "to break, / scatter these pink-stalks" (*CP* 20) and "Garden," in which she calls for it to "cut apart the heat, / rend it to tatters" (25), betray the danger as well as the vitality of H.D.'s quest for

> a new beauty
> in some terrible
> wind-tortured place
>
> (21)

outside the gardens of civilized convention. The wind, as a traditional figure for inspiration, might be expected to fill the poet with knowledge, power, and visionary insight, yet in *Sea Garden* it all too often brings a longed-for amnesia instead ("O to blot out this garden / to forget" [21]) and, at worst, complete annihilation.

Art, of course, is often said to thrive upon opposition (see, e.g., Blake: "Without Contraries is no progression"). Hence, in "Storm" the wind-torn branches and leaves partake of a strange and vibrant beauty (*CP* 36), while in "Sea Lily" a fragile reed (symbol of music and thereby of poetry) becomes "doubly rich" as a result of the storm's buffeting and in the end is borne triumphantly upon the very wind that has threatened to destroy it (14). In "The Wind Sleepers," however, the poet flees the wind's sting, and in "Mid-day," similarly, even the mildest breeze seems to be more than she can withstand:

> A slight wind shakes the seed-pods—
> my thoughts are spent
> as the black seeds.
> My thoughts tear me,
> I dread their fever.
> I am scattered in its whirl
> I am scattered like
> the hot shrivelled seeds.
>
> (10)

Like Lawrence in "Song of a Man Who Is Not Loved"—who feels "a big wind blowing / Me like a gadfly into the dusk" and concludes, "I am too / Little to count in the wind that drifts me through" (*LCP* 222)—the poet of "Mid-day" declares herself "anguished" and "defeated" by the dreadful force that even this "slight wind" heralds (*CP* 10). Yet, far from merely reciting the wind's effects, H.D. also calls into question its provenance: Is she the victim, she asks, of some outside force ("the wind"), or merely of her own inner turmoil ("my thoughts," "their fever")? The question is one that echoes in various forms throughout H.D.'s poetry. Continually invoking and problematizing the destructive powers of sexuality, she persistently debates, even following her own infrequent experiences of visionary consciousness, whether such visions have been projected through her by some omniscient Other or have welled up from an unknown source deep within her own psyche.

In the volumes of poetry following *Sea Garden* H.D. goes on to explore in even greater detail the paradoxical nature of the poet-prophet's stance as both creative agent and receptive vessel. In poem after poem, extending her classical imagery to include a whole array of mythological figures, she chronicles not the idyllic lifestyles and magnificent heroism of the ancient Greeks so much as their agonies, losses, and betrayals, focusing especially on modes of victimization: of women by men; of mortals by gods; of the powerless, always, by the powerful. Despite their Greek mask, many of these poems reflect H.D.'s own experiences at the time of their composition: by early 1919, at the age of thirty-two, she had survived the uncertainties of the Great War as well as the painful losses, either through death or emotional estrangement, of her brother, her father, her stillborn first child, her husband, and such close friends as John Cournos, D. H. Lawrence, and Cecil Gray. Much of her poetic enterprise during this period, then, concerns her attempt to transform personal tragedy into a literature of survival.

Yet, if H.D.'s poetry tries to bring order to experience, it also exhibits an acute awareness that, in Shakespeare's phrase, "The lunatic, the lover, and the poet / Are of imagination all compact": the "spontaneous overflow of powerful feelings," in other words, can bear a perilous likeness to the gushings of a madman. Indeed, far from "swooning" with the "girlish enthusiasm" that William Tindall described as a hallmark of Imagist poetry, H.D. clear-sightedly warns of the dangers that a more ominous form of enthusiasm—literally, possession by a god or divine Other—can entail. As a devout scholar of Greek literature, she was no doubt familiar with Plato's *Phaedrus*, in which Socrates describes four forms of inspiration, or what he tellingly calls "divine madness": prophetic (linked with Apollo); ritual, or telestic (Dionysus); poetic (the Muses); and erotic (Aphrodite and Eros) (52). All are associated with superhuman power or pleasure, yet all suggest as well a lack of control that, if unchecked, can lead to destruction.

In her poetry of the 1920s and 1930s H.D. confronts and problematizes in turn each of Socrates' four modes of divine madness: erotic possession in *Hymen* (1921) and *Heliodora* (1924); Dionysian ecstasy in *Red Roses for Bronze* (1931); prophetic vision in *A Dead Priestess Speaks* and other poems; and the Muse-inspired poetic enthusiasm in virtually every aspect of her investigations. Only with *Trilogy*, composed during World War II, would she move beyond Socrates' association of inspiration with the dangers and intoxications of divine possession, finally evolving a new, more optimistic poetics that would affirm the redemptive possibilities of visionary experience.

"Love . . . bitter-sweet": *Hymen* and *Heliodora*

The poems of *Hymen* and *Heliodora*, published in the early 1920s, explore in often harrowing detail the workings of the divine madness provoked, according to Socrates' schema, by Eros and Aphrodite. Neither volume, to be sure, focuses exclusively on the negative aspects of erotic desire: some poems, such as "Evadne," cheerfully celebrate sexual love (*CP* 132); others, such as "Hymen" and "Leda," associate marriage and sexuality with a measured, abstract grace (101–10, 120–21); and others still, such as "Lethe" and the Sapphic "Fragment 113," reject sexuality (or at least heterosexuality) altogether: "Neither honey nor bee for me" (131, 190). The majority of these poems, however, persistently enact situations of emotional manipulation and entrapment, reflecting the poet's wary conviction that possession, whether of the divine or the sexual kind, can lead to a frightening, debilitating loss of self.

Throughout both volumes H.D. not only celebrates powerful goddesses such as Artemis and Demeter but also lends her voice to such abused, abandoned, and silenced women from the past as Iphigenia, Eurydice, Ariadne, and Penelope. In addition, she rehabilitates a number of women traditionally regarded as evil temptresses—figures such as Phaedra, Helen, and Circe—by showing that they, too, have in their own ways been victims of divine and human machinations. Only Aphrodite, perpetrator of the erotic madness that claims throughout H.D.'s work so many tragic victims, receives no such redemptive treatment. Instead, H.D.'s poetic relationship with the goddess of love is characterized by a profound ambivalence, as she tries to reconcile the agony of unrequited passion and the bitterness of loss with the creativity and joy sparked by erotic desire.

This vexed stance toward Aphrodite is perhaps most explicitly enacted in a series of verses loosely based on fragments from Sappho, patroness of love poets and particularly of female poets. For instance, in "Fragment Forty-one" (". . . thou flittest to Andromeda"), the poet insists that, although Aphrodite has tortured her by allowing her lover to fall in love with another woman, she herself has always remained a faithful devotee of the goddess:

> I too have followed
> her path.
> I too have bent at her feet.
>
> (*CP* 181)

In "Fragment Sixty-eight" ("... even in the house of Hades"), similarly, the poet continues to honor Aphrodite even though she has been "trapped" and "slain" by her:

> though I break,
> crushed under the goddess' hate,
> though I fall beaten at last,
> so high have I thrust my glance
> up into her presence.
>
> (189)

While she does not exempt from blame the lover who has deserted her—"What can death mar in me / that you have not?" (188)—she implies that Aphrodite, above all, is responsible for her pain: the poet has been victimized as much by the vindictive goddess who plagues her with erotic desire as by the mortal man who has rejected her. H.D.'s tendency to blame love rather than the lover bears out Adrienne Rich's assertion that female poets seldom protest male oppression directly:

> Until recently this female anger and this furious awareness of the Man's power over her were not available materials to the female poet, who tended to write of Love as the source of her suffering, and to view that victimization by Love as an almost inevitable fate. Or, like Marianne Moore and Elizabeth Bishop, she kept sexuality at a measured and chiseled distance in her poems. ("When We Dead Awaken: Writing as Re-Vision," *On Lies* 36).

Indeed, by placing a female in the role of rapist—Aphrodite, after all, violates the poet's peace of mind, if not her body—H.D. suggests, problematically, that the anguished love poet is the victim less of an invasive, external Other than of an internalized, female destructive force. As in "Mid-day," then, in which "my thoughts" and "I" become separate and antagonistic entities, the poet, tortured by her own emotions and desires, becomes possessed, in a sense, by herself.

"Fragment Forty" ("Love ... bitter-sweet") offers one explanation why the poet, despite the pain that erotic desire has caused her, continues to worship at the shrine of love, which is both "bitter" and "sweet," both "honey" and "salt" (*CP* 173). Love here is personified not by Aphrodite but, instead, by her son Eros, a capricious and elusive god;

the poem addresses the impossibility of imprisoning him or, by extension, of sustaining any form of romantic love for long. In a series of comparisons recalling the flower and sea imagery of *Sea Garden*, the poet admits her astonishment that her lover's unfaithfulness, a manifestation of Eros's cruelty and power, has not crushed and destroyed her:

> I had thought myself frail;
> a petal,
> with light equal
> on leaf and under-leaf.

> I had thought myself frail;
> a lamp,
> shell, ivory or crust of pearl,
> about to fall shattered,
> with flame spent.

(174–75)

As in *Sea Garden*, however, the very force that threatens to annihilate the poet actually lends her strength: "to sing love," she courageously asserts, "love must first shatter us" (175). To some extent, of course, the poet's determination to put a brave face on the matter smacks of pure survivalism: having been both "deserted" and "shattered" by love, she seeks to make the best of her pain, transforming bitterness into sweetness, bitter experience into art. On the other hand, however, the conclusion of "Fragment Forty" reflects a very real belief on H.D.'s part— one shared, as I have shown, by precursors including Goethe and Blake as well as by Rilke and Lawrence—that adversity and contradiction are necessary preconditions for creativity. Forcefully demonstrating that erotic madness need not necessarily lead to a loss of self-control and thence to self-destruction, H.D. shows instead that possession begets self-possession: just as she can craft well-wrought poems from Sapphic fragments, so she can forge art from agony, triumph from despair. The poet plaintively asks in "Fragment Thirty-six" what she would do if her beloved were to leave her:

> were you lost,
> what rapture

could I take from song?
what song were left?

(166)

The poems of *Hymen* and *Heliodora* assure us, however, that many songs will be left after the loving is over.

All the same, H.D. keeps us vividly aware of the danger that the process might become reversed: that the agony of sexual desire (or, for that matter, the ecstasy of sexual fulfillment) could overtake and over-whelm both the artist and the art. If, at times, the poet of *Hymen* and *Heliodora* seems to crave such self-annihilation, it is because the burden of art and emotion has become too heavy. Thus, in "Cassandra" the eponymous prophetess's appeal to Hymen to slake her unwanted sexual passion can be read, simultaneously, as an appeal to Apollo either to relieve her of her undesired visionary powers or to allow those powers to crush her:

> Hymen, O Hymen king,
> what bitter thing is this?
> what shaft, tearing my heart?
> what scar, what light, what fire
> searing my eye-balls and my eyes with flame?
> nameless, O spoken name,
> king, lord, speak blameless Hymen.
>
> Why do you blind my eyes?
> why do you dart and pulse
> till all the dark is home,
> then find my soul
> and ruthless draw it back?
> scaling the scaleless,
> opening the dark?
> speak, nameless, power and might;
> when will you leave me quite?
> when will you break my wings
> or leave them utterly free
> to scale heaven endlessly?

(*CP* 169–70)

Cassandra's desire to be destroyed if she cannot be left alone results in a Semele-like death wish:

> May Love not lie beside me
> till his heat
> burn me to ash?

(171)

"Servitude," in Gary Burnett's gloss, "controls all of the poem's options" (*H.D.* 78); poetic, prophetic, and erotic possession are all equally implicated in Cassandra's plea for a lover who might "bear with me / the kiss of your white fire" and share her triple burden of vision, passion, and speech:

> is there not one,
> Phrygian or frenzied Greek,
> poet, song-swept, or bard,
> one meet to take from me
> this bitter power of song[?]

(*CP* 171)

"Cassandra" voices H.D.'s conception of poetry, like prophecy, as an agonizing yet inescapable force, one that both energizes and threatens to destroy. Cassandra longs to find a poetic and erotic peer, someone who "can equal me / in ecstasy, desire" (170). Yet the poem also implies that such a slaking of her sexual thirst would result in the loss of her visionary and expressive powers.

In *Eros the Bittersweet*, a delightful essay in erotic paradox, Anne Carson reminds us that the Greek word *eros* denotes a "'want,' 'lack,' 'desire for that which is missing'": thus, Carson playfully argues, "eros is a verb," an active emotional construct that must nonetheless always be represented as "deferred, defied, obstructed, hungry, organized around a radiant absence— . . . eros as lack" (17–18). Eros, or desire, in fact signifies an absence so powerful that it takes on the role of a presence, so that the romantic pairings that generally characterize human sexuality—dualities, if not always necessarily of male and female, then at least of lover and beloved, self and an erotic Other—triangulate into complex constellations that include as a third party desire itself: eros as a force both motivational and mediatory. Stated in Derridean terms,

difference always fractures into *différance*, the endless deferrals of signi-
fication—for "le signe représente le présent en son absence" (Derrida,
Marges 9)—that make sexual consummation an ultimately unsatisfying
experience: intimate contact with another invariably leads to a con-
sciousness of one's own finiteness, motivating, in turn, new fabrica-
tions of desire, new manufacturings of bittersweet lack. Susan Gubar,
discussing the role of unfulfilled desire in H.D.'s Sapphic verse, has
gone so far as to argue that H.D.'s "poetic abandon," the inspired pas-
sion that fueled her poetics, depended for its intensity upon "erotic
abandonment":

> While it is certainly true that H.D. writes obsessively about her
> desire for the mastery of such men as Pound, Aldington, and
> Lawrence, her poetry is motivated less by their presence than by
> their absence. . . . For H.D., then, inspiration and abandonment (by
> men) are inextricably intertwined. ("Sapphistries" 57)

After all, as Carson notes, even the perfect two-person spheres from
which, according to Platonic myth, all human life once emerged were
not content with their "prelapsarian oneness": "They got big ideas and
started rolling toward Olympus to make an attempt on the gods. . . .
They began reaching for something else. So much for oneness" (68;
Symposium 191d). As H.D. puts it in "Epigrams": "Love has no charm /
when Love is swept to earth" (*CP* 172).

René Girard has argued that every literary fiction is triadic in its
structure: all plots are built from an inner architecture consisting of
subject, object, and mediator (2). Throughout H.D.'s poetry, and partic-
ularly her Sapphic verse, emotional triangulations of the kind Girard
describes occur frequently, resulting not only in the classic love trian-
gles of romance novels and soap operas (lover plus beloved plus a jeal-
ousy-inducing, plot-furthering third party)[6] but also in the more com-
plex interactions that ensue when the trouble-causing romantic
interloper is not a human but Eros, a god—and an absent, invisible god
at that. Yet, if "that bitter, bitter creature, Eros" frequently serves as
H.D.'s triangulating Other (*Notes on Thought and Vision* 65), the ques-
tion of where he (or, in the case of his female counterpart Aphrodite,
she) comes from remains: Is desire an internal force or one imposed
upon the lover from outside? H.D., as I have already shown, cannot
quite make up her mind (or bring into harmony what, in "Fragment

Thirty-Six," she will call her "two minds"). On the one hand, like the inspirational wind of *Sea Garden*, sexual desire represents a dangerous power that can crush and destroy the poet if it is not safely harnessed. To this extent it makes sense for H.D. to blame her pain and even her expressive failures upon a cruel external Other, eros personified as vindictive deity; then, if she can resist despair and produce poetry despite the agonies imposed by love, her creative victory appears that much more impressive. On the other hand, however, eros also remains, like that threatening yet exhilarating wind of inspiration, a creative necessity for the poet; in addition to transforming desire into art (for "to write," says Roland Barthes, "is a mode of Eros" [xvi]), she must also learn, if required, to create the desire that creates poetry.

As a frightening yet necessary creative force, desire resembles inspiration. In a sense, in fact, desire *is* inspiration, for various forms of lack—the longing for a lost love, the impulse to redress an ancient myth's unfairness, the ambition to express an emotion more perfectly than it has ever been expressed before—motivate virtually all creative endeavor. As Derrida puts it in *Writing and Difference*, "Only *pure absence*—not the absence of this or that, but the absence of everything in which all presence is announced—can *inspire*, in other words, can *work*, and then make one work" (8). The converse, however, does not hold equally true; inspiration is not desire, for, where eros signifies eternal emptiness, inspiration implies a fullness, fulfillment. Thus, if the lover strives not for union with the desired Other so much as for an endless suspension of desire—"For his delight is in reaching; to reach for something perfect would be perfect delight" (Carson 69)—then divine inspiration, or the flooding of the self with the essence and energies of another, represents precisely the movement of closure that kills desire and makes poetry, particularly love poetry, impossible. This paradox is not, however, an unresolvable one; the trick is to welcome inspiration as one welcomes love yet to hold it, like desire, always at a distance, submitting influence, like ardor, to the rigors of one's own emotional and artistic discipline. This will become H.D.'s strategy in her later, self-confidently prophetic works, as she employs various mechanical metaphors—the radio, the receiving station, the film projector—to explain how her mind can function as an instrument both of passive receptivity and of controlled precision. Meanwhile, however, particularly in her Sapphic verses, H.D. opts to err on the side of cautious internalization, hinting that, despite her invocations of and tirades against powerful gods such as Eros and Aphrodite, her painful yet productive erotic conflicts are largely self-imposed.

H.D.'s "Fragment Thirty-six," which bears as its epigraph the Sapphic lines "I know not what to do: my mind is divided," offers a particularly vivid demonstration of how sexual desire can induce a violent internal conflict. Trying to choose between awakening her beloved or praising him in song7—"is song's gift best? / is love's gift loveliest?" (*CP* 165)—H.D. literalizes the psychic battle between love (desire fulfilled) and song (desire deliciously suspended) by representing her "two minds" as wrestlers poised for stylized yet vicious combat:

> My mind is quite divided,
> my minds hesitate,
> so perfect matched,
> I know not what to do:
> each strives with each
> as two white wrestlers
> standing for a match,
> ready to turn and clutch
> yet never shake muscle nor nerve nor tendon;
> so my mind waits
> to grapple with my mind,
> yet I lie quiet,
> I would seem at rest.
>
> (167)

Even more so than in H.D.'s earlier poem "Mid-day," the poet's self, the "I" of the poem, seems separate from her mind, or, in this case, from her two minds, destructive and self-destructive entities (personified, oddly, as men) that prepare to annihilate each other while the poet merely "lie[s] quiet" and observes. As so often in H.D.'s poetry, the image is simultaneously one of powerlessness—the poet, helpless to affect the outcome of their struggle, can only watch the wrestlers fight it out—and of determined control: far from succumbing to the emotional paralysis that the situation threatens to engender, the poet rises above the conflict and transforms it into art. Thus, she effectively resolves her own dilemma—love or song?—by enacting the triumph of artistic expression over transient physicality, thereby bearing out Anne Carson's assertion that erotic action is nearly always displaced, through the process of triangulation, by "a ruse of heart and language" (17). The poet, in other words, invariably chooses eros sublimated (song) over eros fulfilled (sexual love), a tendency continued in the following stanza, in which H.D. shifts her imagery from the Olympic arena to her beloved seashore:

> as a wave-line may wait to fall
> yet (waiting for its falling)
> still the wind may take
> from off its crest,
> white flake on flake of foam,
> that rises,
> seeming to dart and pulse
> and rend the light,
> so my mind hesitates
> above the passion
> quivering yet to break,
> so my mind hesitates
> above my mind,
> listening to song's delight.
>
>   (CP 167)

Desire here remains suspended and sustained, a fragile yet productive arc (flaking with foam, shimmering with light), a wave forever unbreaking, enshrined already in song and "song's delight."

The image of one mind, or one part of the poet's mind, hovering tentatively above another recalls H.D.'s 1919 essay "Notes on Thought and Vision," one of her earliest attempts to articulate a theory of creativity that might permit, in turn, a poetics of self-possession. At the beginning of the essay H.D. posits a tripartite division of self into body, mind, and a vaguely Emersonian "over-mind" (later she will switch to the more Freudian terms *sub-conscious, conscious,* and *over-conscious mind,* instead) to explain the interactions of multiple psychic states within a single human being (*Notes* 17, 49). In contrast to Lawrence, who so often divides his world into bipolar opposites (male/female, active/passive, systole/diastole), or Rilke, who in the *Sonnets to Orpheus* yearns for a continuous oscillation between two complementary principles, H.D. tends to break her imaginative universe into units of three; thus, figures such as her "Hermes of the Ways" achieve their power, as I have shown, not just by traversing two disparate realms but by establishing a third realm that, although dependent on the other two for its definition, partakes fully of neither. In "Notes on Thought and Vision," as she shifts the meanings of her terms and definitions practically from one paragraph to the next, the conceptual trinities that H.D. posits may seem slippery, unwieldy, and even, like Lawrence's gender classifications, downright self-contradictory. Nonetheless, her consistent effort to avoid a rigidly dualistic cosmological schema, the kind of system that almost invariably comes to include "male" and "female" among its primary oppositional pairings, bears witness to the complexity as well as the confusion of her thinking on the subject of artistic creativity.

More so perhaps than any other of H.D.'s works, "Notes on Thought and Vision" strongly emphasizes the roles of sexuality and sexual desire in artistic production, presenting love in a far more positive light than do most of her poems from the same period. Although she stresses in the opening lines of the essay that "men and women of highest development" will aim for an equilibrium of all three "states or manifestations of life" (body, mind, and over-mind) at once, H.D. accords special attention to the body, or what, a few pages later, she will come to call the "love-brain":

> Men and women of temperament, musicians, artists, especially, need these [physical] relationships to develop and draw forth their talents. Not to desire and make every effort to develop along these natural physical lines, cripples and dwarfs the being. To shun, deny and belittle such experiences is to bury one's talent carefully in a napkin. (17)

Describing the over-mind, that hyperconscious yet strangely unconscious perceptive state that gives rise to creative vision, first in terms of a cap over one's head and then as a "closed sea-plant, jelly-fish, or anemone" that seems to send long feelers trailing through the body, H.D. notes that such heightened vision can manifest itself physically as well as mentally:

> I first realised this state of consciousness in my head. I visualise it just as well, now, centered in the love-region of the body or placed like a foetus in the body. (19)

Having herself recently given birth to a child, H.D. links creative consciousness not, like Rilke in his seven "phallic hymns" or Lawrence in *Fantasia of the Unconscious*, with the fertilizing force of male sexuality but, rather, with a productive, reproductive organ specific to women: "The brain and the womb are both centres of consciousness, equally important" (21). Yet, despite her emphasis throughout "Notes on Thought and Vision" on what she calls "vision of the womb," H.D. avoids the kind of biological determinism that this passage could easily be misread as espousing. "Vision of the womb," for H.D., is only one manifestation of the "love-vision" that she associates with the physical aspects of creative consciousness; though centered, for women, in the uterus, such vision can also spring from "the corresponding love-region of a man's body" (20).

Citing for classical authority Socrates, whose "whole doctrine of vision was a doctrine of love," H.D. argues in "Notes" that visionary insight depends upon the energizing force of erotic desire: "We must be 'in love' before we can understand the mysteries of vision." Moreover, she asserts (much as Carson intimates in *Eros the Bittersweet*) that sexual desire must remain unconsummated if it is to be sublimated into art:

> The love-region is excited by the appearance or beauty of the loved one, its energy not dissipated in physical relation, takes on its character of mind, becomes this womb-brain or love-brain that I have visualised as a jelly-fish *in* the body.

Every lover, according to H.D.'s romantic/erotic schema, must "choose one of the same mind as himself, a musician, a musician, a scientist, a scientist, a general, a young man also interested in the theory and practice of arms and armies" (*Notes* 22), in order to achieve the "sympathy of thought" that leads to a productive interchange of ideas. Yet, just as H.D. emphasizes here similarities rather than differences of temperament as the constituent elements of creativity (in contrast to the "without Contraries is no progression" school of thought with which she elsewhere, particularly in the violent verses of *Sea Garden*, seems to agree), her association of love with creative vision remains strikingly free of notions of sexual dualism: although she argues that "there is no great art period without great lovers" (21), H.D. gives no indication that such lovers must be heterosexual (in fact, her examples of two scientists or two soldiers loving each other suggest, if anything, a male homosexual paradigm). Thus, even so gender-specific a concept as "vision of the womb" is not made to rely upon the traditional creativity-as-birth metaphor, which assumes some form of male-female interaction as a prerequisite for artistic (re)production. Creativity, she suggests, results from sexual desire but not, even in a metaphorical sense, from heterosexual intercourse.

"Notes on Thought and Vision" does not, to be sure, avoid heterosexual metaphors entirely; for instance, whereas early in the essay H.D. pictures the body and the intellect, the love-mind and the over-mind, as two lenses of an opera glass that can only "bring the world of vision into consciousness" when focused together (23), later she explicitly (hetero)sexualizes this process of mind-body harmonization: "But as it takes a man and woman to create another life, so it takes these two forms of seed, one in the head and one in the body to make a new spiritual birth" (50). Nonetheless, even if one agrees with Barbara Guest's statement that "some of the 'Notes' read like D. H. Lawrence at his philosophic worst" (120), H.D.'s essay reflects a nonessentialist mode of thinking that would remain largely foreign both to Lawrence and to Rilke. Although she insists on the need for Otherness, in the sense of sexual partnership, as a component of creativity, she avoids conventional conceptions of maleness and femaleness as mutually energizing and fertilizing forces.

Even when, in a series of 1920 epigrams entitled "Helios and Athene," H.D. more obviously anatomizes creative destiny, it is in order to declare Athene, who possesses both male and female characteristics, to be a mediatory figure on the order of Rilke's Orpheus or H.D.'s own Hermes:

> The Love of Athene is symbolized by the arch of wings, for Demeter by the cavern or grot in the earth, and for Phoebus in the very essential male power. Love for Athene is the surrender to neither, the merging and welding of both, the conquering in herself of each element, so that the two merge in the softness and tenderness of the mother and the creative power and passion of the male. In her hand is the symbol of this double conquest and double power, the winged Nike. (*CP* 330)

Although Athene, like Artemis, is a virgin goddess, she has had vicarious experience of love through her insight into both male and female sexuality, both masculine "creative power and passion" and motherly "tenderness." Athene's "double conquest and double power" might be read as referring, then, not so much to her hermaphroditism—she is, after all, still clearly a female figure—as to her bisexuality: her knowledge, like that of Tiresias, of the erotic secrets of both sexes.[8]

"Notes on Thought and Vision" and "Helios and Athene" were composed during two of the many holidays that H.D. would spend together with Bryher, the wealthy young Englishwoman who, having fallen in love with H.D., had recently rescued her from grave illness and psychological despair. H.D.'s relationship with Bryher (eventually, it would become one primarily of emotional rather than physical interdependence, to the extent that H.D.'s daughter would later describe her mother and foster mother as "platonic lesbians")[9] was not her first homosexual experience; as her autobiographical novel *HERmione* makes clear, her passionate love affair with Frances Gregg ("Fayne Rabb") during her college days in Pennsylvania had already had a profound effect upon her sexual self-definition.[10] Yet it may well have been H.D.'s recent reaffirmation of her own bisexuality, especially so soon after the painful dissolution of her marriage to Richard Aldington, that encouraged her to avoid—even while "Helios and Athene" relies upon traditional gender stereotypes in its celebration of the goddess—strictly heterosexual metaphors in her discussions of poetic creativity. Whereas Lawrence's repression of his own homosexual tendencies seems to have led, in other words, to an increased misogyny and a "poetics of machismo," H.D.'s bisexuality apparently diminished the risk of ideological rigidity. This is not to say, however, that her thinking would henceforth eschew all patriarchal constructions of gender; as Rachel Blau DuPlessis has vividly demonstrated, H.D. would continue for the rest of her life to conceptualize poetic experience along strongly heterosexual lines ("Romantic Thralldom").

"Notes on Thought and Vision," then, represents less an evolutionary milestone than a single, rather isolated moment in H.D.'s thinking about creativity and gender. But the essay also echoes several of the major themes of *Hymen* and *Heliodora:* H.D.'s insistence on sexual love, though not necessarily on heterosexuality, as a key to poetic production; her emphasis on erotic desire rather than erotic fulfillment, since sexual consummation implies a loss of control, whereas desire can be channeled or sublimated into art; and her use of female figures such as Cassandra and Sappho as the at times plaintive, at times forceful articulators of the poet's own literary anxieties, sexual longings, and "vision of the womb." If the poems of *Hymen* and *Heliodora* do not, for the most part, address issues of poetic inspiration directly, they do express virtually all the paradoxical fears and desires that complicate and energize any prophetic poet's enterprise. H.D.'s yearning for a force greater than herself to absolve her of expressive responsibility, her terror that such possession might lead to a loss of identity, and her concerted attempt to bring body and mind (love-brain and over-brain) into some kind of visionary focus reflect concerns and ambivalences that would continue to surface in her poetry for the next forty years.

Dionysian Ecstasies, Delphic Projections

Whereas *Hymen* and *Heliodora* take as their central theme erotic passion, H.D.'s subsequent poetry shifts its main focus to two of the other forms of divine possession described in Plato's *Phaedrus*. Specifically, in *Red Roses for Bronze* (1931) H.D. explores the ritual enthusiasm that Socrates associates with Dionysus, while in *A Dead Priestess Speaks* and other poems from the late 1920s and 1930s she turns her attention to the prophetic fervor induced by Apollo, the god of poetry, instead.

Of Socrates' four modes of divine madness, Dionysian ecstasy is the one that most readily indicates an utter lack of self-control. At the same time, however, the ritual nature of telestic madness suggests a planned rather than a spontaneous frenzy, since the consumption of alcohol or other mind-altering substances provides, paradoxically, a conscious means to an uncontrolled state of consciousness. E. R. Dodds notes that, in contrast to "the Apolline mediumship [of the Pythia or Sibil] which aims at knowledge," Dionysian experience is pursued for its own sake, "the mantic or mediumistic element being absent or quite subordinate." Apolline mediumship is "the rare gift of chosen individuals"; Dionysian ecstasy, in contrast, "is so far from being a rare gift that it is highly infectious" (69). It represents divine inspiration, in other words, in its most degenerate form.

Dionysus already makes his appearance in H.D.'s work in such early poems as "The God" (1916), in which the wine god (representing the more prosaic human personage of Richard Aldington) suffuses both the wine-dark landscape and the fascinated poet herself with his rich yet sinister essence:

now I am powerless
to draw back
for the sea is cyclamen-purple,
cyclamen-red, colour of the last grapes,
colour of the purple of the flowers,
cyclamen-coloured and dark.

(CP 47)

Here Dionysus represents an ominous force but one that is also fascinating, intoxicating, erotic. In the poems of *Red Roses for Bronze*, in contrast, H.D. portrays Dionysian influence and ecstasy as nothing short of terrifying. "Choros Translations from *The Bacchae*," for instance, replays the most gruesome section of Euripides' tragedy, as the Bacchantes,

driven mad,
mad,
mad
by Bacchus.

(224)

first dance themselves to a sacred frenzy and then join Agave in tearing her innocent son Pentheus to shreds. Whereas the female figures of *Hymen* and *Heliodora* are frequently possessed by Aphrodite, a female goddess who in part represents their own self-destructive psyches, H.D.'s Bacchantes are driven from ecstasy to madness to murder by a specifically male god, who favors the use of women as the vehicles of his power.[11] Indeed, Bacchus/Dionysus embodies as well as enacts the dangers of direct revelation, having been born from a union that resulted in a mortal woman's tragic annihilation by Zeus, as H.D. was grimly aware: "It was *de rigueur* for an Olympian not to appear to a mortal direct. Therefore Selene who requested this, was burned to ash" (*Notes* 38).

Red Roses for Bronze opens with a desperate but ultimately failed bid for the kind of artistic control that might make recourse to divine inspiration, and hence to Dionysian madness, unnecessary. In the volume's title piece the poet, figured as sculptor, seems determined to master herself and her erotic agonies by mastering the man who has caused them. Like a sort of female Pygmalion, she longs to mold a new, more loving, more dependable lover to replace the old one who has failed her:

> If I might fashion
> eyes and mouth and chin,
> if I might take dark bronze
> and hammer in
> the line beneath your underlip
> (the slightly mocking,
> slightly cynical smile
> you choose to wear)
> if I might ease my fingers and my brain
> with stroke,
> stroke,
> stroke,
> stroke,
> stroke at—something (stone, marble, intent, stable, materialized)
> peace,
> even magic sleep
> might come again.
>
> (CP 211)

In a much earlier poem called "Pygmalion" H.D. calls into question the poet-sculptor's ability even to master his or her own creation; Pygmalion, although he can carve images of the gods from stone, remains uncertain whether he shapes them or they, ultimately, shape him:

> Now am I the power
> that has made this fire
> as of old I made the gods
> start from the rocks?
> am I the god?
> or does this fire carve me
> for its use?
>
> (50)

"Red Roses for Bronze," similarly, shows how the poet's attempt to act out her anger and her desire—to "stroke, / stroke, / stroke, / stroke at" her lover's face in a gesture both violent and gently erotic—ends in a sort of creative stalemate: the poem, written entirely in the subjunctive ("*If* I *might* take a weight of bronze . . ."), describes less the poet's actual mastery of her lover and her emotions than her anguished realization that such control still eludes her.

The short, strung-out, repetitive verses of "Red Roses for Bronze" are echoed again and again in poems throughout the volume, as H.D. finally abandons the exquisite linguistic precision that first brought her fame as an Imagist. The problem is that she fails to replace such disciplined technique with a redeeming sense of confidence; although her poetic voice, powerful in its desperation, might be said to have prophetic resonances, hers is the tortured prophecy that borders on the discourse of madness. Gary Burnett has tried to redeem the stylistic shortcomings of *Red Roses for Bronze* by arguing that, just as H.D. would increasingly employ mechanical metaphors to describe her visionary experiences, here she uses "simple mechanical repetition" in order to create "a new perception" through language (*H.D.* 104). Burnett's defense of the volume is ingenious but, I think, unconvincing; H.D.'s repetitions are "mechanical" only in the negative sense of seeming automatic and robotic, demonstrating no real imaginative control over her material. When, in "Chance Meeting" (another poem addressed to an unfaithful lover), the poet describes an oracle, or seer, "that speaks numb and unheeding what he says," one can hardly help associating such a lack of expressive self-consciousness with H.D. herself.

Like the Cassandra of her own earlier poem, H.D., in verse after verse throughout *Red Roses for Bronze*, begs various divine figures to grant her the self-annihilation that comes with a dulled or altered consciousness. In "Wine Bowl," for instance, she describes how she longs to drown her poetic vision in a wine bowl crafted with her own hands, to replace her own verses with songs praising the god's instruments of possession, the grape and the wine bowl and the wine:

> I will challenge the reed-pipe
> and stringed lyre,
> to sing sweeter,
> pipe wilder,
> praise louder
> the fragrance and sweet
> of the wine-jar.
>
> (*CP* 242)

Although the wine bowl and wine jar could be read here, as in Lawrence's early poem "Mystery," as symbols of female sexuality, the poem nonetheless makes clear that it is, in fact, Dionysus rather than the poet whose song will cast its erotic spell over those who hear it; the male god, not the female poet, bears the true power of enchantment. Thus, the poet finds herself caught once again in the classic dilemma of the prophet, longing for a voice more forceful than her own to speak through her yet realizing that her speech (and in this case, perhaps, her sexuality as well) must thereby become dependent upon the agents of her possession, the blood-red wine and the wine god.

In "Choros Sequence from *Morpheus*" H.D. eventually rejects both Dionysus and his sleep-inducing cousin Morpheus, exclaiming that she will worship Apollo, god of poetry, instead. Yet, despite this renewed affirmation of the poet's craft, H.D.'s need to move in a new direction, to find a new form of expression that might both allow for a greater sense of self-confidence and accommodate a wider range of feeling, is still painfully apparent. Not until "The Mysteries," the final poem of *Red Roses for Bronze*, are we offered any indication of what this new direction will be. Formally, like so many other poems in the volume, "The Mysteries" is short lined and diffuse; H.D. continues to "heap up repetitions," in Louis L. Martz's description, "that cry out after emotion, but do not create it" (*CP* xxiii). Thematically, however, the poem is different, more optimistic in tone than most, progressing, like "Choros Sequence from *Morpheus*," from initial despair toward hope. Its subtitle, appropriately, is "Renaissance Choros"; indeed, the poem's very placement in *Red Roses for Bronze* is suggestive of rebirth, for it follows immediately after H.D.'s "Epitaph," the gravestone she places on her previous poetic endeavor:

> So I may say,
> "I died of living,
> having lived one hour";
>
> so they may say,
> "she died soliciting
> illicit fervour";
>
> so you may say,
> "Greek flower; Greek ecstasy
> reclaims for ever

one who died
following
intricate songs' lost measure."

(300)

"The Mysteries" seems to begin where "Epitaph" leaves off, inside
the grave:

Dark
days are past
and darker days draw near;
darkness on this side,
darkness over there
threatens like a spirit
like massed hosts.

(CP 300)

In this place and time of darkness and despair, there is nothing but evil:

only the emptiness,
pitfall of death,
terror,
the flood,
the earthquake,
stormy ill.

(300)

Soon, however, the prophetic voice of doom that uttered the poem's
opening lines is banished by another, a gentle but equally authoritative
voice of hope:

then voice within the turmoil,
that slight breath
that tells as one flower may
of winter past
(that kills
with Pythian bow,
the Delphic pest;)
one flower,

slight voice,
reveals
all holiness
with
"peace
be still."

(300–301)

Prophetic utterances can come in many forms; generally, however, one expects some show of physical or emotional intensity, a booming or a raving. But the "slight voice" of H.D.'s poem is not without ancient precedent: it recalls, like Rilke's poem "The Comforting of Elijah" (*SW* 1:563–64), the passage in the Old Testament in which Elijah is sent to stand upon a mountaintop and receive God's commands:

> And, behold, the Lord passed by, and a great and strong wind rent the mountains, and brake in pieces the rocks before the Lord; but the Lord was not in the wind: and after the wind an earthquake; but the Lord was not in the earthquake; and after the earthquake a fire; but the Lord was not in the fire: and after the fire a still small voice. (1 Kings 19:11–12)

Whether or not H.D. was familiar with this passage when she wrote "The Mysteries," the poem is distinguished from her earlier work by its use of biblical as well as classical imagery. On the surface, perhaps, considering the proper names that occur in the poem (Adonis, Demeter, Iacchus), the Greco-Roman mode seems stronger; read in the context of H.D.'s earlier work, this is a poem about the Eleusinian Mysteries, rites of love and fertility sacred to the nature goddess, Demeter.[12] The "still small voice" affirms, like Demeter herself, the cycles of nature and natural renewal, which require only a gentle catalyst: "one flower may slay the winter" (*CP* 301). Yet the slight "voice within the fever" that echoes through the poem is not that of Demeter nor of one of her acolytes; it is Christ's voice, and his language comes straight out of the New Testament:

"behold
the lilies
how they grow,

behold how fair . . .
king may never boast
so beautiful a garment."

(302)

"behold the dove,
the sparrow,
not one dies
without your father."

(303)[13]

Christ has entered the poem "to sanctify / the fervour / of all ancient mysteries": to embrace, in other words, a heterodoxy that recognizes both in Demeter's fertility rites and in the Christian rite of communion a shared belief in cyclical resurrection:

"The mysteries remain,
I keep the same
cycle of seed-time
and of sun and rain;
Demeter in the grass
I multiply,
renew and bless
Iacchus in the vine;
I hold the law,
I keep the mysteries true,
the first of these
to name the living, dead;
I am the red wine and bread."

(CP 305)

For H.D., as for the German poet Friedrich Hölderlin in his famous elegy "Brot und Wein" (114–19), bread and wine have become doubly potent substances, symbolizing not only the body and blood of Christ but also the immanence of the Greco-Roman gods, specifically Demeter and Dionysus/Bacchus. Thus, H.D. brings together pagan and Christian religious belief in a single, simple image of physical sustenance and spiritual transformation. Her use here of wine as a redemptive symbol comes, to be sure, as rather a surprise in light of the deep ambivalence toward Dionysian ecstasy expressed in poems such as "Choros Translations from *The Bacchae*" and "Wine Bowl," which warn of the seductive attractions and possessive perils of intoxication. Whereas wine represents, throughout most of *Red Roses for Bronze*, both a dangerous loss of expressive control and the poet's problematic desire for such abandon, with "The Mysteries" its signification becomes reversed; now it symbolizes, instead, the poet's power over her sources of poetic inspiration, her newfound ability to marshal compelling religious symbols to her own ends.

"The Mysteries" both affirms and builds upon ideas first expressed by H.D. more than a decade earlier in "Notes on Thought and Vision," which ends with a contemplation of Christ's relationship to the Eleusinian mysteries of nature and the body: "Christ . . . was the body of nature, the vine, the Dionysus, as he was the soul of nature" (*Notes* 53). Herself a native of Bethlehem, Pennsylvania—a coincidence that later made her wonder whether she unconsciously desired to be "the founder of a new religion" (*Tribute* 37)—H.D. would increasingly turn in the 1920s and 1930s to ruminations on her own Christian heritage, a reappraisal that would eventually culminate in *The Gift* (a 1943 memoir of her childhood) and *The Mystery* (an unpublished 1951 novel about the Moravian sect in America). Thus, the affirmation of life and heterodox myth with which "The Mysteries" concludes charts the direction of much of H.D.'s future work. In particular, it anticipates many of the poems that she would compose after 1933–34, the years during which, in what was to be the most significant turning point in her poetic career, H.D. underwent two brief but intense periods of psychoanalysis with Sigmund Freud in Vienna.[14]

Susan Stanford Friedman, in *Psyche Reborn: The Emergence of H.D.*, has already so exhaustively documented the poetic consequences of H.D.'s encounters with Freud that there is little need for me to rehearse her arguments in much detail here. Friedman's thesis can be summed up, briefly, as follows: H.D.'s study of the occult (astrology, numerology, Tarot, Kabbalah), which began in the 1920s and continued throughout her life, had already begun to convince her by the early 1930s that "spiritual reality cannot be learned through reason alone. Intuitional, visionary, and experiential apprehension of spiritual reality is essential" (*Psyche* 12). Freud, of course, was a strong proponent of reason, privileging science over art and religion, empirical reality over subjectivity. Yet, as Lionel Trilling pointed out in his 1950 essay "Freud and Literature," Freud performed a great service to creative writers by showing how poetic imagery resembles dream imagery—how, in other words, the generation of metaphor can be understood as a universal rather than an exclusively "literary" process. H.D. exploited Freud's findings on dreams and universal myth while essentially ignoring his emphasis on reason. Thus, she transformed his theories, which regarded the unconscious largely as a source of danger, into a creative cosmogony of her own making, affirming the role of the unconscious as a source of vision—"the Delphi of the mind, the wellspring of art and religion" (*Psyche* 70). H.D.'s sessions with Freud served to strengthen rather than undermine her newly developed belief in the superiority of intuitive vision. She became, in other words, what Harold Bloom would call a "strong reader" of Freud, willfully misreading even his most adamant statements to suit her own purposes (Bloom, *Anxiety*).

In her 1935 poem "The Master" H.D. grants Freud direct credit for having brought about the release of her newfound prophetic voice: "And it was he himself, he who set me free / to prophesy" (*CP* 458). Yet, even well before her first sessions with "the Master" in 1933, H.D. had begun to portray poetic prophecy—the mode of "divine madness" that Socrates, in *Phaedrus*, associates with Apollo—in a guardedly positive light, integrating Apollonian images into some of the mechanical metaphors that she would increasingly use to explain, describe, and justify her paradoxical stance as a prophetic poet. In particular, she came to associate Apollo with what Adalaide Morris calls the "concept of projection," a term uniting the vocabularies of three fields of inquiry that would play especially important roles in H.D.'s poetic practice: psychoanalysis, alchemy, and film. As "the master metaphor of H.D.'s technique," the concept of projection informed H.D.'s transitions "from Imagist to clairvoyant, to film theorist, analysand, and prophetic poet" (Morris 413).

H.D., although she had used the term as early as 1919 in "Notes on Thought and Vision," first began to employ "projection" as a specifically mechanical metaphor when, through the influence of Bryher and Bryher's husband, Kenneth Macpherson, she became deeply involved in avant-garde filmmaking in the late 1920s. Rewriting traditional conceptions of Apollonian enthusiasm, she came to extol Apollo as the god not only of poetry and prophecy but also, in his attribute as sun deity and hence as light god, of the cinema. Her 1927 essay "The Cinema and the Classics," for instance, claims the cinema as the site where the modern Apollo plies his inspirational trade: "In the hands of the avant-garde, film repossesses the visionary consciousness of Athens, Delphi, and Eleusis." (The essay cautions, to be sure, that "mechanical efficiency, technique carried to its logical conclusion do not make divinity"; H.D. had in mind sound cinema, which she feared would destroy the "mystery" of silent film).[15] Two 1927 poems entitled "Projector" and "Projector II" even more explicitly link the powers of film with Apollo:

> light
> who is god
> and song.

(CP 350)

In contrast to her earlier Sapphic "Fragment Thirty-Six," in which she figured her own mind (her desire, her song) as a wave poised but forever unbreaking, H.D.'s "Projector" poems celebrate above all the cinema's ability to flood the intellect and sweep the mind beyond such abstract self-restraint:

> This is his gift;
> light,
> light
> a wave
> that sweeps
> us
> from old fears
> and powers
> and disenchantments;
> this is his gift,
> light
> bearing us aloft,
> enthusiastic,
> into realms of magic;
> old forms dispersed
> take fresh
> shapes
> out of nothingness;
> light
> renders us spell-bound,

enchants us
and astounds.

(354–55)

H.D.'s glorification here of film—even tawdry Hollywood gets redeemed as the "holy wood" of Apollo (*CP* 358)—is a problematic one, for her chief fascination with the medium seems to lie in its ability to transport the viewer to "realms of magic," to offer "visions of streams / and path-ways" in which "our spirits walk . . . with shadow-folk / and ghost-beast" (353): in other words, to provide not so much a clearer view of reality as an escape from it. If the "astounded" and "enchanted" viewer is "borne aloft" with enthusiasm, it is enthusiasm in William Tindall's deprecatory sense ("girlish enthusiasm" [56]) rather than in Plutarch's more exalted one ("divine inspiration [that] casteth body, mind, voice and all far beyond the ordinary habit" [qtd. in Prescott 265]). H.D.'s "Projector" poems, then, although fascinating in their attempt to reconcile classical notions of prophecy and hermetic conceptions of magic with the latest developments of modern technology, read all too much like some of Lawrence's more unfortunate mediocrities, as the extravagance of the poet's praise for the cinema "sweeps away" much of the complexity of her thought, imagery, and language.[16]

All the same, H.D.'s celebration of Apollo and of the "visionary consciousness" to which the cinema grants access reflects an important change in her thinking about visionary experience in general. The cinematographic metaphor provides a "safe" way—one that she would eventually learn to exploit more effectively—of explaining how the poet can accept Apollonian influence (i.e., divine inspiration) as a fertilizing force yet still retain some degree of expressive autonomy. Asked by the *Little Review* in the spring of 1929 how she most liked to spend her time, H.D. replied:

I myself have learned to use the small projector, and spend literally hundreds of hours alone in my apartment, making the mountains and village streets and my own acquaintances reel past me in the light and light and light.[17]

Apollo, god of the "light and light and light," may be the patron of the cinema, of poetry, and of prophetic insight, yet it is still H.D. who "projects" and thereby controls the visionary image.

H.D. returns to a more ambivalent view of Apollo in poems such as her 1931 "Sigil," in which the poet initially declares her special selection by Apollo—

> God marked me to be his,
> scrawled, "I, I, I
> alone can comprehend
> this subtlety"
>
> (*CP* 415)

—but then, like the Cassandra of her earlier poem, begs the god to overwhelm her with divine frenzy:

> bring back the ultimate light
> on Delphic headland;
>
> take me,
> O ultimate breath,
> O master-lyrist,
> beat my wild heart to death.
>
> (417)

With its obsessive self-declaration—"I, I, I"—coupled with the poet's anguished wish for self-destruction at the hands of a powerful male god, "Sigil" anticipates Sylvia Plath's much later poem "Daddy," in which self-affirmation ("Ich, ich, ich, ich") takes on tones of self-disgust ("ick!"), as the poet explores in graphic and disturbing detail her own fascination with her male interlocutor's destructive powers:

> Every woman adores a Fascist,
> The boot in the face, the brute
> Brute heart of a brute like you.
>
> (223)

H.D. would never escape entirely from her desire for such "enthrallment" to a powerful male, whether god, hero, or lover. Seldom, however, would she portray Apollonian possession in quite such masochistic terms as in "Sigil."

In fact, Apollo is probably the most multifaceted and therefore the most self-contradictory of the many gods and goddesses in H.D.'s pantheon, for he represents not only poetry and prophecy, modes of discourse traditionally associated with irrationality and madness, but also the opposing qualities of light, reason, and order. Indeed, Apollo himself could be said to embody the paradox at the heart of any poetics of prophecy, for he symbolizes both artistic control and inspired ecstasy, both formal craft and spontaneous expression, both the obscuring effects of poetic language and the revelatory effects of divine illumination. In her 1933 poem "Delphi" H.D. depicts Apollo as the source of all poetic inspiration; by accepting and acknowledging him as her patron, she moves toward an explicit recognition that poetic inspiration can serve as a manifestation of divine reason as well as of divine madness.

"Delphi" is, however, like most of H.D.'s meditations on Apollo, a deeply ambivalent poem. The poet laments that she belongs neither to the world of ordinary mortals, to whom she will always appear mad, nor to that of the gods, whose close proximity could kill her:

> you will write in the city
> of fir-trees and loam,
> in the fields
> you will sing of the market;
> you will be
> among prophets,
> a satyr;
> when the note of the flute
> calls to dance,
> you will walk
> drunk but not
> with that mixed wine;
> his tune is his own;
> in his, not in your time,
> ecstasy will betray you;
> if he cares,
> he will flay;
> if he loves,
> he will slay you.

(CP 405–6)

As in earlier poems such as "Cassandra," H.D. depicts divine inspiration in eroticized terms that remind us of all the mortal women destroyed, in Greek and Roman mythology, by a god's sexual passion: Daphne, Semele, Psyche, to name only a few. Yet "Delphi" moves beyond notions of prophecy as a traumatic, rapelike experience, emphasizing the poet's reciprocal desire for the god and above all her special selection, her exceptional ability to perceive the voice of Apollo even in ordinary events:

> yet one day
> he will speak
> through a child or a thrush
> or a stray in the market;
> he will touch
> with the arm of a herdsman
> your arm,
> he will brush
> with the lips of a brother
> your lips;
> you will flame into song.

> (402)

The poetic doctrine expressed here—that everyday life can take on, to the trained eyes of the visionary, a revelatory significance not apparent to ordinary mortals—is hardly a new one for H.D.; even her earliest Imagist technique privileged close observation, the elaboration of seemingly minor visual details into insights of visionary relevance. Now, however, she attributes such insight above all to her special status as Apollo's priest. Just months after "Delphi" was published, in 1933, H.D.'s work with Freud would only serve to confirm for her what the poem already intimates: the prophetic poet's role need not be passive and esoteric but can be based, instead, on an active apprehension and explication of ordinary experience. A decade later, in *Trilogy*, such revisionary hermeneutics—the art of inspired interpretation, linked not only with Apollo but also with one of H.D.'s earliest patrons, the messenger god, Hermes—would become H.D.'s primary visionary strategy, as she learned to read even the ruins of bombed-out London as an encoded "hieroglyph" promising resurrection and renewal.

From Possession to Self-Possession: *Trilogy*

Although poetry is traditionally associated with spontaneous expression and emotional intensity, even H.D.'s earliest work betrays her vivid awareness that the successful lyricist must suspend and exploit passion rather than succumb to it. By the 1940s she would apply similar principles to the concept of inspiration, deliberately seeking ways of gaining access to revelatory experience and then of channeling it into measured articulation. H.D.'s extensive readings in mysticism and the occult during the 1930s, as well as her exhilarating, challenging encounters with Freud, sparked her final transformation into the confident poet-prophet of *Trilogy*, for they persuaded her to trust in the importance of intuition, to invite rather than flee from visionary apprehension. Above all, Freud encouraged H.D. to recognize and celebrate her own role as a gifted translator of what she would come to call "the hieroglyph of the unconscious" (H.D., *Tribute* 93).

H.D. hoped to legitimize visionary experience both by revealing the mystical basis of Freud's supposedly "scientific" work—"it's a sort of scientific-mystery, Elusinian [*sic*] up to date, this [psychoanalysis]"[18]—and, conversely, by treating mystical revelation as a science. "I am not, as you know, a sloppy theosophist and horoscope-ist," she wrote to Bryher, regarding Freud's disapproval of her interest in astrology, or "star-stuff"; "but you know, I *do believe in these things and I think there is a whole other-science of them*. And that is where, in a way, S.F. and I part company."[19] Yet H.D.'s attempts to reconcile spirituality with rationality run along gendered lines that closely parallel Freud's own association of the former with femininity and the latter with masculinity: "the mother represents the emotional, creative or dream-self," she would later write of her own family, "while the father represents the intellectual, critical or constructive self" (*Sword* 144).

H.D. was delighted when Freud ascribed to her the attributes of both sexes: "He says, 'you had two things to hide, one that you were a girl, the other that you were a boy.' It appears I am that all-but extinct phenomina [*sic*], the perfect bi—."[20] The previous year she had responded with similar enthusiasm when he informed her, as she reported to Bryher in a passage typed entirely in red ink, that "*all women are deeply rooted in penis-envy, not only the bi-sexual or homo-sexual woman. The advanced or intellectual woman is more*

frank about it. That is all." H.D. was so excited by Freud's theory—
"Now this strikes me as being a clue to everything"—that she begged
him to make it public: "I screamed at him, 'but the supreme compli-
ment to [red ink begins] WOMAN would be to trust women with this
great secret."[21] While H.D.'s uncritical acceptance of Freud's penis
envy doctrine may trouble feminist readers today, Freud's gender ide-
ology provided her, however paradoxically, with an important means
to self-empowerment, for it allowed her to see herself as an
unabashedly bisexual figure who, like the Athene of her own earlier
"Helios and Athene," was privy to the secrets of both sexes and could
thus, by sublimating sexuality into art, fuse "female" spirituality and
"male" science:

> I have tried to be man, or woman, but I have to be both. But it will
> work out, papa [Freud] says and I said, now in writing. Mstn.
> [masturbation] with me, only breaks down the perfection, I have to
> be perfect, in balance, I may get that in writing, and will become
> more abstract toward the writing of life, now I know WHAT I am. O,
> I am so very grateful and happy, Fido.[22]

H.D.'s conviction that "I have to be both" man and woman would
not, to be sure, last forever. Later works such as *Helen in Egypt* still
insist on creative bipolarity and the need for a male brother/
lover/father figure to complement, supplement, and, to return to the
old sex-as-creativity metaphor, fertilize the female poet's art; but that
male figure is always portrayed as an external Other, not an internal-
ized, constituent element of the female poet herself. During the early
1940s, however, H.D. would briefly achieve the kind of creative gender
balance that her sessions with Freud had convinced her to strive for,
speaking with the voices of male and female seers alike and thereby
demonstrating her ability to transcend gender boundaries altogether.
She would also finally conquer—though only, as it turned out, for a
short time—her fear of inspiration as a source or a form of madness,
affirming, instead, the ultimate sanity and even the scientific, rational
basis of her vocation as prophetic poet.

In the Old Testament, as I have noted, prophets traditionally act as
historical witnesses, interpreting present events for "their own day and
generation," rather than necessarily forecasting future doom (von Rad
112). Jewish hermeticists fulfill a similar, if less dramatic, function,

reading the hidden in the apparent by attending to the *"bat qol"* or "daughter of a voice," which serves for Talmudic scholars as a sort of internalized, intellectualized muse.[23] Both Hebrew prophecy and Jewish mysticism, then, typically rely not on direct revelation so much as on the inspired interpretation of encoded signs. H.D., familiar through extensive reading with both of these visionary modes, had already learned from Freud to see herself as a gifted translator of dreams and visions; with *Trilogy* she would turn her skills to the interpretation of material reality, taking on a new role as an inspired observer of the historical here and now. *Trilogy* is not without its moments of unmediated revelation; for the most part, however, H.D. attends to the "god in the details," holding herself open to inspiration in the form of a "still, small voice."

Set in war-torn London, *Trilogy* opens with a visionary experience of the most violent, direct, and terrifying kind:

> so, through our desolation,
> thoughts stir, inspiration stalks us
> through gloom:
>
> unaware, Spirit announces the Presence;
> shivering overtakes us,
> as of old, Samuel:
>
> trembling at a known street-corner,
> we know not nor are known;
> the Pythian pronounces—we pass on.
>
> (CP 510)

Here divine inspiration is a dangerous external force, one that, like the war itself, "stalks" and brutally "overtakes" the unwilling poet. Soon, however, wondering "what saved us? what for?" (511), the poet rallies to an affirmation of her role as an active interpreter and privileged initiate:

> Yet we, the latter-day twice-born,
> . . . .
> we are the keepers of the secret,
> the carriers, the spinners

of the rare intangible thread
that binds all humanity

to ancient wisdom.

(521–23)

The image of the poet as a spinner of words is one that recurs frequently in H.D.'s writing, so often, in fact, that Susan Stanford Friedman has entitled her massive study of H.D.'s prose *Penelope's Web*, in keeping with H.D.'s own description of her novelistic technique: "It is obviously Penelope's web that I am weaving" (*Tribute* 153). Although Friedman uses the image specifically as a metaphor for H.D.'s prose fabrications, the theme of spinning and weaving finds its way into much of her poetry as well (see, e.g., "At Ithaca" and "Ariadne" [*CP* 163–64, 330–35]) and becomes especially prominent in *Trilogy*, which was written during a period when H.D. herself was spending much of her spare time weaving fanciful tapestries (or, as she wrote to Viola Jordan in a fortuitous misspelling, doing "typestry stitching").[24] Mircea Eliade notes that many cultures have specifically associated spinning with female power (the Greek Fates, the witch in "Sleeping Beauty," and the spider in E. B. White's *Charlotte's Web* all come to mind): "there is a secret link between the feminine initiations, spinning, and sexuality" (*Myths* 215). But the spinning image has its negative, disempowering side as well, for it recalls the fate of Arachne, whose pride and impudence in weaving a tapestry depicting the gods' crimes against mankind caused her to be turned into a spider by H.D.'s favorite goddess, Athene (Ovid, *Met.* 6:1–150). In *Majic Ring*, written while *Trilogy* was still in progress, H.D. asks whether she, too, might be exposing herself to such danger:

> I have dared to wonder if my spinning of this tale or "yarn" was not on a par with that of Araché [*sic*], whose subtlety and whose craft, rivalling that of the Goddess, caused her to be damned forever as a spider.

"But," she adds in a delicately self-affirmatory gesture, "there is nothing so beautiful as a spider-web at dawn, hung with exquisite small globes of dew or diamonds":

And if I catch something of the evanescent *light that never was* in this web, in these circles of time and these circles of 4th dimensional myth and thought and vision, I need not fear the wrath of the grey-eyed Goddess, for my object is like Theseus', to slay a Monster of black-superstition and peril and to restore her kingdom, and beside me, has stood her friend and enemy, Anax Apollo, Helios, Lord of Magic and Prophecy and Music. (*Majic Ring* 155–56)

Throughout *Trilogy*, as in her earlier poetry, H.D. invokes many outside sources of inspiration, including not only "Apollo, . . . Lord of Magic and Prophecy and Music," and Athene, "the grey-eyed Goddess," but also a wide range of heterodox religious figures, from the Egyptian Amen-Ra to the Christian Virgin Mary to a series of apocryphal angels. Yet she also frees herself of any real dependence on such figures by emphasizing her own creative and interpretive autonomy. Specifically, she takes on for herself the hermeneutic and hermetic functions, respectively, of Hermes, who translates (in the word's etymological sense of "carrying over") divine messages to humankind, and of Hermes Trismegistus, the ancient alchemist whose ability to transform ordinary substances into gold H.D. figures as emblematic of the poet's craft.

Like Hermes Trismegistus, "thrice-master" of magic, astrology, and alchemy, or the Delphic Pythia, whose three-legged tripod represents the fusion of religion, art, and medicine in prophetic utterance,[25] H.D. tries, in her three-part *Trilogy*, to transcend bipolar dualities by breaking them into more complex yet ultimately more stable units of three. Invoking powerful figures from both male and female prophetic and religious traditions (Samuel, John of Patmos, Christ; the Pythia, the Virgin Mary, Mary Magdalen), she offers herself as an Athene-like hermaphroditic figure who, speaking with the voices of both sexes, charts a new path of heterodox prophecy between them. While she does not seek to overthrow traditional male-female stereotypes, H.D. merges them together in new, doubly potent symbolic combinations; for instance, with the "Flowering of the Rod" that serves as an image for London's rebirth from the ashes of war, she collapses male-female symbolic hierarchies by crowning with flowers, symbols of female sexuality, a phallic staff associated with the male prophet Aaron. The flowering rod, which in the Old Testament marks Aaron's ordination as a priest and later helps Moses bring forth water from the desert,[26] has always symbolized both special selection and fertility, but only within a purely patriarchal tradition; indeed, D. H. Lawrence exploits the masculinist elements of the image in his 1922 novel *Aaron's Rod*, the title of which refers to the protagonist's flute (and hence to his powers as artist) but also to his phallic self-sufficiency. H.D., in contrast, emphasizes the rod's hermaphroditic element: permutating *rod* into *rood* and thence to "the flowering of the reed," she unites images of precision (rod and reed are biblical instruments of measurement) and emotion (the reed symbolizes music and thereby poetry), thus bringing together a further set of bipolar opposites (logos/pathos) in a single figure for prophetic power.

Similarly, H.D. both accentuates and collapses the dichotomy between past and future when, in "The Flowering of the Rod," she summons a new era of hope and promise that seeks to break free of historical contingency altogether by endlessly repeating history's most triumphant moments. Geoffrey Hartman has noted (following Martin Buber's distinction) that the purpose of prophecy, as opposed to the apocalyptic mode, is to "renew time rather than hasten its end"; prophetic poetry "founds or repairs time" by "utter[ing] time in its ambiguity: as the undesired mediation, which prevents fusion, but also destruction" ("Poetics of Prophecy," 24, 27). In a poem called "May 1943," written not long after *Trilogy* was begun, H.D. enacts what Hartman calls the prophet's "burdened relation to time" (23) when she attempts to "mend a break in time" with her poet's pencil (*CP* 493).[27] And a year and a half later, in the final section of *Trilogy*, she takes that project one step further by alchemically uniting past and future in a "Golden Age" of the present:

> I have gone forward,
> I have gone backward,
>
> I have gone onward from bronze and iron
> into the Golden Age.
>
> (584)

With *Trilogy*, then, H.D. at last acknowledges prophecy, which can entail messages of both doom and rebirth, as a positive, life-affirming vocation. This, in turn, allows her to redeem and celebrate the four modes of inspiration—erotic, Dionysian, prophetic, and poetic—that

Socrates, in *Phaedrus*, identified as forms of divine madness. Now, in place of the Aphrodite who in *Hymen* and *Heliodora* so often drives men and especially women to erotic madness—"for venery stands for impurity / and Venus as desire / is venereous, lascivious"—H.D., the alchemist of words, presents an etymologically purified love goddess, "Venus whose name is kin / to venerate" (553–54). Rather than a frenzied Bacchante, driven, in *Red Roses for Bronze*, to ritual murder, the poet becomes a visionary herald of resurrection, intoxicated not by the reason-shattering wine of Dionysus but by the New Testament wine that symbolizes spiritual rebirth:

> I am so happy,
> I am the first or the last
>
> of a flock or a sward;
> I am *full of new wine*.[28]
>
> (583)

Finally, instead of Apollonian madness, possession by the "master-lyrist" who can beat the poet's "wild heart to death," H.D. offers us poetic prophecy as a form of wisdom, reason, and even mathematical logic:

> It is no madness to say
> you will fall, you great cities,
>
> (now the cities lie broken);
> it is not tragedy, prophecy
>
> from a frozen Priestess,
> a lonely Pythoness
>
> who chants, who sings
> in broken hexameters,
> . . . .
> it is simple reckoning, algebraic,
> it is geometry on the wing.
>
> (584–85)

H.D.'s earlier poetry does not, as I have already noted, deal as explicitly with the Muse-inspired poetic madness as it does with erotic, Dionysian, and prophetic forms of ecstasy. In *Trilogy*, however, H.D.

redeems even Socrates' fourth and final mode of inspiration, claiming a gentle yet powerful mother goddess as her own sane, purifying muse.[29] Appearing to her as in a dream or vision, this Lady in White, Bona Dea, Guardian Angel, and Virgin Goddess presents herself to the poet, unencumbered by the trappings of an androcentric Father/Son tradition ("the Lamb was not with her, / either as Bridegroom or Child" [571]), to offer a new form of divine inspiration independent of religious orthodoxy:

> she carries a book but it is not
> the tome of the ancient wisdom,
>
> the pages, I imagine, are the blank pages
> of the unwritten volume of the new;
> . . . .
> but she is not shut up in a cave
> like a Sibyl; she is not
>
> imprisoned in leaden bars
> in a coloured window;
>
> she is Psyche, the butterfly,
> out of the cocoon.
>
> (570)

Trilogy, although it has been condemned by some critics for being too simplistic in its syncretist view of religion and by others for being too esoteric, is undeniably a work of lyrical delicacy and imagistic complexity. But perhaps its greatest strength lies in the splendid self-assurance of H.D.'s voice and vision, which carries the reader even past moments of potential strain or tedium. Although she does not by any means identify herself only with powerful figures—on one occasion she describes herself as an "indigestible" shell, on another as a worm[30]—the poet leaves behind, at least temporarily, the unfortunate victims of divine possession who haunted her earlier works. Instead, with supreme self-confidence, she exploits and expands both female and male prophetic traditions. Like Rilke and Lawrence, she attempts to tap into the best of both sexual worlds yet refuses to succumb to the weaknesses of either.

The Mechanics of Inspiration

After *Trilogy* and until her death in 1961, H.D. would continue to explore issues of spiritual and gender identity, laying claim to specifically female forms of power by asserting the triumph of love over war, of spiritual experience over mere rational existence. Influenced by the syncretist philosophies of such writers as Robert Ambelain and Denis de Rougement, she would increasingly come to associate inspiration not with a rapelike violation but, instead, with a mystical, transcendent union of opposites. The calm, measured products of her later years— important, epic works such as *Helen in Egypt* and *Hermetic Definition*— are celebrated by many as the culminating masterpieces of her career, largely because of their pioneering efforts to rewrite male myths and epics from a feminist perspective. Yet they lack the prophetic resonances of *Trilogy*, which brings together so many different voices and cultural archetypes in stating its own syncretist message of present-day redemption.[31] The obvious but rather facile explanation that prophecy thrives only on contradiction and tension—for instance, on the violence, heroism, hope and despair of wartime—strikes me as inadequate to explain *Trilogy*'s uniqueness among H.D.'s work. A postscript is needed here to clarify why she moved so quickly beyond prophecy to a more contemplative mode of discourse.

Like Rilke (and unlike Lawrence, who, despite an early interest in theosophy, generally took care to distance himself from any spiritualist involvement), H.D. was an inspired poet in deed as well as in word; that is, she actually underwent a number of visionary experiences that had, at least in retrospect, a profound effect on her creative self-definition. Four of these events occurred in 1919–20, quite early in her poetic career, shortly following the end of the war, the dissolution of her marriage, the birth of her daughter, and the beginning of her relationship with Bryher, in whose steadying company three of the four incidents took place. The first was the "jelly-fish state" that she experienced in the Scilly Isles in 1919 and described in "Notes on Thought and Vision" as well as in the much later "Advent," her account of her 1933 psychoanalysis with Freud. The second "vision" occurred on board ship while she and Bryher were on their way to Greece in the spring of 1920; while standing on deck with a man named Peter Van Eck (Peter Rodeck in "real life"), she sighted an island and a group of dolphins, only to learn afterward that dolphins, island, and perhaps Van Eck himself had all apparently been figments of her imagination. The third and fourth visionary episodes occurred in Corfu later that spring, when, shortly after having been told that it would be too dangerous for two women to travel alone to Delphi, H.D. had her own "Delphic" vision and saw a series of simple images (a head, a chalice, a lamp resembling the Pythia's tripod at Delphi, and a more complex and fluid picture of Niké, Winged Victory, climbing a ladder) "write themselves" on the wall of her hotel. Soon afterward, on one of their last evenings in Corfu, she enacted for Bryher a series of hallucinated dance scenes, taking on the imaginative identity first of a tree, then of an Indian medicine man, then an Indian girl ("Minne-ha-ha"), a female mountain spirit, a Californian woman singing in Spanish, a lisping island maiden, a Japanese girl, a Greek mountain boy, a Tibetan "priest of some high mystery," and, finally, a Lady in a tower, wearing fabulous jewels "full of traditional occult power" and named, like the earth mother, Rhea. These tableaux, H.D. would later speculate, originated in "the high regions of mystery and magic, of religious affinities, of hidden, secret storehouses of revelation and inspiration and healing" (*Majic Ring* 247).[32]

What is perhaps most striking about the events of 1919–20 is that, although H.D. describes her jelly-fish state in "Notes on Thought and Vision" and alludes to the Peter Van Eck incident in such autobiographical novels as *Palimpsest* and *Hedylus*, virtually no reference to these obviously significant and deeply impressive episodes finds its way into her poetry of the period in which they occurred, except insofar as the poems of the 1920s betray a particularly deep distrust of visionary experience. In contrast to Rilke's inspirational "hurricane" at Duino, then, which resulted directly in two separate cycles of brilliantly accomplished poems, H.D.'s encounters with visionary consciousness led to no immediate poetic breakthrough; in fact, most of her written attempts to make sense of these otherworldly occurrences date from two decades or more after the time that she actually underwent them. "I have had some spiritual experiences," H.D. confided in a 1919 letter to John Cournos, probably soon after her Scilly Island trip: "I am not able to think of myself as a *person* now. I must move, act, and do as it is *moved* upon me to do and act."[33] Yet not until many years later, as she struggled to make retrospective sense of the shattering experiences of World War I, would she articulate a strategy whereby she might overcome such losses of self and shape them into viable art: "I will write these notes and re-write them," proclaims her alter ego, Julia, in *Bid Me to Live*, "till they come true" (176).

H.D.'s own recuperative process of "writing and re-writing" the 1919–20 visions—which included the production of an autobiographical novel, *The Gift*, that ruminates on the gift of visionary apprehension bestowed upon her by her mother and Moravian grandmother—took place mostly during and immediately following World War II, the period when she also composed her prophecy-affirming *Trilogy* and, not coincidentally, immersed herself more deeply than ever before or after in an unabashed quest for direct revelatory experience by means of spiritualist séances. In the early years of the war, having recently joined the London Society for Psychical Research in order to use the society's library and attend lectures there, H.D. had come into contact with a Eurasian psychic named Arthur Bhaduri, who eventually began to assist in weekly séances with H.D., Bryher, and Bhaduri's mother, May. In October 1943, following a lecture on spiritualism by Lord Hugh Dowding (chief air marshal of the Royal Air Force [RAF] during the Battle of Britain and author of the spiritualist treatise *Many Mansions*), she wrote to Dowding and asked if she could join his spiritualist "circle"; although he replied that he had no room for her, she maintained a correspondence with him over the next several months, meditating on the increasingly important roles that several images associated with him (a Viking ship, a lone eagle) played in her own group's séances.[34] Some time later H.D. began to conduct séances on her own at home, using a small three-legged table that had once belonged to William Morris and that was connected in her mind both with Morris's spiritualist interests and with the Pythia's tripod at Delphi.[35] In the late summer of 1945 she received messages from a group of RAF pilots who had been killed in the Battle of Britain, warning her of the dangers to the environment that would result, or so she interpreted their communications, from the atom bombs recently dropped on Hiroshima and Nagasaki. Dowding, to whom she promptly relayed these messages, met with her several times but refused to accept or even to discuss the warnings from "his" pilots; when, in February 1946, he wrote to her to condemn her revelations as "trivial and uninspiring,"[36] H.D. was devastated, taking his letter as "an ultimate 'repudiation,' a rejection of her that was superimposed on a series of betrayals by ideal male figures, many of whom were connected in some way with war" (Friedman, *Psy-

che 175). Soon thereafter, partly as an immediate result of Dowding's rejection, H.D. suffered a serious mental breakdown that led to a long period of illness and recuperation at a Swiss "Nervenklinik."

H.D. recalls these events both in a bizarre unpublished roman à clef called *The Sword Went Out to Sea* (1947) and in such subsequent memoirs as the *Hirslanden Notebooks* (1947–49) and "H.D. by Delia Alton" (1949–50). But the most detailed account of the 1943–44 séances themselves can be found in *Majic Ring*, an extraordinary unpublished document cataloged at the Beinecke Library as a "novel" but which in fact consists, at least in part, of copies of the actual letters that H.D. sent to Dowding in November and December of 1943.[37] Eventually, she stopped mailing her long epistles to Dowding ("He is tired," she wrote ruefully on 17 December [104]), but she continued until April 1944 to keep a detailed journal of subsequent séances with Bryher and Bhaduri. Only later would she transform *Majic Ring* into a novel by altering such factual details as her own age and changing all the names: Bryher would become "Gareth," Bhaduri "Ben Manisi," Lord Dowding "Lord Howell," and Hilda D. Aldington herself, in a variant on her own name that she would frequently invoke in connection with prophetic and mystical experience, "Delia Alton."[38]

During the period of her spiritualist involvement with Bhaduri, H.D. often worried about the possible perils of tampering with the unknown. In a 1942 letter to her friend Viola Jordan, who had expressed concern over H.D.'s newfound psychic interests, she wrote apologetically, "I have little attacks [of spiritual interest] at times, like the horoscopes"—"but," she added in a note of self-directed caution, "I think any sort of medium stuff (in excess) does drain ones [*sic*] vitality and is dangerous."[39] Similarly, in "Writing on the Wall," her 1944 memoir of her earlier sessions with Freud, she hints that Freud might have been right to classify her 1920 Corfu vision as a "dangerous symptom," a sign, perhaps, of "megalomania":

> We can read my writing, the fact that there was writing, in two ways or in more than two ways. We can read or translate it as a suppressed desire for forbidden "signs and wonders," breaking bounds, a suppressed desire to be a Prophetess, to be important anyway, megalomania they call it—a hidden desire to "found a new religion." . . . Or this writing-on-the-wall is merely an exten-

sion of the artist's mind, a *picture* or an illustrated poem, taken out of the actual dream or daydream content and projected from within (though apparently from outside), really a high-powered *idea*, simply over-stressed, *over-thought*, you might say, an echo of an idea, a reflection of a reflection, a "freak" thought that had got out of hand, gone too far, a "dangerous symptom." (*Tribute to Freud* 51)

Yet, despite such expressions of doubt and danger, most of her works from the World War II years, including "Writing on the Wall" itself, are concerned primarily with affirming the purpose and value of H.D.'s past visionary experiences and thereby justifying her present involvement in spiritualism.

This is especially true of *Majic Ring*, in which H.D. looks back at her 1920 experiences in Greece and explains why she was unable to make sense of them at the time:

> I did not know anyone in the psychic-research world and anyhow, I think that I was afraid that my own experience or my own philosophy would not stand up to the proddings of the inexpert, of the unilluminated. I was right, of course. But it left me alone in my world, enclosed in a chrystal [*sic*] ball. (145)

Although she does not mention the wall picture episode that she would soon afterward dissect in "Writing on the Wall," she spends seemingly endless pages going over the significance of her other two Greek "visions": the illusory island/dolphin sighting on board ship with Peter Van Eck and the dance "tableaux" that she performed for Bryher on Corfu. She redeems the loss-of-control aspect of the dance scenes— "I was 'possessed' like someone in a Gospel story"—by arguing that she remained, nonetheless, a self-conscious agent throughout the event: "Though I was 'possessed,' I in turn possessed the mood, was aware of my surroundings; this was no trance state" (208). Similarly, she endows the Van Eck vision with prophetic rather than merely hallucinatory qualities by etymologically associating the dolphins with Delphi, seat of inspiration; thus, the dolphins come to represent, like Van Eck himself, H.D.'s "guide and inspiration," while the islands are interpreted as a vision of "the promised land, the islands of the blest, the islands of Atlantis or of the Hesperides," and even "the kingdom of heaven" (160–63). Finally, she goes so far as to regard the dance and dolphin episodes together as instances of divine revelation:

> Perhaps the woman on the boat going to Greece, in the early spring of 1920, did see God. Possibly, the girl and the woman [Bryher and H.D.] did see projections of the white light that is final illumination. (309)

In the notes that she kept on her wartime séances H.D. recalls how an apotheosized Freud spoke to her on 19 October 1944 ("the Master" had died in 1939) through the medium of Bhaduri:

> "Respect for you—attached—mind keen at end—you are placing yourself at disposal of a greater mind—you are the instrument— you will prove the work of this Master (Freud) did not represent a finality but a THRESHOLD. Not science, only lever that opened door—way cleared, then work begins."[40]

Majic Ring is full of similar "instrumental" metaphors, describing the poet as a projector casting her memories and visions, "like a roll of film that had been neatly stored in my brain," onto a screen (127), the poet as a wireless set (11–13) or receiving station (246, 287–88) picking up signals from the unknown. In Corfu, in 1920, H.D. had relied on her companion, Bryher, to provide the stable, logical, "masculine" half of the visionary equation:

> If my being had flowered and quivered and responded to that wind of inspiration, like the branches of a paper-birch or like the strings of a harp, hers had remained the static lode-stone, the north-star, the steel of the magnetic horseshoe, around which the iron-fillings collect in different patterns. . . . I am not the whole machine. Gareth's intense psychic quality is concealed, she is like the inner springs and wheels, or the careful wrapping around live-wire" (*Majic Ring* 238, 246)

In fact, H.D. repeatedly credits Bryher (who eventually repudiated H.D.'s occult interests by denying that they had ever existed)[41] with having facilitated, indeed made possible, her visionary experiences: in the Scilly Isles, for instance, it is Bryher who says, "Let it come," when a hesitant, resistant H.D. begins to have her "jelly-fish experience" (*Tribute* 130); in the Corfu "writing on the wall" scene she urges H.D. to "go on" with her vision and even "carries on the 'reading'" when H.D. becomes too exhausted to continue (48–56); and during the Corfu dance tableaux she once again encourages a tired, confused H.D. to "go on" with her dances and descriptions (*Majic Ring* 198). Yet, despite such emphasis on the partnership aspect of visionary apprehension, H.D.'s image of the poet as a receiving station would eventually allow her to combine notions of passive reception and of active scientific ordering in a single, hermaphroditic image describing the vatic energies of Freud's "perfect bi" alone:

> Delia [H.D.] is only receiving messages like a receiving-station. She herself is conditioned to this, by her mystical visionary Moravian background and by her father's scientific trend and devotion to abstract truth. (288)

With her use of mechanical metaphors to explain the workings of divine inspiration, H.D. tries in *Majic Ring* to domesticate visionary experience, to render a mysterious unknown force familiar and comprehensible. She seeks to rationalize the irrational by invoking, paradoxically, not scientific knowledge but scientific ignorance: "We know so little about the actual cross-currents of projected thought and emotion, and in any case, it is not necessary to be a watch-maker in order to tell the time" (65). Later, in works such as *The Sword Went Out to Sea* and "H.D. by Delia Alton," she employs similar terms to describe the rationality and logic of her RAF messages: "It seemed in the end, as natural as receiving a letter or a telegram. . . . I don't know how a telephone does work, nor wireless nor radio" (199). Unlike her earlier projection metaphor, then, which left the issue ambiguous, the image of the wireless effectively resolves the question of whether divine revelation comes from outside or from within the poet: throughout *Majic Ring* inspiration is clearly an external force that the inspired poet, sensitive and attuned to such influences in ways that ordinary mortals are not, must pick up, translate, and pass on to the masses. H.D.'s new conviction that inspiration comes from outside, validated by her séance experiences, must have been in its way a comforting one, for it absolved her of responsibility or blame for her visions, indicating that they really *were* visions and not, as Freud had argued, "dangerous symptoms" of some inner conflict or even of madness. All the same, when her break-down came in 1946, it was internal rather than external forces that brought it about (although the accumulated strain of having lived through the London Blitz no doubt played a role as well); H.D.'s ideal-ization of Lord Dowding and her feverish dependence on his approval ultimately had far more shattering effects upon her than did the RAF boys' messages of doom.

What *Majic Ring* makes clear, at any rate, is that H.D., precisely during the period when she was writing *Trilogy*, was both more opti-mistic about visionary revelation and more firmly convinced of the reality and importance of otherworldly inspiration than at any other time in her life. Although she had suppressed her earlier psychic expe-riences, her séances with Bhaduri convinced her that such visions had to be communicated, not only through prose meditations but also and especially through her poetry. In fact, many of the central figures of *Trilogy* are projections of visionary images that first appeared to H.D. about the time of the séances; for instance, the redemptive god Amen-Ra in "The Walls Do Not Fall" (CP 523–24) is based on a mysterious alabaster-skinned "Master" whom she saw in a dream "during the big raids," and the Bona Dea who affirms female creativity in "Tribute to the Angels" closely resembles a Lady in White who manifested herself to H.D. at two séances in November 1943 (*Majic Ring* 57, 100).

Such visionary experiences led H.D. to believe, at least for a time, that her whole purpose as a poet was to reveal the secrets of psychic communication that she had learned during her séances:

> Maybe, my whole urge toward self-expression has led me to this point—maybe, I am now able to express this quite difficult, indeed almost impossible philosophy of communion or communication. For actually very little acceptable writing has been done on the subject; although there are libraries of books open to any psychic-research worker, very little has been done by modern poets or writers. (*Majic Ring* 113)

H.D.'s statements here implicitly refute Joseph Riddel's assertion that *Trilogy* should not be interpreted "in terms of prophecy or mystical rev-elations, as an archaeological uncovering of the secrets concealed in ancient words or texts"; the poem, Riddel argues, "proceeds not by opening or unconcealing, but by layering" (159–60). Certainly, *Trilogy* does operate, perhaps more so than any of H.D.'s other works, in a palimpsestic mode: practicing her own brand of hermeticism, the poet reshapes and reinscribes each word, image, and sign almost as soon as she decodes it. Yet H.D. herself clearly perceived her enterprise as a revelatory rather than an obfuscatory one:

> There is endless exploration to be done by some gifted person who has time and health and power of concentration and of imagination. . . . Personally, I feel that my peculiar service to this work, lies in the general evocative and creative channels. (*Majic Ring* 92–93)

H.D.'s major works from the war years—*Majic Ring*, "Writing on the Wall," *The Gift*, and especially *Trilogy*—repeatedly seek to define and affirm the poet's role as an interpreter, through the "evocative and creative channels" of her writing, of visionary consciousness. H.D. would never, to be sure, entirely relinquish her fear that revelatory experience might lead to or even serve as a manifestation of madness. "All this may seem to you crazy," Bhaduri warns her in *Majic Ring*:

> You will write and think how crazy it is. You may think you are crazy. You will wonder about it. You will live to achieve so much. It may seem crazy, but it is *all* a big work. It is no delusion. (276)

H.D.'s use of mechanical metaphors allowed her, at least for a time, to conceptualize inspiration as a form of visionary receptivity that neither mandates traditionally feminine passivity nor leads inevitably to "craziness." But, following her repudiation by Lord Dowding and her 1946 breakdown, H.D. completely abandoned her participation in séances and psychic phenomena, presumably because her involvement in "medium stuff" had turned out to be, as she had earlier feared, so draining and dangerous. At the same time, she also began her shift away from the prophetic mode of *Trilogy*, which grounds visionary experience in the paradoxes of history and tradition, to the more contemplative, mystical mode of *Helen in Egypt*, which revolves around Helen's attempts to achieve access to "the ultimate Mystery" (204) by embracing and transcending the dualisms of Love and War (32), of time and infinity (200), of Athens (the intellect) and Eleusis (the mysteries [212]), of lyre and sword (227), of Daemon and goddess (260), and even, finally, of poetry and pure being: "She herself is the writing" (22). *Trilogy*, then, remains her most vigorous, intellectually complex, and poetically coherent attempt to convert what she perceived as otherworldly inspiration into what the world perceives as art.

PART 2

Myths

Chapter 4

Orpheus, Eurydice, and the Poetics of the Turn

Woman as the goddess in the machine of the human psyche is a heroine who will drive us, like a female chauffeur, through all the avenues of hell, till she pitches us eventually down the bottomless pit.
                    —D. H. Lawrence, "Education of the People," 1919

I am a woman in the prime of life
driving her dead poet in a black Rolls-Royce
through a landscape of twilight and thorns.
                    —Adrienne Rich, "I Dream I'm the Death of Orpheus," 1968

In D. H. Lawrence's macabre vision of gender relations (echoed more bitterly than defiantly by Adrienne Rich) the modern Orpheus has become the hapless pawn of his powerful, hellish bride. But things have not always been so. Throughout most of literary history, in fact, although Eurydice has stood stolidly at the center of the Orpheus myth, she has seldom been its real subject, the "chauffeur" who drives the legend. Instead, for the most part, she has passively embodied such problematic abstractions as femininity, Otherness, and death, symbolizing at worst the witchy dark side of women—Eurydice is "in the prime of life," as Rich notes, only when she is dead—and at best the otherworldly inspiration relentlessly pursued by her famous husband. Orpheus, in contrast, has always been a figure of extraordinary richness and complexity, embracing nearly half a dozen archetypically potent situations within a single myth. In his most positively suggestive roles Orpheus is celebrated as the mystical priest, founder and patron of the Orphic cult; the consummate poet, whose song can charm trees, stones, and even the dark denizens of the underworld; and the great romantic hero whose love transcends and, briefly, conquers death. On a less triumphant note, however, he is also remembered as the overambitious quester whose failure to rescue Eurydice has come to symbolize the futility of trying to outwit death.

As the dismembered victim of jealous maenads, Orpheus represents, more ambivalently still, both the imperfect mortal whose song has failed to charm and the deathless poet whose music issues even from the lips of his decapitated head. In this final manifestion he becomes, like his Egyptian counterpart, Osiris, a physically incoherent being who yet retains all the integrity of identity, thus enacting, as twentieth-century writers as diverse as Anouilh, Valéry, Goll, Rilke, Benn, Blanchot, and Ashbery have recognized, the situation, anguished yet articulate, of the modern poet.[1] To a poetic generation frantically scrambling to shore fragments of meaning against its spiritual ruins, Orpheus guarantees, in Walter Strauss's analysis, "the possibility of reassembling the shattered fragments" of the fractured self (18).[2] Orpheus embodies both the powers of art and the limitations of art, both the possibility of conquering death and the futility of the attempt. Indeed, it is the very ambivalence of the myth he inhabits that accounts for its special appeal to modern poets. As intercessor between life and death, between humanity and the gods, between "the radiant solar enlightenment of Apollo and the somber subterranean knowledge of Dionysus" (Strauss 18), Orpheus is the ultimate go-between, the fallible hero who nonetheless attempts to fuse irreconcilable opposites and to bridge the gap between the possible and the forbidden. His characteristic moment, symbolizing both his success and all his failures, is located in his turn, his enigmatic backward glance at Eurydice: the gesture by which he attempts, and necessarily fails, to embrace the world of light and the world of darkness in a single all-encompassing regard.

From Eurydice's point of view, of course, Orpheus' turn, however admirable and ambitious its motivations, has an unambiguously unpleasant result: she is packed off to the underworld, refused the chance at life that moments before had been so tantilizingly dangled before her. Bearing none of Orpheus' symbolic baggage, defined and manipulated by his powerful gaze, Eurydice is, comparatively speaking, a mythological nobody. Her only obvious archetypal significance resides in a negative role: that of woman-as-Other, woman-as-death, woman as the "dark continent" that Freud found both so threatening and so irresistible. If, as many scholars believe, the Orpheus/Eurydice myth originally ended with Orpheus' successful completion of his mission, then Eurydice must at one time have personified, like Persephone, rebirth and regeneration: the successful passage from winter into spring and from death into life.[3] But by the time she finds her way into

Virgil's *Georgics* and Ovid's *Metamorphoses*, the earliest recorded versions of the myth,[4] Eurydice has already been demoted from a death-defying figure of fertility to an impotent pawn of the powers that be, forever relegated—except in such happy ending revisions of the tale as the operas by Peri, Monteverdi, and Gluck[5]—to the underground realm of darkness and death.

If, for many readers, Eurydice's fate seems frustrating and unfair, for others it has provided the very secret of her appeal. Rilke, for instance, in his 1904 poem "Orpheus. Eurydike. Hermes," portrays Eurydice as the embodiment of pure feminine mystery, possessing an otherworldly knowledge and power far superior even to that of her archetypal poet-husband. Orpheus, meanwhile, proves notably unsuccessful in his role as a mediator between life and death. Indeed, even in his initial embodiment as romantic hero, bravely leading Eurydice toward life, he appears dazed and distracted—"seine Sinne waren wie entzweit" ("his senses seemed to be split in two")—in contrast to his silent bride, who, suffused with death "wie eine Frucht von Süssigkeit und Dunkel" ("like a fruit with sweetness and darkness"), has already achieved an inviolable perfection. Eurydice is "in sich" and "voll von ihrem grossen Tode" ("in herself," "filled with her great death"), yet she has also been utterly emptied of her previous subjective existence, "ausgeteilt wie hundertfacher Vorrat" ("shared out like a hundredfold provision"). Rooted in and at one with death and the underworld, she is "jenes Mannes Eigentum nicht mehr" ("no longer that man's possession"), a being of pure Otherness (*SW* 1:542–45).

By the end of the poem Eurydice has become so completely immersed in her new state that Orpheus' turn does not move her or even register upon her:

> Und als plötzlich jäh
> der Gott sie anhielt und mit Schmerz im Ausruf
> die Worte sprach: Er hat sich umgewendet—,
> begriff sie nichts und sagte leise: *Wer?*
>
> (SW 1:545)

> [And when suddenly
> the god stopped her and with pain in his cry
> spoke the words: He has turned around—,
> she understood nothing and said softly: *Who?*]

Following this understated denouement—Orpheus' dramatic turn is reduced to a pitiful gesture, barely perceived or comprehended—Eurydice executes with dizzying swiftness a dismissive turn of her own, descending back toward the darkness of the underworld that, in Rilke's view, so richly empowers her. Orpheus, meanwhile, having failed to capture her essence or comprehend her mystery, fades to a faraway, faceless figure by the entrance gates: "irgend jemand, dessen Angesicht / nicht zu erkennen war" ("someone or other, whose countenance / could not be recognized" [SW 1:545]). Far from an act of condemnation or of self-empowerment, Orpheus' turn is revealed as having been one of utter longing, of hope that he too might partake of the secrets of Eurydice's dark realm. Thus, "Orpheus. Eurydike. Hermes," in addition to forcefully articulating what Strauss calls "Rilke's familiar mythology of maidens or women, prematurely dead, who find their highest fulfillment in nonfulfillment, in . . . a kind of inviolate chastity" (173), also communicates the male poet's envy of Eurydice, his own desire to achieve a similar purity and fulfillment of purpose. The poem suggests that Eurydice's very passivity, her acceptance of and consummation in death, constitutes an achievement that Orpheus can only hope to emulate.

Nearly twenty years later in the *Sonnets to Orpheus*, however, Rilke would develop a very different view of Orpheus, representing him as a successful intercessor between life and death and celebrating the Orphic turn itself, the moment of transformation from one state of being into another, as the supreme poetic gesture. Rilke's mandate in the *Sonnets* is not to rescue Eurydice but, rather, to tap her as a source of inspiration, "to know what Eurydice knows, to understand it, and to transpose it into song" (Strauss 183)—an accomplishment far outstripping that of his earlier Orpheus, whose lament for his bride springs as though unwilled from his lyre. The Orpheus of Rilke's *Sonnets*, in other words, having learned whatever secrets the underworld has to teach him, has been freed from most of his previous uncertainties; Eurydice, in contrast, remains locked in her role of archetypal female, still associated with passivity and death, consigned forever to the realm of inviolable Otherness that Rilke himself, Orpheus-like, has finally achieved the power to sing. In fact, all women, as Rilke indicates in a series of "Gegen-strophen" originally intended as part of the fifth Duino Elegy, can be seen as endlessly duplicated versions of Eurydice:

Blumen des tieferen Erdreichs,
von allen Wurzeln geliebte,
ihr, der Eurydike Schwestern,
immer voll heiliger Umkehr
hinter dem steigenden Mann.

(*SW* 2:137)

[Flowers of the deeper realm,
beloved of all roots,
you, Eurydice's sisters,
forever full of holy turning
behind the ascending man.]

If, for Rilke, Orpheus' wife is a being of pure Otherness, both bride and inviolable virgin, then Maurice Blanchot takes the level of abstraction even further by identifying Eurydice not as a flesh-and-blood woman, not even as an archetypically representative one, but, rather, as the nocturnal center at the core of all artistic endeavor. In "Le Regard d'Orphée," an essay appropriately located at the center of his 1955 *L'Espace littéraire*, Blanchot portrays Orpheus as the emblematic modern poet, while Eurydice is the dark essence that he struggles to draw back with him to the light-realm of expressive art:

Eurydice est . . . l'extrême que l'art puisse atteindre, elle est, sous un nom qui la dissimule et sous un voile qui la couvre, le point profondément obscur vers lequel l'art, le désir, la mort, la nuit semblent tendre. (179)

[Eurydice is . . . the greatest extreme that art can attain, she is, beneath a name that conceals her and a veil that covers her, the profoundly obscure point toward which art, desire, death, and night seem to strain.]

Orpheus' turn, for Blanchot, is an act both of error and inspiration, generating art through the very failure of the artist:

Il perd Eurydice, parce qu'il la désire par delà les limites mesurées du chant, et il se perd lui-même, mais ce désir et Eurydice perdue

et Orphée dispersé sont nécessaires au chant, comme est nécessaire
à l'oeuvre l'épreuve du désoeuvrement éternel. (181)

[He loses Eurydice because he desires her beyond the measured
limits of song, and he loses himself, but that desire and lost Eu-
rydice and dispersed Orpheus are all necessary for song, just as the
ordeal of eternal idleness is necessary for work.]

Although one might term Blanchot's account of the Orpheus myth a
romance of sorts, since Eurydice remains the object of the poet's most
profound desire, the pathos and human drama apparent even in Rilke's
highly mythologized version have disappeared here completely.
Orpheus, to be sure, still represents the human poet in all his power
and imperfection, but Eurydice has been reduced from a woman to a
wound, a dark, unrecoverable core of meaning—or, precisely because
it is unrecoverable, of meaninglessness.

Klaus Theweleit, exploring Orpheus' fate in modernist and post-
modern culture, asks to what extent

the sacrifice of women, which is one of the bases of artistic pro-
duction in patriarchal societies, is not just a symbolic one, but one
that goes on in the lives of real couples, . . . one that concerns living
men and especially living women directly. ("Politics of Orpheus,"
156)

Theweleit argues that the Orpheus/Eurydice myth must be under-
stood as a fable not only of artistic ambition but also of the deep-seated
gender conflict in which artistic endeavor is grounded: "Frauen sind in
der Vorstellungen und Verfahrensweisen patriarchaler Gesellschaften
zu einem Teil *selber* immer Hades" ("Women, in the conceptions and
procedures of patriarchal societies, are to a certain extent *themselves*
always Hades" [*Orpheus (und) Eurydike* 104]). Writers such as Rilke and
especially Blanchot merely take to its logical extreme a process of
abstraction already thousands of years old when they reduce Eurydice
first to "the eternal feminine," then to a silent Other, and finally to a
core of unattainable darkness. Indeed, by masking the complex emo-
tional dynamics of the myth, their accounts replay the very terms of the
conflict: Orpheus' transformation into the paradigmatic modern poet
takes place only, so to speak, over Eurydice's dead body.

Not until fairly recently have female writers, infiltrating both the literary marketplace and the canon in ever-increasing numbers, actively rejected Eurydice's traditional role as long-suffering wife, abandoned lover, patient muse, and death-filled archetype. No longer content to serve merely as the passive sources of male inspiration, female poets have set out to find creative outlets of their own. But, if Eurydice has begun to find her own voice in twentieth-century poetry,[6] the modern Orpheus has not always responded with good grace to the mutiny of his once-silent consort. One of the more colorful skirmishes in the textual/sexual war of literary modernism was fought by Lawrence and H.D., whose personal and poetic interactions replayed the complex gender dynamics, the turns and returns, and the shifting leader-follower patterns that characterize the Orpheus/Eurydice myth.[7]

H.D. outlines the terms of the conflict in a central scene of her autobiographical roman à clef *Bid Me to Live*, as Rico, a famous writer, offers Julia, the novel's protagonist, some advice on one of her poems:

> I don't like the second half of the Orpheus sequence as well as the first. Stick to the woman speaking. How can you know what Orpheus feels? It's your part to be woman, the woman vibration, Eurydice should be enough. You can't deal with both. (51)

Julia, understandably annoyed, rebuts with a reflection on Rico's double standard:

> Rico could write elaborately on the woman mood, describe women to their marrow in his writing; but if she turned round, wrote the Orpheus part of her Orpheus-Eurydice sequence, he snapped back, "Stick to the woman-consciousness, it is the intuitive woman-mood that matters." He was right about that, of course. But if he could enter, so diabolically, into the feelings of women, why should not she enter into the feelings of men? (62)

Julia's angry question focuses not only on the specific unfairness of Rico's advice but also on that of the myth her poem invokes. If Rico, as Orphic poet, may fix and penetrate "the woman-consciousness" with his piercing male gaze, why may not she, as Eurydice, also "turn round" and focus her artistic attention upon the thoughts and feelings of a man?

The scene describes, in thinly fictionalized form, the emotional dynamics of H.D.'s brief but turbulent relationship with Lawrence, which began in 1914 and culminated in the 1917 encounters detailed in the novel. If the exchange between Rico and Julia echoes one that actually took place between Lawrence and H.D., then it appears that H.D. heeded Lawrence's advice: her 1916 poem "Eurydice," written at a time when she was regularly exchanging manuscripts with Lawrence, is angry, defiant, and revisionary, but it does, indeed, "stick to the woman speaking."[8] Playing a willing Eurydice to Lawrence's charismatic Orpheus, H.D. apparently had hoped that her friend and fellow poet could draw her, as Julia is briefly drawn by Rico, out of the emotional hell of her daily wartime life and into "another dimension" of poetic existence (*Bid Me to Live* 68–69). Like the Eurydice of her own poem, she responded not with resignation but with bitterness and anger to what she perceived as his eventual turn against her. Whether or not *Bid Me to Live*, in which Rico first tacitly encourages and then coldly rejects Julia's tentative romantic advances, accurately recounts what "really happened" between Lawrence and H.D., the novel in any case presents events as H.D. later chose to interpret them: clearly, she felt that Lawrence, warning her not to pursue him into the terrain of emotional cross-dressing that he himself had so successfully navigated, had betrayed her on personal and artistic grounds alike.

Thus, although it is tempting to contemplate their literary relationship solely through the filter of their physical and emotional interactions, as several critics have seen fit to do,[9] the creative give-and-take between Lawrence and H.D. reached well beyond the private sphere of their correspondence and occasional meetings; in fact, it played itself out primarily in the unsheltered realm of art, as each grappled publicly, in writing, with the anxiety of the other's influence.[10] H.D.'s interest in Lawrence, to be sure, had more to do with his forceful personality and what she perceived as his symbolic Orpheus/Osiris role than with his actual accomplishments as novelist or poet. In her old age she would list him as one of the seven male "initiators" who, she felt, had most crucially influenced her poetic and personal development (*Compassionate Friendship* 24), while much earlier, in a 1916 letter that almost certainly refers to Lawrence, she granted him an even more potent role, confiding to John Cournos that "there is a power in this person to kill me":

> I mean literally. For the spiritual vision, his thoughts, his distant passion has given me, I thank God—because vision is of God! I

thank God! But . . . there is another side—if he comes too near, I am afraid for myself! I do not mean physically—. . . . I mean in a more subtle way.[11]

Lawrence, similarly, looked to H.D. less for poetic influence as such—although he consistently admired and praised her poetry[12]—than for some "more subtle" form of inspiration and initiation. When Cecil Gray, "Cyril Vane" of *Bid Me to Live*, wrote a letter in late 1917 accusing Lawrence of "allowing himself to become the object of a kind of esoteric female cult . . . a Jesus Christ to a regiment of Mary Magdalenes," Lawrence replied with a defense both of his own role as visionary messiah and of his "women's" initiatory function:

> As for me and my "women," I know what they are and aren't, and though there is a certain messiness, there is a further reality. Take away the subservience and feet-washing, and the pure understanding between Magdalen and Jesus went deeper than the understanding between the disciples and Jesus, or Jesus and the Bethany women. But Jesus himself was frightened of the knowledge which subsisted between the Magdalen and him, a knowledge deeper than the knowledge of Christianity and "good," deeper than love, anyhow. . . .
>
> It seems to me there is a whole world of knowledge to forsake, a new, deeper, lower one to *entamer*. And your hatred of me, like Frieda's hatred of me, is your cleavage to a world of knowledge and being which you ought to forsake, which, by organic law, you must depart from or die. And my "women," Esther Andrews, Hilda Aldington [H.D.] etc, represent, in an impure and unproud, subservient, cringing, bad fashion, I admit,—but represent none the less the threshold of a new world, or underworld, of knowledge and being. . . . The old world must burst, the underworld must be open and whole, new world.—You want an emotional sensuous underworld . . . : my "women" want an ecstatic subtly-intellectual underworld, like the Greeks—Orphicism—like Magdalen at her feet-washing—and there you are.[13]

Accepting the role not only of Christ, Lawrence also paints himself here as Orpheus, descending to that "new, deeper, lower . . . world, or underworld, of knowledge and being" to which H.D., as Magdalen/Eurydice, can, he believes, show the way. For Lawrence, as for Rilke and Blanchot, the underworld is female: a dangerous but alluring realm in which mystery and intuition are privileged over conventional wisdom and reason. Orpheus, as archetypal male poet, descends into that world in hopes of capturing and bringing to utterance all the secrets of the unknown. Whether one interprets his journey in psychoanalytical terms as a descent into the unconscious or in sexual terms as the descent into the body of the woman—a kind of physical "harrowing of hell"[14]—the quest remains, above all, one for mastery: over the Other within or merely over the other across the breakfast table.

Like Rilke, who in the *Sonnets to Orpheus* lauds Orpheus as an intercessor between the irreconcilable realms of life and death, Lawrence emphasizes the ambition rather than the danger of the Orphic quest by presenting it, in such early essays as his 1914 *Study of Thomas Hardy*, as an ultimately successful one:

> For a man who dares to look upon, and to venture within the unknown of the female, losing himself, like a man who gives himself to the sea, or a man who enters a primeval, virgin forest, feels, when he returns, the utmost gladness of singing. (104)

At times he implies, to be sure, that the voyage of sexual discovery should be mutual and interactive:

> What is true of men is so of women. If we turn our faces west, towards nightfall and the unknown within the dark embrace of a wife, they turn their faces east, towards the sunrise and the brilliant, bewildering, active embrace of a husband. (105)

Yet, by equating femininity with darkness, passivity, and the will-to-inertia, while holding men to represent light, action, and the will-to-motion, Lawrence establishes a sexual cosmogony in which only the male can claim real credit for creativity, artistic power, and utterance:

> In every creature, the mobility, the law of change, is found exemplified in the male, the stability, the conservatism is found in the female. In woman, man finds his root and establishment. In man, woman finds her exfoliation and florescence. The woman grows downwards, like a root, towards the centre and the darkness and

the origin. The man grows upwards, like the stalk, towards discovery and light and utterance. (127)

Lawrence, who often solicited help from women in his own literary endeavors, was willing enough, and indeed deemed it necessary, to employ women as guides to the realm of the unknown. He took care, however, to distance himself from those aspects of femininity that he found undesirable or potentially damaging to his masculine ego. By describing H.D., for instance, as "impure and unproud, subservient, cringing," he was able to suggest that she, despite the potency of her Magdalen/Eurydice role, was nonetheless also "feminine" in all the worst ways, betraying symptoms of an emotional "messiness" in which he wanted no part. As Orpheus, he would gladly follow his Eurydices down to their underworld; he refused, however, to value too highly their contribution to his quest or to grant them, worse yet, reciprocal access to his own upper world of male privilege. Although Lawrence as Orpheus might emerge from the underworld in possession of all its secrets— hence, his ability to "write elaborately on the woman mood, describe women to their marrow in his writing"—Eurydice was to remain locked in her role of archetypal female, associated, if not with trivial emotionality, then with the mute, inactive Otherness of passivity and death.

H.D., writing her poem "Eurydice" in 1916, probably had not yet read Lawrence's *Study of Thomas Hardy;* though already completed by 1915, the essay was not to see publication until 1936. She was, however, almost certainly familiar with the basic tenets of her friend's gender ideology, and both her poetry and her later prose attest that she clearly recognized the dangers of the sexual stereotyping that Lawrence's philosophy, like the Orpheus/Eurydice myth itself, sought to universalize and justify. Written during the painful disintegration of her marriage to Richard Aldington, "Eurydice" can be read on the most obvious biographical level as H.D.'s personal cry of rage and despair against an unfaithful husband, also a poet and once a mentor, who has drawn her toward happiness only to turn and reject her:

So you have swept me back,
I who could have walked with the live souls
above the earth,
I who could have slept among the live flowers
at last;

so for your arrogance
and your ruthlessness
I am swept back
where dead lichens drip
dead cinders upon moss of ash.

(CP 51)

Embedded here too, however, is H.D.'s response to Lawrence, who had told her to "stick to the woman speaking": in other words, to remain, like Eurydice herself, in the dark realm of the female, the realm of "the woman vibration." Although H.D. may have bowed to Lawrence's polemic in cutting out the Orpheus section of her poem, she no doubt recognized that his advice itself constituted an Orphic turn, a betrayal of confidence that was at the same time a condemnation. Her Eurydice executes an Orphic turn of her own—or, if you will, a "Eurydicean" turn away from patriarchal convention—when she rejects the familiar myth of Orpheus as the faithful lover whose glance back at his wife signals at once his aspiration and his human imperfection. Orpheus' backward glance, this Eurydice suggests, is more a gesture of greed—

So for your arrogance
and your ruthlessness
I have lost the earth
and the flowers of the earth

—than one of love or even of pure passionate need.

At the same time, H.D. also rejects the image of Eurydice as the passive object of her heroic husband's quest, allowed, while Orpheus charms the underworld with his music, no creative voice of her own. Decades later, in *Helen in Egypt,* H.D. would confront epic tradition by depicting the restless quest of Helen of Troy, one of Western mythology's most enduring emblems of the woman-as-object, not for bloody heroism but for subjective understanding and spiritual fulfillment. "Eurydice" is only slightly less ambitious: H.D.'s heroine, rather than accepting her fate in silence or lamenting vaguely to the gods,[15] cries out defiantly against all male oppression, offering a manifesto for a feminist poetics appropriating hell, the negative space of literary marginality into which the female poet has been driven, as a source of power:

Against the black
I have more fervour
than you in all the splendour of that place,
against the blackness
and the stark grey
I have more light.

. . . .

At least I have the flowers of myself,
and my thoughts, no god
can take that;
I have the fervour of myself for a presence
and my own spirit for light;

and my spirit with its loss
knows this;
though small against the black,
small against the formless rocks,
hell must break before I am lost;

before I am lost,
hell must open like a red rose
for the dead to pass.

(CP 54–55)

Eurydice's determination to reign in hell if she cannot write poetry in heaven is not, perhaps, the most satisfying solution possible to the creative dilemma in which Orpheus has placed her. But it is a courageous one, and the apocalyptic imagery of the final stanza—in which hell, in a demonic revision of Robert Burns, threatens to open "like a red rose"—suggests that Eurydice's "flowers of myself" are powerful blooms, indeed.[16]

If "Eurydice" represents, at least in part, H.D.'s response to Lawrence's Orphic pretensions, to the sexual politics that govern his poetic practice, then Lawrence's "Medlars and Sorb-Apples" can be read as his turn against her turn: Orpheus' counterresponse to Eurydice's mutiny. The poem, which appears in the 1923 volume *Birds, Beasts and Flowers*, was written in Italy in 1920, nearly three years after Lawrence's friendship with H.D. had, for reasons that her letters and memoirs only hint at, effectively ended.[17] By this time the Lawrence who wrote "The Crown" and *Study of Thomas Hardy*—essays that, despite their insistence on gender polarity, strongly advocated an emotional and creative alliance between the sexes—was well on the way to becoming a bitter, polemical misogynist, as the complex sexual dynamics of *The Rainbow* and *Women in Love* gave way to the woman-bashing, protofascist energies of *Aaron's Rod, Kangaroo,* and *The Plumed Serpent.* If, as Hilary Simpson has argued, the political inroads made by feminists during and after the Great War were at least partially responsible for the abrupt change in Lawrence's thinking, then Eurydice's rebellion against Orpheus could be said to have inspired a furious backlash.

Whatever the cause of his reactionary shift, Lawrence, who in 1917 named H.D. among the women indicating "the threshold of a new world, or underworld, of knowledge and being," had by 1919 abandoned any belief that the sexes should move toward each other or that, worse yet, men should follow women anywhere. Instead, he reaffirmed a traditional model of male leader and obedient female follower: "Man must either lead or be destroyed. Woman cannot lead."[18] Woman, he insists in such essays as *Fantasia of the Unconscious* (1923) and "Education of the People" (1919), must remain in the underworld of Otherness. And man, for his part, should "reduce her once more to a naked Eve, and send the apple flying" (*Fantasia* 188), driving her "back . . . to the old mindlessness, the old unconsciousness" (*Phoenix* 623):

> Break off the old polarity, the merging into oneness with others, with everything. . . . Break clean away from the old yearning navel-string of love, which unites us to the body of everything. Break it, and be born. Fall apart into your own isolation; set apart single and potent in singularity for ever. One is one and all alone and ever more shall be so. Exult in it. . . . Exult in your own dark being. (634)

"Medlars and Sorb-Apples" is about just such a navel string–breaking birth experience, about the exultation of achieving the state of "dark being" that is the self's final loneliness. But it is also, in however disguised a form, a poem about sexual politics: Orpheus' last damning word to Eurydice. The poem opens with a passionate apostrophe to the medlars and sorb-apples of the title:

> I love you, rotten,
> Delicious rottenness.

I love to suck you out from your skins
So brown and soft and coming suave,
So morbid, as the Italians say.

(LCP 280)

Since Lawrence himself tells us, in the prose preface to the "Fruits" section of Birds, Beasts and Flowers, that "fruits are all of them female" and that, "when they break and show the seed, then we look into the womb and see its secrets" (277), these opening lines would seem to present themselves as an unambiguous sexual metaphor, with the "delicious rottenness" of the fruit symbolizing the female mystery that, when "sucked out" by the male poet, exudes a pungent, deathlike sweetness—the secret, frightening but powerful, of the female underworld. But Lawrence quickly undermines such a reading by associating the "brown morbidity" of the medlars and sorb-apples not with women or feminine mystery but, instead, with the potent masculinity of "white gods":

What is it, in the grape turning raisin,
In the medlar, in the sorb-apple,
. . . .
What is it that reminds us of white gods?

Gods nude as blanched nut-kernels,
Strangely, half-sinisterly flesh-fragrant
As if with sweat,
And drenched with mystery.

(280)

Having thus dispensed with the poem's potential female Other, the poet descends to the underworld swiftly and neatly, striding "down the strange lanes of hell" without the aid of a Eurydice figure to serve either as "threshold," goal, or guide:

Sorb-apples, medlars with dead crowns.
I say, wonderful are the hellish experiences,
Orphic, delicate
Dionysos of the Underworld.

A kiss, and a spasm of farewell, a moment's orgasm of rupture,
Then along the damp road alone, till the next turning.
And there, a new partner, a new parting, a new unfusing into
    twain,
A new gasp of further isolation,
A new intoxication of loneliness, among decaying, frost-cold
    leaves.

(LCP 280–81)

The orgasmic imagery of the poem invites us to recall the familiar Lawrentian dictum that it is in sex that we become most aware of our isolation, of life's proximity to death. But this "orgasm of rupture" does not entail the "death-agony," the "Osiris-cry of abandonment," that it does in such other *Birds, Beasts and Flowers* poems as "Tortoise Shout" (*LCP* 367, 364). Here, leave-taking and loneliness are not painful but "intoxicating," "exquisite," and "perfect," as the soul becomes

ever more vividly embodied
Like a flame blown whiter and whiter
In a deeper and deeper darkness
Ever more exquisite, distilled in separation.

(281)

"Medlars" is above all, then, a poem about self-discovery, self-accomplishment, and the rapture of achieving self-fulfillment through a kind of mystic self-intoxication: an incantatory "Orphic farewell, and farewell, and farewell" (*LCP* 281). Yet with the invocation of Orpheus—linked here, as he probably was in his earliest mythological manifestations, with the wine god, Dionysus—Lawrence cannot help but bring at least the shadow of Eurydice into the poem. She has been left unnamed, to be sure, and her image has been refracted into that of the endlessly multiplied "new partner" who is always already waiting, ripe for the next farewell, at "the next turning": at every turn of the road, or, in a slightly different reading, every time Orpheus turns. In contrast to Orpheus, "distilled in separation," this Eurydice is scattered and substanceless, much like the young bride of Rilke's "Orpheus. Eurydike. Hermes," who upon entering the underworld is immediately

aufgelöst wie langes Haar
und hingegeben wie gefallner Regen
und ausgeteilt wie hundertfacher Vorrat.

(*SW* 1:545)

[loosened like long hair
and given forth like fallen rain
and distributed like a hundredfold provision.]

Despite Eurydice's physical absence, however, her voice still echoes clearly through the poem:

So, in the strange retorts of medlars and sorb-apples
The distilled essence of hell.
The exquisite odour of leave-taking,
Jamque vale!
Orpheus, and the winding, leaf clogged, silent lanes of hell.

(*LCP* 281)

"*Jamque vale*," as Lawrence must have known, are among Eurydice's last words to Orpheus in Virgil's *Georgics*, the earliest recorded account of the myth.[19] Whether the poem, then, is about loneliness discovered through sex or about the close kinship of sex to death or about the self's euphoric farewell to the fetters of its earthly consciousness, it is also about a man's desire to experience the intoxicating mysteries of the underworld in the company only of the "white gods" who represent his own distillation into perfection, his own more accessible Otherness. This Orpheus soundly rejects Eurydice, both as archetype and as individual, in favor of "the *ego sum* of Dionysos / The *sono io* of perfect drunkenness." His descent now is no longer into "the unknown within the dark embrace of a wife" (*Study of Thomas Hardy* 105) but into an "intoxication of final loneliness": the known, egoistic depths of the self.

Although feminists are quick to point out that the persistent historical association of the feminine with darkness, intuition, and passivity oppresses women more than it honors them, implicitly barring them access to the privileged male realms of reason, action, and political power,[20] one can argue that Lawrence's pre-1918 gender ideology did pay some form of homage to women, for it offered them a space of their own, a narrow venue of power, so that a poet such as H.D. could stake out her fragment of poetic turf, if in no other way, at least by articulating "the woman vibration." If Lawrence, as Orpheus, felt confident enough to descend to Eurydice's underworld, at least he admitted that he needed her help to get there. In his postwar "male comradeship" phase, however, Lawrence grants all power, all privilege, and all action to men, "the leaders, the outriders" (*Phoenix* 665). He begins by appropriating the underworld, the realm of Otherness that he once exclusively associated with women, as the domain of the emphatically male white gods who represent his phallic consciousness. Critics such as Cornelia Nixon have described Lawrence's "male comradeship" phase as a "turn against women," thereby implying that Lawrence executed the kind of destructive Orphic turn that H.D. reacted against in "Eurydice," stereotypically consigning women to an artistically limited and politically powerless underworld. But, in the misogynist phase that followed hard on the war years, Lawrence did not turn *against* women, fixing them with his damaging, dismissive Orphic gaze, so much as turn *away* from them, refusing even to acknowledge their contribution to his own artistic empowerment.

Thus, in his 1923 *Fantasia of the Unconscious* Lawrence no longer professes to seek a "new world" associated with feminine mystery but calls, instead, only for masculine energy and enlightenment. In a passage recalling his 1913 poem "She Looks Back," a virulent tirade against mother love in which he castigates Frieda for longing for the young children she had abandoned for his sake (*LCP* 205–8), Lawrence exhorts his male contemporaries:

> You've got to know that you're a man, and being a man means you go on alone, ahead of the woman, to break a way through the old world into the new. And you've got to be alone. And you've got to start off ahead . . . and never look back. Because Lot's wife, looking back, was turned to a pillar of salt, these miserable men, for ever looking back to their women for guidance, they are miserable pillars of half-rotten tears. (*Fantasia* 189)

Lawrence transfers onto modern man the consequences of a woman's mythical transgression, suggesting that a taboo peek backward will result not merely, as for Orpheus, in the loss of the desired Other but also, as for Lot's wife, in self-condemnation. Thus, he portrays

Orpheus' turn—the poet's ambitious attempt to see into the worlds of light and darkness, life and death, male and female, simultaneously— as a gesture not of artistic ambition but, rather, of "feminine" weakness.

For Lawrence of the early 1920s, with his bitter attacks on feminism and his disturbing fascination with male-dominated, protofascist modes of government, vision marched in a straight line, with no ambiguous glances to the right or left; Orpheus remained a useful model only so long as he never looked back. Shortly before his death, to be sure, Lawrence reaffirmed at least some of the "tenderness" and other feminine values that he had a few years earlier so strenuously rejected. But he never renewed his personal contact with H.D., whose accusations in "Eurydice" he had so effectively deflected with the self-absorbed *"sono io"* of "Medlars and Sorb-Apples." As H.D. herself later recalled, his last letter to her represented a definitive turn away: "'I hope never to see you again,' he wrote" (*Tribute* 134).[21]

Nonetheless, Lawrence did cast a final glance—a conciliatory rather than a damning one—in H.D.'s direction, or so, at least, H.D. herself came to believe. When, after Lawrence's death, Stephen Guest delivered to her a copy of *The Man Who Died* (*The Escaped Cock*) with the words, "Lawrence wrote this for you" (*Tribute* 134), H.D. was clearly flattered by Guest's suggestion that Lawrence had modeled his priestess of Isis, who ministers to and regenerates the risen Christ/Osiris, after her.[22] In *Tribute to Freud* she chronicles how, during and after her 1933–34 psychoanalytic sessions with Freud, she came to recognize Lawrence not only as Orpheus to her Eurydice, leader to her follower, but also as Osiris to her Isis: the twin brother initial sharer who had inspired her artistically but whose shattered image she must now in turn gather up, reconstruct, re-member.[23] Although she refers to Lawrence's many female "disciples" as a "choros of Maenads" (133),[24] thereby suggesting that their hagiographic accounts tear Lawrence/ Orpheus to pieces rather than reconstituting him, H.D. grudgingly admits, "I envied these women who have written memoirs of D. H. Lawrence, feeling that they had found in him some sort of guide or master" (140–41). Her own recollections present the voice not of an adoring follower but, instead, of an ambivalent equal. "I am almost afraid to speak," she confesses in her 1935 poem "The Poet," almost certainly written with Lawrence in mind: "[I] certainly won't cry out, 'hail,' / or 'farewell' or the things people do shout."[25] Rejecting Eurydice's traditional, final *"jamque vale"*—"and now farewell"—H.D.

would in fact go on to write about Lawrence extensively, just as she would obsessively reconstruct and reexamine, both in fictionalized form and in her journals and memoirs, her relationships with such other problematic figures in her life as Frances Gregg, Ezra Pound, and Richard Aldington.

Bid Me to Live—begun in 1927, heavily revised over several decades, and finally published in 1960—represents H.D.'s most sustained attempt to put Lawrence/Osiris back together again, shaping a new image from the shards of memory. As she would do with Freud in her 1956 *Tribute to Freud*, she gains control over Lawrence's powerful image by placing him within a mythological framework of her own making, associating him with a range of symbolic and historical figures whose significance she herself can fix and manipulate—reducing Rico, for instance, from the great Lawrentian poet-lover to "an Orpheus head, severed from its body" (*Bid* 51). Claiming her own position as Lawrence's literary and symbolic equal, she goes on to portray him as Dis, the ruler of the underworld, and herself as Persephone, who, like Orpheus, can pass between the realms of life and death:

> Tenderness. That was it, not flame and seething passion, the dark-god he spoke of. Or if a dark-god, then one truly, Dis of the under-world. . . . He had called her Persephone. . . . He was burnt out too, and white, but there was no dark flame now, none of his dark-god, unless he were Dis of the under-world, the husband of Persephone. Yes, he was her husband. (141)

In depicting him as Persephone's "burnt-out" husband, H.D. invites a no-longer-threatening Lawrence to share the creative space that she, in "Eurydice," had long ago claimed as her own—to join her, that is, in her "tender" female underworld, now a place of refuge and strength. She covertly acknowledges the gentler, conciliatory tone of such late poems as Lawrence's "Bavarian Gentians,"[26] in which the dying poet, plucking, perhaps, one of the "flowers of myself" that H.D. bravely grew in "Eurydice," gingerly bears a torchlike blue gentian down to

> the sightless realm where darkness is awake upon the dark
> and Persephone herself is but a voice
> or a darkness invisible enfolded in the deeper dark
> of the arms Plutonic.
>
> (*LCP* 697)

"Lead me then, lead the way," urges Lawrence, the Orphic poet who once wanted only to be followed. For, although he makes his final journey alone—"let me guide myself . . . down the darker and darker stairs"—the Lawrence of "Bavarian Gentians" does not succumb to the "intoxication of final loneliness" that closed "Medlars and Sorb-Apples." Instead, he seeks with his "torches of darkness" to discover and illuminate, "[shed] darkness on," Pluto and Persephone, "the lost bride and her groom": the male and female deities of darkness as they lie at last in conjugal embrace.

Toward the end of *Bid Me to Live* Julia defiantly reminds Rico, and perhaps herself as well, that "Rafe [Aldington] is not the Marble Faun, not even a second-rate Dionysus. . . . He is not Dionysus, you are not Orpheus. You are human people, Englishmen, madmen" (163–64).[27] Yet, although she unceremoniously hauls a mythologized and self-mythologizing Lawrence/Orpheus/Dis up from Eurydice's murky underworld, H.D. nonetheless ends her novel with an affectionate tribute to his memory, gently condemning his "mad" gender ideology but also acknowledging the initiatory, even inspirational role he has played in her work. From Lawrence's 1912 love poem "Gloire de Dijon" she appropriates the term *gloire*, which she uses to describe her own artistic aspirations, the ineffable visionary aura that she was straining to capture in her writing. The *gloire*, as Julia explains to Rico, represents the resolution of the conflict between them; it symbolizes Orpheus and Eurydice, Osiris and Isis, Dis and Persephone, together—maleness and femaleness fused in a single artist and a single work of art:

> Perhaps you would say I was trespassing, couldn't see both sides, as you said of my Orpheus. I could be Eurydice in character, you said, but woman-is-woman and I couldn't be both. The *gloire* is both. (176)

Like the mythical Orpheus at his most ambitious moment, H.D. tries, with the image of the *gloire*, to "see both sides": to encompass at once the world of man and the world of woman in the range of her own artistic vision. In the end, however, she turns away from the transcendent male-female *gloire* and back to the realm of human common sense: "No, that spoils it; it is both and neither. It is simply myself sitting here, . . . propped up in bed, scribbling in a notebook, with a candle at my elbow" (177).

Chapter 5

Leda and the Poetics of Violation

A shudder in the loins engenders there
The broken wall, the burning roof and tower
And Agamemnon dead.
                              Being so caught up,
So mastered by the brute blood of the air,
Did she put on his knowledge with his power
Before the indifferent beak could let her drop?
                    —William Butler Yeats, "Leda and the Swan," 1925

How did Yeats imagine it like that,
his feathered glory, her thigh's betrayal,
her soul pulsing to his heartbeat?
A semen-smelling man, his glove
at her throat, the blood-flow,
the broken wall,
the monumental time of his whimpering,
his after-reek she can't wash off,
her gentle lover pleading
forget, trust me,
and the tears of impossibility between them.
                    —Phyllis Stowell, "Leda," 1988

In a revealing misspelling, W. B. Yeats once called the rape of Leda "a classic enunciation":[1] a divine annunciation, that is, akin to the Virgin Mary's visitation by the Holy Spirit, but one with the explicitly articulatory character of a prophetic pronouncement. His sonnet "Leda and the Swan," accordingly, focuses less on Zeus's erotic or political motivations for the attack than on Leda's capacity to translate such divine immanence into human understanding: "Did she put on his knowledge with his power / Before the indifferent beak could let her drop?" (*Poems* 212). Although the poem, which thematizes divine revelation, presumably was not born of it—in fact, the early drafts demonstrate that "painstaking effort rather than a single flash of inspiration" characterized the poem's genesis (Ellmann 176)—Yeats chose to couch his descriptions of its origins in largely visionary terms: despite his initial conception of the poem as a political allegory, he explains, "bird and lady" eventually "took such possession of the scene that all politics went out of it" (*Cat and Moon* 37). In contrast to Leda, who remains silent throughout the poem, Yeats himself succeeded in channeling possession into self-possession, inspiration into articulation, and spiritual annunciation into poetic enunciation. All the same, his attribution of visionary origins to the poem implies a certain identification with Leda's receptive stance. But, as Lawrence Lipking notes, the "recasting of the self into a woman's passive state does not come easily to a man" (137); read as a fable of divine inspiration, then, the Leda myth offers a model of poetic creativity that is, particularly for male writers, as problematic as it is compelling.

Inspiration, at its best, signifies a positive, generative influence, a fertilizing encounter of human and divine energies. But if poets and mystics throughout history have figured creative and religious inspiration in terms of sexual union and shared sexual ecstasy, the dark side of inspiration is violation: a violent overwhelming of self by Other that finds its sexual analogy in rape. As the Leda myth itself dramatizes, the rape analogy is an uncomfortable one for male and female writers alike, for it posits a sexual cosmogony that characterizes the inspiring Other as male, while the experience of the inspired poet is explicitly feminized.[2] For women, of course, rape is no merely abstract concept; even if no woman lives in actual fear of being violated by a swan (or, one would hope, by Zeus in any form), tales such as the Leda myth, in which human contact with the divine is couched in the vocabulary of sexual conquest, can serve as all-too-accurate metaphors both for female poets' real-life experiences of male domination and for their anxieties of male literary influence. One has only to recall Ezra Pound enthusiastically "slashing" H.D.'s pen name and poetry in a London tea shop or the Australian writer Mollie Skinner weeping bitterly as she read D. H. Lawrence's heavily rewritten version of her own novel *The Boy in the Bush* to recognize how age-old patterns of sexual subjugation can find disturbing echoes in the processes of literary production.[3] Female writers confronting the Leda myth, then, might reasonably be expected to identify, at least on some imaginative level, with Leda and her plight; that is, one can hardly imagine a woman writing about the myth solely from Zeus's point of view, except perhaps with heavy irony. Indeed, contemporary female poets such as Olga Broumas, Phyllis

Stowell, Mona Van Duyn, Kathleen Fraser, and Dorie LaRue have almost uniformly spoken, in their accounts of the myth, either through or on behalf of Leda.[4]

For male writers, however, the issue becomes more complicated. Although modernist literature is replete with examples of what Sandra M. Gilbert and Susan Gubar have termed "sexchanges"—literary appropriations of opposite gender roles and disguises—male identification with Leda requires a kind of emotional cross-dressing that few men, given especially Leda's status as victim, have been willing to undertake or sustain. Yeats, Rilke, and Lawrence, in particular, all frequently courted and laid claim to outside inspiration by actively cultivating such "passive" traits as sensitivity, receptivity, and intuition, qualities that all three explicitly associated with a "feminine" mode of being and to which all repeatedly attempted, using a variety of personal and poetic strategies, to gain some form of access. Yet these same poets proved conspicuously unwilling, in their literary responses to the Leda myth, to place themselves fully in the imaginative role of the female, perhaps because they recognized in Leda's plight the central paradox of their own visionary enterprise: Leda's "knowledge and power" are achieved only through her powerlessness, her unwilling submission to another's will and desire.

So dramatic and so memorable is Yeats's famous sonnet that most twentieth-century readers have come to think of it as the definitive account of the Leda myth. Certainly, we cannot easily imagine "Leda and the Swan" beginning in any other way than with a "sudden blow," an emphatic collision that collapses the origins of Western civilization into a single, startling moment of divine presence. In Yeats's early drafts, however, the poem begins much more tentatively: "The swooping godhead is half hovering still, / yet climbs upon her trembling body"; "A swoop upon great wings and hovering still . . ."; "A rush, a sudden wheel, and hovering still . . ." (Ellmann 176–79). Not until the poem's final version, in fact, does Yeats himself stop hovering around his subject matter and opt for a startling, violent impact. Yeats's poem is the intertext through which readers today necessarily view the Leda myth; certainly, no contemporary Leda poem in English can possibly be free of its influence. But it is important to remember that many of Yeats's modernist contemporaries, including Rilke, H.D., and probably Lawrence, wrote their Leda poems without having read "Leda and the Swan" and that Yeats himself wreaked important violence on the myth when he chose to foreground the painful, destructive aspects of Leda's rape by Zeus. In fact, prior to the publication of Yeats's poem in 1925,[5] Leda is seldom depicted as the unwilling victim of a brutal, "indifferent" attack.

Instead, legions of painters and sculptors from Greek antiquity onward have represented Leda's encounter with the swan mostly in terms of romantic playfulness and/or sexual acquiescence.[6] Late-nineteenth- and early-twentieth-century writers, similarly, generally portray Leda's story not as a violent drama of pursuit and violation but, rather, as a peaceful idyll (or, in the case of Alfred Jarry's 1900 *opérette bouffe*, as a bumbling comedy) of male ardor and willing female abandon. Remy de Gourmont's innocent Leda, for instance, succumbs gladly to the charming, passionate swan, "si royal et si mâle" ("so royal and so male" ["Leda," *Divertissements* 149–51]); Oliver St. John Gogarty's Leda finds herself "stirred with wonder" by the swan's "alban beauty" ("To the Liffey with the Swans," 50); John Gray's Leda affords "swift assistance" to her "feathered lord" ("Leda," 82–85); and the disconcertingly blue-skinned nymph of Pierre Louÿs's well-nigh pornographic novelette *Lêda* swoons with delight when the swan penetrates her with his beak "comme s'il mangeait ses entrailles" ("as if he were eating her entrails" [28–30]). Only T. Sturge Moore ("Agathon to Lysis," 119) and a youthful Aldous Huxley ("Leda," 1–18) so much as hint that Leda's fascination with the swan might be tempered by fear and suffering. More recent poets, too, often fail to follow Yeats's more sympathetic example; Lawrence Durrell, for instance, asserts baldly that "the flapping of the wings excited Leda" ("Swans," 50), and even Robert Graves, whose 1958 poem "Leda" at least injects a modernist sense of sinister brutality into the story, stresses above all the bestial desire and perverse complicity of the woman whose Ledaesque behavior he describes:

> Heart, with what lonely fears you ached,
>   How lecherously mused upon
> That horror with which Leda quaked
>   Under the spread wings of the swan.
>
> Then soon your mad religious smile
>   Made taut the belly, arched the breast,
> And there beneath your god awhile
>   You strained and gulped your beastliest.

Pregnant you are, as Leda was,
    Of bawdry, murder, and deceit;
Perpetuating night because
    The after-languors hang so sweet.

(Poems 115)

Bram Dijkstra has advanced several explanations—besides the obvious aesthetic one that swans and maidens look rather decorative together—for the Leda myth's persistent favor among fin de siècle artists. On the one hand, he suggests, pastoral depictions of Leda as the swan's acquiescent lover characterize women as "other-than-human" creatures who, craving still the "animal pleasures" that men have transcended, are to be despised as well as feared. On the other hand, the swan-god's "assertive act of rape" allows male artists to control such dangerous femininity by returning Leda to woman's supposedly "predestined position of abject submission to male authority" (316–17). Similar motivations might account for the myth's popularity in literary works of the same period: most of these either express, as in de Gourmont's 1899 novel *Dream of a Woman*, a man's well-founded anxiety toward a femme fatale who, so long as her bestial desires remain unfulfilled, can be neither fathomed nor possessed by mortal man (16–20), or they enact, as in Louÿs's 1898 *Lêda*, a male fantasy of female sexual abandon. Gabriele D'Annunzio's 1913 novella "Leda without Swan" in a sense does both, balancing the narrator's sexual angst vis-à-vis a real-life Leda against his voyeuristic mastery of a sculptural one. "I went . . . to see that dismembered voluptuousness," the protagonist recalls of a Leda statue dropped by careless workmen, concluding with evident relief: "The parts that expressed pleasure most intensely are intact" (180).

The iconoclastic event described in D'Annunzio's story takes place late in 1899; his smashed Leda sculpture, entering the new century fragmented yet still charged with imaginative potency, thus serves as a strikingly appropriate symbol for the Leda myth's own transition into modernism, and especially for modernist writers' peculiar ambivalences concerning Leda's simultaneous passivity and power. That Yeats, in particular, was extremely sensitive to the paradoxes of Leda's position is evident in "Leda and the Swan," a poem that has inspired, precisely due to its ambiguities, more diverse and often contradictory explications than perhaps any other short lyric of its era.

Robert Snukal, asserting that "Leda is being raped, not only by a god, but by history as a god" (167–68), takes the most obvious line of interpretation, emphasizing both the historical and mythical dimensions of the event. Other critics, however, have insisted on tracing far more convoluted trajectories of authority and vision. Despite Yeats's own account of how the poems' protagonists came to "possess" his imagination, for instance, such readers as Kenneth Burke, Bernard Levine, Brenda S. Webster, and the poet Laurence Lieberman have suggested that the swan represents the poetical apotheosis of Yeats himself, so that the poem in effect dramatizes the poet's violent possession of his muse: "in his early poems, there are the white birds, which are 'seminal' aspects of himself; these become deified in taking the form of Zeus, as a swan; and in this form they again descend to earth" (Burke n. 257). Leo Spitzer argues that the poem, in portraying Zeus's rape of Leda, itself enacts a violation of the reader—"the reader, too, . . . [is] helpless and numb like the girl: we, too, feel the helplessness, the terror, the horror of closeness imposed" (273)—while W. C. Barnwell, advancing precisely the opposite interpretation, insists that "we as readers" can be seen "as the rapists that repeat again and again the drama of sexual encounter through reading the poem itself" (62). Finally, several critics have identified the poem's real rapist as Leda herself. C. F. MacIntyre, for instance, expresses the wish (though not specifically in reference to Yeats's poem) "that Dante had put Leda in his seventh circle, where she richly belonged for having violated nature" (141), while Bernard Levine, in a particularly improbable reading, distorts the poem's syntax and punctuation in order to demonstrate that Zeus, who is apparently so "staggered" by Leda's great beauty that he is compelled to rape her, is actually more of a victim than she is: for instance, "the girl may be construed as struggling in such a way as to have forced 'her nape' into 'his bill'. . . making *him* helpless" (117). John F. Adams, similarly, claims that Leda "actively participates in the sexual experience" (53), to the extent that she "takes a kind of mastery over the man": "There is almost a suggestion of the infant in this god's heart beating against the captive but still maternal breast of Leda, a feeling which is not, I believe, unusual for the female in her sexual climax" (55). Adams admires the poem above all for its profound insights into "the female's passive role in sex" and "the mystery of woman's passive pleasure in being violated" (54); little wonder, then, that he pronounces

"Leda and the Swan," a work that he finds "almost embarrassingly personal" (49), to be "primarily a poem for men" (58).

Whether the poem portrays history's rape of humanity, the poet's rape of the muse, the poem's rape of the poet, the poem's rape of the reader, the reader's rape of the poem, or even Leda's rape of nature and of Zeus, most commentators would agree—although in doing so they tend to ignore the gender contradictions implicit in any identification of a female rape victim with generic "man"—that Yeats's sonnet enacts, above all, the divine imposition of a mythic design upon human existence. The poem privileges Leda's rather than Zeus's point of view, yet the poet identifies himself fully with neither, standing as an observer, detached yet empathetic, whose role is to enunciate to his audience the rape's historical significance as annunciatory event. Yeats, himself a believer in the kind of revelatory parousia that "Leda and the Swan" thematizes, would place the poem in a central position of *A Vision*, his 1925 occult tour de force setting forth the bizarre cosmological schema that had, he claimed, been revealed to him through his wife's automatic writing. His accounts of *A Vision*'s origins describe a gendered genealogy of inspiration, his wife acting as a fertile but uncomprehending vessel for the voices from beyond that Yeats, as authoritative male, would subsequently interpret and systematize. "Leda and the Swan" suggests a similarly gendered creative hierarchy: the poet, clarifying the historical significance of Leda's rape, himself seems privy to the "knowledge and power" of which Leda, described in the poem as "staggering," "helpless," "terrified," and "vague," is as yet but dimly aware.

Yeats's Leda, however, though "mastered" both by Zeus and by the poet, is by no means a wholly passive figure. Her womb, the "there" where Zeus's shuddering loins "engender" Troy's destruction,[7] microcosmically contains not only "Agamemnon dead," Mycenae's future king inscribed within a yet-to-be-lived past, but also "the broken wall, the burning roof and tower": the city of Troy at the instant of its demise. As a locus, then, both of human potentiality and historic process, Leda's body encompasses as well as participates in the whole cycle of birth, destruction, and regeneration that her rape initiates, embracing if not necessarily reconciling the dialectically opposed forces—humanity and divinity, spirit and flesh, motion and stasis, male and female, Love and War—that inhabit and energize the poem.[8]

Similarly, in "The Mother of God," another poem about a divine insemination, Yeats indicates that Mary nurtures in her womb not only Christ but the cosmos:

> The threefold terror of love: a fallen flare
> Through the hollow of an ear;
> Wings beating about the room;
> The terror of all terrors that I bore
> The Heavens in my womb.

> (*Poems* 244)

That Mary bears "the Heavens" in her body, while Leda incubates "broken" and "burning" buildings and a king who is always already dead, indicates both the limitations and the scope of each woman's function as a passive yet indispensable instrument of historical change. Although they gestate what they cannot control, both Leda and Mary fulfill the prophet's, or prophetic poet's, designated function of transforming godly annunciation into human enunciation by rendering a divine will intelligible and incarnate. Whether or not they "put on" the god's knowledge, then, these women surely participate in, perhaps even supersede, his power.

Given especially Yeats's own lifelong fascination with séances, automatic writing, and other forms of attempted contact with the unknown, one can hardly help but wonder whether he—who would claim in 1936 that he had "looked out of [the] eyes" of "the woman in me" and "shared her desire"[9]—did not on some level himself long to take on the receptive "female" role, with all its visionary immediacy, that was filled in the Greek myth by Leda, in Christian lore by Mary, and in real life by his wife.[10] Yet "Leda and the Swan" amply documents the dangers of such a direct and unmediated access. Poised uncertainly between identification and impartiality, the poem, with its emphasis on the rape's destructive consequences and its grimly vivid depiction of the attack itself—from violent impact to shuddering orgasm to callous postcoital indifference—betrays every bit as much fear of the "sudden blow" as desire for Leda's resulting visionary stature.

While Yeats's poem focuses on Leda's role as visionary victim, Rilke's earlier "Leda" (1907–8) presents the rape from an opposite, though similarly paradoxical, perspective. Like Yeats, Rilke was often to link creative inspiration specifically with the feminine receptivity and traditionally female sexual passivity that Leda most obviously represents, declaring in 1904 that "das tiefste Erleben des Schaffenden ist weiblich—denn es ist empfangendes und gebärendes Erleben" ("the deepest experience of creativity is feminine—for it is a receptive and birth-giving experience").[11] Later, however, in a 1912 letter, Rilke would employ decidedly less exuberant if equally feminized language to describe the onslaught of poetic inspiration that he had recently undergone at Duino: "I feel as if I were being physically torn to pieces," he complains, because—and note here how closely his account parallels the sexual sequence of Yeats's sonnet—"the spirit rushes in and out so brusquely, comes so wildly, and departs so abruptly."[12]

Rilke would spend much of his life trying to cultivate in himself— whether by repeatedly articulating his own aesthetic of femininity, by establishing friendships and love affairs with artistic women, or by translating the love poetry of female writers from Louise Labé to Elizabeth Barrett Browning—those receptive, feminine traits that he believed to be the necessary characteristics of a successful poet. His own poem about the Leda myth, however, despite his explicit association of religious and creative inspiration with the physical and emotional experiences of women, largely avoids any close identification with the story's female protagonist. Instead, the poem offers an emphatically male point of view; in fact, it reverses the terms of the rape-by-the-Other metaphor, suggesting that, if the myth is to be read as a fable of poetic inspiration, then it is Zeus rather than Leda who stands in the role of the poet, so that the story enacts not the poet's violation by an inspiring Other but, rather, his own visionary "penetration" of his poetic object:

> Als ihn der Gott in seiner Not betrat,
> erschrak er fast, den Schwan so schön zu finden:
> er ließ sich ganz verwirrt in ihm verschwinden.
> Schon aber trug ihn sein Betrug zur Tat,
>
> bevor er noch des unerprobten Seins
> Gefühle prüfte. Und die Aufgetane
> erkannte schon den Kommenden im Schwane
> und wußte schon: er bat um Eins,

das sie, verwirrt in ihrem Widerstand,
nicht mehr verbergen konnte. Er kam nieder
und halsend durch die immer schwächre Hand

ließ sich der Gott in die Geliebte los.
Dann erst empfand er glücklich sein Gefieder
und wurde wirklich Schwan in ihrem Schooß.

                                                    (SW 1:558)

[When the god entered him in his need,
he was almost surprised to find the swan so lovely:
confused, he let himself vanish within him.
But soon his deceit swept him onward to his deed,

before he had even tried the feelings
of that new existence. And the woman, undone,
already recognized the comer in the swan
and knew already: he wanted that

which she, confused in her resistance,
no longer could conceal. The god alit
and, necking through her ever-weakening hand,

released himself into his beloved.
Then, at last, he delighted in his plumage
and became truly swan in her lap.][13]

Rilke's version of the Leda story departs significantly from mytho-
logical precedent: rather than transforming himself into a swan, Zeus
actually enters a swan's body, making for an opening line—"When the
god entered him in his need"—with confusing and even homosexually
suggestive connotations.[14] Documenting not just one but two acts of
penetration, the poem recalls the kind of triangulated sexual economy
described by such explicators of literary homoerotics as Eve Sedgwick,
who, in *Between Men*, traces displacements of male homosexual desire
onto the body of a shared woman, and Wayne Koestenbaum, whose
Double Talk posits male literary collaboration as a covertly homosexual
act mediated through a shared text characterized as female. Although
Leda's body is undeniably shared by the poem's two male figures,
however, the swan, too, serves an important mediatory function of its
own, for it shields Leda from the unfortunate fate of Semele, whose

human form could not survive the intensity of Zeus in his unmasked sexual glory. In fact, the swan takes on an almost hermaphroditic character, occupying both the male role of rapist and the traditionally female role—filled, for Yeats, by powerfully passive women like Leda and Mary—of mediatrix.

By reversing the Leda myth's expected trajectory of revelation, Rilke suggests in his poem that it is neither the swan nor Leda who garners true knowledge and power from the rape but, rather, Zeus, the rapist. As an allegory of poetic inspiration, then, the story reads something like this: the poet (Zeus) must enter the body of literary language and poetic perception (the swan) before he can fully master his poetic object (Leda), yet only after that mastery has been achieved does he really "delight in his plumage" and become "truly swan," truly poet. If, in other poems from the same period, such as "Alkestis" and "Orpheus. Eurydike. Hermes," Rilke portrays women as potent and inviolable beings whose dark, mysterious powers he, as male poet, clearly envies and desires, in "Leda" such revelatory Otherness seems to be mostly the province of the swan. As in Yeats's sonnet, however, Leda's body, and more specifically her womb, turns out to be the hidden center of the poem: the poem's final word, *Schooß*, though usually translated as "lap," also means "womb," so that Leda, far from serving as a mere instrument of Zeus's desire, provides and indeed circumscribes the site of his creative transformation. "Inside a woman," as Lawrence Lipking notes, "is also where men take form" (128); even in adulthood, in Rilke's understanding of the creative process, a man must reenter the realm of the female before he can emerge as poet. Infantlike, Zeus can be reborn or metamorphized, rendered "truly swan," only in Leda's lap/womb, the maternal, internal recesses of her body.

Rilke's "Leda" depicts poetic inspiration not as a rawly revelatory act but as an event composed in and mediated by language, a meaning figured by the plumage of the swan, whose feathers (*Feder*) are also, of course, writing instruments.[15] As Rilke's poem makes particularly evident, much of the poetic appeal of the Leda myth stems not only from its classic situation, graphically enacted, of human intercourse with the divine but also from the swan's potential as a multivalent literary symbol: swans are graceful, like the rhythms of poetry; white, like an unwritten page; romantic, singing only at the moment of death.[16] For Rilke, then, the swan represents both the cloak of language and, in a 1906 Thing-poem called "The Swan" (*SW* 1:510), the mysterious, still

grace that humankind achieves only in death. Yeats, similarly, in his
1919 "The Wild Swans at Coole," uses swans to evoke memory and the
ideals of youth; later, in his 1931 "Coole Park and Ballylee," they
become a majestic yet highly ironic emblem of the human soul (*Col-
lected Poems* 129, 239–40). Elsewhere in the rich imagistic vocabulary of
Symbolist poetry, the swan symbolizes the poet who, like Baudelaire's
albatross, stumbles awkwardly and ridiculously on land among men
yet soars gracefully in his own medium; alternately, the swan is poetry
itself, as in Mallarmé's sonnet "Le vierge, le vivace et le bel aujour-
d'hui," in which *le cygne* (the swan) homonymically suggests *le signe*
(the sign), its frozen captivity in a lake of ice recalling both the fascina-
tion with perfection and the danger of sterility implicit in Mallarmé's
own crystalline aesthetic of "poésie pur" (90).[17] As the bird of Apollo,
the god of poetry, the swan evokes order, reason, and grace. Yet its role
in the Leda myth renders it an unpredictable, Dionysian creature as
well, so that the swan participates in, even embodies, one of the essen-
tial paradoxes of lyric poetry, which equally privileges "spontaneous
overflow" and structured artifice.

Whereas Rilke highlights the beauty and serenity that constitute
the swan's Apollonian aspects, D. H. Lawrence seems to have been
intrigued, above all, by its Dionysian potential. Like Mallarmé's swan,
Lawrence's acts as a symbol of poetic language and poetic power; yet
his is a wild, unmastered creature that represents not the domesticated
purity of a Symbolist idyll but, rather, a cosmic principle both sinister
and regenerative:

> Far-off
> at the core of space
> at the quick
> of time
> beats
> and goes still
> the great swan upon the waters of all endings
> the swan within the vast chaos, within the electron.
>
> For us
> no longer he swims calmly
> nor clacks across the forces furrowing a great gay trail
> of happy energy,

nor is he nesting passive upon the atoms,
nor flying north desolative icewards
to the sleep of ice,
nor feeding in the marshes,
nor honking horn-like into the twilight.

But he stoops, now
in the dark
upon us;
he is treading our women
and we men are put out
as the vast white bird
furrows our featherless women
with unknown shocks
and stamps his black marsh-feet on their white and marshy flesh.

("Swan," LCP 435–36)

Lawrence's swan, as this 1929 poem is quick to emphasize, defines itself primarily through its abnegation of previous literary traditions: it does not "honk hornlike into the twilight," as we might expect Yeats's clamorous memories to do, nor does it "swim calmly" like Rilke's death swan, nor does it fly north, like Mallarmé's *cygne*, "desolative icewards / to the sleep of ice." In its unfettered form, forceful diction, and unconventional imagery the poem itself, in fact, seems to partake of the swan's vibrant energy, as Lawrence, striving not for intricate artifice but for raw power, sounds a vehement rejection of the Symbolist aesthetic that governs Mallarmé's elaborate verbal labyrinths and Yeats's and Rilke's immaculate versifications.

As early as 1915, in an essay called "The Crown," Lawrence had named the swan as a potent symbol of both earthly physicality and heavenly abstraction, both still beauty and eternal change:

The swan is one of the symbols of divine corruption with its reptile feet buried in the ooze and mud, its voluptuous form yielding and embracing the ooze of water, its beauty white and cold and terrifying, like the dead beauty of the moon, like the water-lily, the sacred lotus, its neck and head like the snake, it is for us a flame of the cold white fire of flux. So that, when Leonardo and Michaelangelo represent Leda in the embrace of the swan, they are painting mankind

in the clasp of the divine flux of corruption, the singing death.
(*Phoenix II* 403).

Later, in his 1919 "Poetry of the Present," Lawrence employs virtually identical metaphors—although his symbolic emphasis has shifted now from swan to swan-white lotus—in his call for a poetics privileging immediacy, flux, and "wind-like transit," the "creative mutation" that he hoped to harness in his "seething poetry of the incarnate Now":

> Let me feel the mud and the heavens in my lotus. Let me feel the heavy, silting, sucking mud, the spinning of sky winds. Let me feel them both in purest contact, the nakedness of sucking weight, nakedly passing radiance. (*LCP* 182–83)

"Swan" attests to Lawrence's continued effort, even a decade later, to capture and, paradoxically, to preserve on paper that state of eternal flux of which the swan itself is both symbol and harbinger. Yet with the poems' allusion, in its final stanza, to the Leda myth, Lawrence suggests that it is the union of bird and female, rather than the swan alone, that most adequately expresses that "purest contact" between earth and sky.

In a 1928 painting called *Leda* Lawrence depersonalizes Leda by showing only her naked torso beneath the body of the swan; in *Singing of Swans*, painted the same year, he depicts two white swans flying overhead as several naked humans of indeterminate gender interact on the ground below (*Paintings* 77, 97; see Figs. 1 and 2). Even more so than Yeats, then, who describes Leda's rape as one in a series of annunciatory events that shape human history, or Rilke, who perceived in Zeus's dual penetrations the revelatory enterprise of the poet, Lawrence universalizes the Leda myth, transposing its action to the present day and suggesting that not just one but many "featherless women" have felt or will feel the stamp of his "vast white bird." In "Swan" he conceives of the poet simultaneously as a participant in— "But he stoops, now / in the dark / upon us"—and an observer of the primal scene between woman and god, woman and beast:

> and we men are put out
> as the vast white bird

Fig. 1. *Singing of Swans.* Watercolor by D. H. Lawrence, 1927–28. 9 × 12 in.

furrows our featherless women
with unknown shocks.

But a second, briefer poem called "Leda" makes it clear that the poet
feels "put out" above all because he himself longs to share more fully in
the women's revelatory experience, to gain access, in Yeats's terms, to
the "knowledge" and "power" generated by the swan's "unknown
shocks":

Come not with kisses
not with caresses
of hands and lips and murmurings;
come with a hiss of wings
and sea-touch tip of a beak

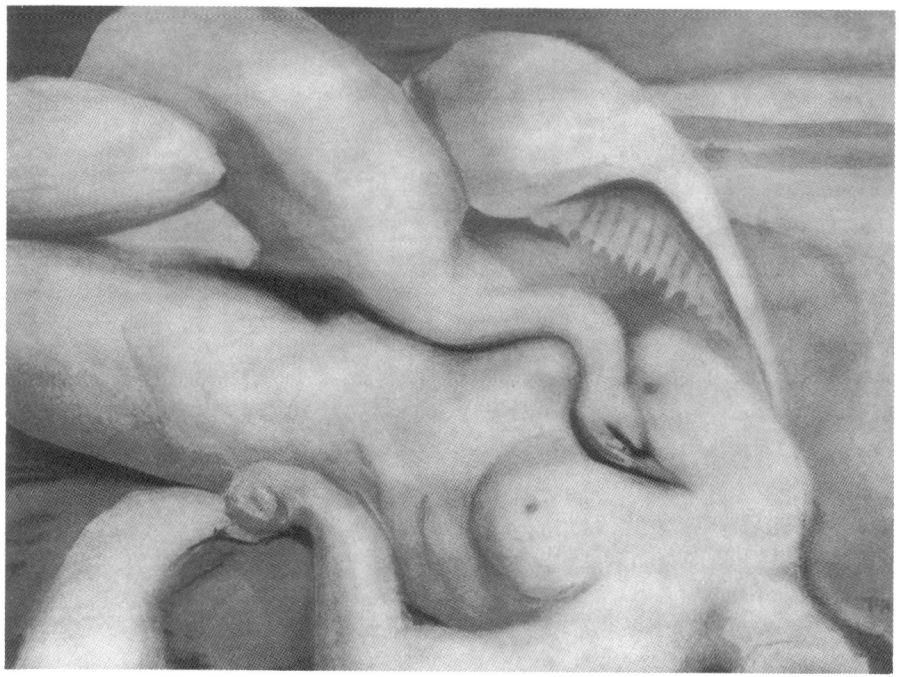

Fig. 2. *Leda*. Watercolor by D. H. Lawrence, c. 1928. 9 × 12 in.

and treading of wet, webbed, wave-working feet
into the marsh-soft belly.

(*LCP* 436)

Lawrence's poetics of inspiration articulates itself here as fiat, a
plea to the inspiring Other not for a kinder, gentler visionary influ-
ence—"come not with kisses, / not with caresses"—but, rather, for a
"sudden blow," an energetic, unmediated impact. The more brutal the
annunciation, he suggests, the more vibrant and intense the resulting
enunciation. Needless to say, Lawrence was hardly alone among mod-
ernist poets in his belief that violence is a necessary precondition for
change; Yeats's fascination with the Leda myth sprang from a similar
conviction, while T. S. Eliot and Ezra Pound proved to be no more
immune to sympathizing, so to speak, with the devil.[18]
    If, in "Swan" and "Leda," Lawrence avoids identifying himself

entirely with the "featherless women" who passively undergo the swan's stamping and furrowing, his Leda poems do focus, nonetheless, on victimization: not on the ordeal of the violated women, however, but on the sexual angst of the left-out, "put-out" men. If man does not regain access to the unscientific, mysterious universal forces that the swan's chaotic energy represents, Lawrence suggests, he risks losing his own sexual identity and being cuckolded, in effect, by a bird—an anxiety familiar to no less a paradigmatic product of literary modernism than Stephen Dedalus, who, in the early chapters of James Joyce's *Ulysses*, irreverently pictures Mary explaining her pregnancy to her incredulous husband: "C'est le pigeon, Joseph" (41). For Lawrence the divine Other effects its ornithological incarnation in the form not of pigeon but of swan (Yeats even posits an inspirational canary).[19] But while Stephen Dedalus, namesake of the inventor of human flight, empathizes with Jesus, whose "father's a bird" (Joyce 19), Lawrence directs his warnings to a modern Joseph: "Do you think, scientific man, that you'll be father of your own babies?" he asks in a poem called "Give Us Gods": "There'll be babies born that are cygnets, Oh my soul!" (*LCP* 437–38). Lawrence goes on to describe "the father of all things"—his cosmic swan "within the vast chaos, within the electron"—brushing past his own body on its way to inseminate the world's women:

> And in the dark unscientific I feel the drum-winds of his wings
> and the drip of his cold, webbed feet, mud-black
> brush over my face as he goes
> to seek the women in the dark, our women, our weird women
>   whom he treads
> with dreams and thrusts that make them cry in their sleep.
>
> (438)

Both anxiously fearful and jealously covetous of Leda's archetypal role as receptive female, Lawrence finally translates his own ambivalence, in a poem called "Won't It Be Strange?," into an almost poignant fear simply of being left out:

> Won't it be strange, when the nurse brings the new-born infant
> to the proud father, and shows its little, webbed greenish feet

made to smite the waters behind it?
. . . .
And when the father says: This is none of mine!
Woman, where got you this little beast?
will there be a whistle of wings in the air, and an icy draught?
will the singing of swans, high up, high up, invisible
break the drums of his ears
and leave him forever listening for the answer?

(438–39)

If Lawrence remained unwilling to identify too closely with Leda's plight as visionary victim, even at the risk of finding himself left "forever listening for the answer" to his prophetic inquiries, he was hardly alone in his hesitation. Similar refusals were exhibited not only by Yeats and Rilke but by at least one female contemporary as well.[20] H.D., whose initially frail literary identity was for so many years defined and manipulated by such strong-willed male mentors as Lawrence, Ezra Pound, and Richard Aldington, was often to channel her desire for literary autonomy, as I have shown, into an almost obsessive fear of inspiration, expressed again and again throughout her early poetry. The nature poems of *Sea Garden* (1916), in which flowers (traditional symbols of femininity) are continually being ripped apart and scattered by the wind (divine inspiration), give way in later volumes to a virtual Arachne's tapestry full of mythical women who have been victimized by men and/or male gods: Eurydice, consigned to the underworld by an "arrogant" Orpheus (*CP* 51–55); Cassandra, abducted by Agamemnon into concubinage and doomed by Apollo to utter prophecies that will never be believed (169–71); Penelope, tediously weaving while Odysseus travels and makes love (163–64); Helen, hated by "all Greece" for her fatal beauty and her role in a war that was not, in fact, her fault (154–55). Yet, despite her obvious preoccupation, in these poems and elsewhere, with female victimization and male power, H.D.'s 1921 poem "Leda" contains no hint either of the suffering or of the violence that generally mark other modernist accounts of the Leda myth.

If male modernists avoid identifying closely with Leda by transforming her, in a sense, from a person into a place—for Yeats she is the site where Troy's fall is enacted; for Rilke her lap/womb provides the only location where Zeus can become "truly swan"; and for Lawrence

her "marshy flesh" and "marsh-soft belly" represent, less than a body
to be penetrated, a landscape to be furrowed, trodden, and stamped—
H.D. dehumanizes her even further by portraying her as a "gold day-
lily," a symbol of traditionally female sexual passivity who seems
wholly lacking in the passion and anguish that characterize so many of
H.D.'s other heroines:

Where the slow river
meets the tide,
a red swan lifts red wings
and darker beak,
and underneath the purple down
of his soft breast
uncurls his coral feet.

Through the deep purple
of the dying heat
of sun and mist,
the level ray of sun-beam
has caressed
the lily with dark breast,
and flecked with richer gold
its golden crest.

Where the slow lifting
of the tide,
floats into the river
and slowly drifts
among the reeds,
and lifts the yellow flags,
he floats
where tide and river meet.

Ah kingly kiss—
no more regret
nor old deep memories
to mar the bliss;
where the low sedge is thick,
the gold day-lily
outspreads and rests

beneath soft fluttering
of red swan wings
and the warm quivering
of the red swan's breast.

(*CP* 120–21)

In the dreamlike, almost eerie calm of its pastoral setting, "Leda" calls
to mind another cryptic poem about a rape, Mallarmé's "L'Apres-midi
d'un faun" (58–62), in which a faun's lascivious attack on two young
nymphs is carefully screened behind the linguistic opacity of a Symbol-
ist idyll—so carefully screened, in fact, that neither the faun nor the
reader can actually determine whether or not the rape was merely a
dream. Like so many of H.D.'s early poems, "Leda" is set in a border-
line region of time and space: in the "dying heat" of the setting sun, at
that ill-defined place "where the slow river meets the tide." Here, how-
ever, that borderline signifies not, as in poems such as "Oread" and
"Hermes of the Ways," a clashing of disparate elements; instead, it indi-
cates an almost uncanny blurring of definitions, a dissolution of reality-
dream distinctions. Reflecting and reflected in the red and gold of the
sunset, swan and lily merge with their natural surroundings and thus,
even before the "kingly kiss" of the final stanza, with one another, dif-
fusing any sense of present or impending violence. Yet the "rich gold"
of the flower and the enigmatic redness of the swan render the poem's
naturalistic, reedy setting a strangely artificial one as well: true to the
Symbolist aesthetic from which her own early Imagist enterprise
evolved, H.D. cannot resist gilding the lily.

H.D.'s poetry and fiction tend to dwell long and hard on themes of
memory, regret, and betrayal and particularly on the kind of sexual and
psychological victimization—female vulnerability exploited by male
power—for which the Leda story provides only one of many mytho-
logical precedents. "Leda," then, in avoiding such themes as adamantly
as it does, becomes instantly suspect by virtue of its omissions: How,
we must ask, could a poet so well versed both in real-life and literary
injustice portray a rape scene that admits no trace of ugliness or terror?
One reply, of course, is that H.D. was merely following fin de siècle
precedent, echoing rather than questioning familiar representations of
the story as a romance rather than a rape; her poem, after all, was pub-
lished two years before Yeats would thematize mythic violence in
"Leda and the Swan," nine years before the publication of Lawrence's

strange, swampy swan poems. Still, H.D.'s poem is not, I would argue, quite so benign as it may at first appear; although the peaceful merging indicated in its first two lines—"Where the slow river / meets the , tide"—may seem a far cry from the "sudden blow" that opens Yeats's sonnet, there is something immediately sinister about the red swan that "lifts red wings / and darker beak" in a measured but threatening gesture. Red can denote a positive and life-giving vitality, yet violence and the stain of blood, martial power, and deadly passion are also encoded in the swan's uncanny ruddiness.

At the same time, however, the bloody violence suggested by the swan's vivid hue is undercut by the calm, muted adjectives that describe its essence and actions: it is soft, warm, fluttering, drifting, and quivering—an oddly feminized rapist. In fact, although the "fluttering" and "quivering" presumably indicate, like the "shudder in the loins" of Yeats's swan, an ejaculatory act of male orgasm, there is something undeniably motherly and brooding about the "warm quivering / of the red swan's breast"; rather than fertilizing an egg to be laid by Leda, it almost seems as though the swan, settling himself softly over her, has transformed the lily maiden herself into a golden egg that he will lovingly incubate. Whereas Rilke and Yeats emphasize the woman's terrified resistance to the swan, H.D.'s peaceful Leda welcomes its "kingly kiss"; she is entranced rather than violently entered, enraptured rather than raped, by the blood-red, hermaphroditic, male yet motherly bird. Like a winged embodiment of Lethe, drowning memory and desire in a blissful amnesia,[21] the swan grants to Leda not prophetic "knowledge and power" but, rather, a grateful loss of both; it functions, in fact, less as a figure of inspiration than as one of anti-inspiration. Thus, if "Leda" does not offer, at least on the surface, the defiant, revisionary "enunciation" of the Leda myth that readers today might hope for and expect, H.D.'s poem does provide, like the male modernists' accounts of the Leda myth, an eloquent commentary both on Leda's passive yet powerful role as a visionary vessel and on the myth's implications as a gendered fable of inspiration. Rather than staging a drama of pursuit and capture that might affirm, even through a reversal of roles, a familiar trajectory of violence,[22] H.D. addresses the Leda myth's potential unpleasantness precisely through her refusal to address it. If inspiration is predicated upon violation, while visionary insight represents a painful burden, then forgetfulness, she suggests, becomes a blessing.

Even more so than Orpheus, then, Leda serves for modernist poets as a compelling yet highly problematic symbol for the visionary poet, caught between power and impotence, between desire and danger. As retold by Rilke, Lawrence, and H.D., both myths reflect anxiety as much as authority, for they intimate that the visionary strategies they chronicle—Leda's silent receptivity, Orpheus' ambitious turn—can be hazardous ones for men and for women alike. Yet these poems tell a more optimistic story as well, for they remind us that conflicts of authority and ideology often make in the end for remarkable poetry and that, even in its most vexed and contradictory moments, a visionary poetics can in turn give rise to a revisionary mythopoetics.

Notes

Introduction

Epigraphs are from Howard 66; Sexton 551.

1. Yeats, "Adam's Curse," *Poems*, 78; Wordsworth, "Preface to the Lyrical Ballads" (2d ed.), in Perkins 321.

2. See, for instance, Fletcher, *The Prophetic Moment: An Essay on Spenser*; Kerrigan, *The Prophetic Milton*; Wittreich, *Visionary Poetics: Milton's Tradition and His Legacy*; Fisher, *The Valley of Vision: Blake as Prophet and Revolutionary*; Harding, *Coleridge and the Inspired Word*; and Weiskel, *The Romantic Sublime*. Hartman, *The Unmediated Vision*, discusses visionary elements in both Romantic and modernist poetry.

3. The *American Heritage Dictionary* defines a prophet, first, as "a person who speaks by divine inspiration or as the interpreter through whom the will of a god is expressed" and, second, as "a person gifted with profound moral insight and exceptional powers of expression"; not until the third definition is a prophet "a predictor; a soothsayer."

4. This division between private sight and public speech does not hold true for all prophetic traditions; in some instances a prophet may serve as the interpreter of signs that are visible to the public at large. See, for instance, Calchal's interpretation of the plague at the beginning of Homer's *Iliad* (1:8–100).

5. See Hesiod, *Theogony*, 1–35; Milton, *Paradise Lost*; Stevens, "To the One of Fictive Music," 87–88; and Merrill, *The Changing Light at Sandover*, 400–406. E. R. Curtius notes that poets have been parodying or satirizing invocations to the Muses at least since Augustan times (232–33); modern poets in particular (Stevens and Merrill being no exceptions) seldom call upon the Muses directly, except in a revisionary or ironic mode.

6. This is not to say that every male poet who claims to have received inspiration from a male god necessarily represents himself as feminized. Particularly in the homoerotic cultures of Greece and Rome, a male poet occasionally invokes a male muse, as when Ovid, at the beginning of the *Amores*, humorously describes himself being pierced by Cupid's phallic arrow.

7. Heraclitus, quoted in Lawrence, *Complete Poems*, 348 (henceforth *LCP*); Goethe, letter to Eckermann, 8 March 1827, quoted in Eliade, *Two and the One*, 79; Blake, *The Marriage of Heaven and Hell* (Perkins 69).

8. I borrow the metaphor of the Möbius strip from Slavoj Žižek, "The Fallen

Object of Ideology" (paper presented at the annual meeting of the Modern Language Association, Chicago, 29 December 1990).

    9. *Collected Poems* (henceforth *CP*), 547–48.

Chapter 1

Epigraphs are from R. M. Rilke, letter to a young girl, 20 November 1904 ("Es ist so natürlich für mich, *Mädchen und Frauen zu verstehen;* das tiefste Erleben des Schaffenden ist weiblich—denn es ist empfangendes und gebärendes Erleben" [*Briefe* 1:104]); and Rich, *The Fact of a Doorframe*, 248.

    1. Conversation with Maurice Betz, 5 January 1925 (Schnack 2:960).

    2. Keats, letter to Shelley, 16 August 1920 (Perkins 1236).

    3. Here and in subsequent chapters all translations, unless otherwise noted, are my own; they have been executed with an eye to communicating the literal meaning of the poems rather than to preserving their formal structure or even, in some cases, their syntactical grace. Throughout this chapter I have followed Stephen Mitchell's precedent in capitalizing *Thing* (Rilke's noun *Ding*) in order to emphasize that word's special place in Rilke's vocabulary.

    4. Stephens, "Zur Funktion sexueller Metaphorik in der Dichtung Rilkes," 531–32; Rilke, *Sämtliche Werke* (henceforth *SW*), 5:638–39.

    5. An inevitable difficulty in translating any of Rilke's "phallic verses" arises from the German language's capacity to express sexuality in strongly euphemistic terms; for the most part Rilke's vocabulary sounds vulgarly anatomistic and prurient only when translated into English. The word *Schooß*, for instance, which can be translated either as "lap" or "womb," actually refers, in the context of this poem, to a place between the two, namely the vagina, which nevertheless remains unnamed. *Scham*, which I have translated here as *sex* and elsewhere as *private parts*, denotes the genitals (both male and female), but only in a guarded sense; the word also means "shame" and thus automatically encodes the concept of prudishness in the vocabulary of sex. Words such as *Glied* (member) and *Samen* (semen or seed) find ready equivalents in English but, nonetheless, retain in German a euphemistic, metaphorical cast that tends to fade in translation. Even in his most schoolboyish moments, in other words, Rilke generally manages to sound infinitely refined and poetic.

    6. See Andreas-Salomé, *Lebensrückblick*, 175.

    7. For a careful and detailed discussion of both the feminist and antifeminist implications of Andreas-Salomé's essay, see Martin 147–69.

    8. Letter to Julie Weimann, 25 June 1902 (Butler 118). This statement may be contrasted to an earlier one made by Rilke in his 1898 Florentine diary: "Eine Frau, welche Künstlerin ist, muß nicht mehr schaffen, wenn sie Mutter wurde. Sie hat ihr Ziel aus sich hinausgestellt und darf im tiefsten Sinne Kunst leben fortan" ("A woman who is also an artist need not create any more once she has become a mother. She has put her goal outside of herself and from now on may, in the deepest sense, live her art" (*Tagebücher* 119).

    9. *Man Does, Woman Is* is the title both of a 1964 book of poetry by Robert

Graves and of one of the poems in the volume (17). Rilke's statements here may also be compared with Graves's assertion in *The White Goddess* that a woman "should write as a woman, not as if she were an honorary man" (391). See also Rilke's lines from the *Buch der Bilder*: "Mädchen, Dichter sind, die von euch lernen / das zu *sagen*, was ihr einsam *seid*" ("Maidens, poets are those who learn from you / to *say* in words what you simply *are*") (*SW* 1:375).

10. Letter to Paula Becker-Modersohn, 12 February 1902 (*Briefe* 1:34).

11. Letter to Clara Rilke, 17 December 1906 (*Gesammelte Briefe* [henceforth *GB*] 2:216).

12. Keats, letter to John Taylor, 27 February 1818 (Perkins 1212).

13. Although Rilke would hint throughout his life, particularly in such works as *Die Weise von Liebe und Tod des Cornets Christoph Rilke* and *Die Aufzeichnungen des Malte Laurids Brigge*, that he sprang from a long line of aristocrats, such claims reflected more wishful thinking than demonstrable fact.

14. Letter to Clara Rilke, 26 October 1907 (*GB* 3:7).

15. The association of volcanoes with certain stereotypically feminine modes of behavior (e.g., emotional volatility, unpredictability, earthbound "naturalness," inarticulate passion) is hardly a new one, having been made humorously by Lewis Carroll, whose White Queen mistakes seven-year-old Alice for a volcano at the beginning of *Through the Looking Glass* (188), as well as more subversively by Emily Dickinson, who, outwardly genteel but inwardly eruptive, identified herself in poem after poem with volcanoes: "Vesuvius at home" (694; also 83, 295–96, 685, 708).

16. Letter to Lou Andreas-Salomé, 26 February 1901 (*Briefwechsel Andreas-Salomé* 41).

17. Letter to Lou Andreas-Salomé, 28 December 1911 (*GB* 3:160).

18. Letter to Lou Andreas-Salomé, 20 January 1912 (*GB* 3:182).

19. Letter to Emil Freiherrn von Gebsattel, 24 January 1912 (*GB* 3:192–93).

20. Letter to Lou Andreas-Salomé, 20 January 1912 (*GB* 3:182–83).

21. Thurn und Taxis-Hohenlohe, *Erinnerungen*, 48–49. To reduce confusion I have placed my own ellipses in square brackets; all others are part of the original text.

22. Letter to Marie von Thurn und Taxis, 12 January 1912 (*Briefwechsel Thurn und Taxis* 90).

23. Letter to Marie von Thurn und Taxis, 16 January 1912 (*Briefwechsel Thurn und Taxis* 92).

24. Letter to Gräfin Manon zu Solms-Laubach, 12 January 1912 (*GB* 3:176).

25. Letter to Annette Kolb, 22 January 1912 (*GB* 3:186).

26. For more on Rilke's appropriations, through the act of translation, of the voices of female poets, see Tucker, "Rilke's Eternal Woman and the Translation of Louise Labé."

27. For a full description of these séances, see Thurn und Taxis, *Erinnerungen*, 72–76. The princess's son Pascha, who was not allowed to see Rilke's questions, apparently operated the planchette; his mother, despite her membership in the SPR, declared herself to be "durchaus kein Medium" ("absolutely no

medium") and merely observed the proceedings. See also B. J. Morse, "Rainer Maria Rilke and the Occult."

28. Letter to Marie von Thurn und Taxis, 29 July 1913 (*Briefwechsel Thurn und Taxis* 304).

29. Letter to Marie von Thurn und Taxis, 21 October 1913 (*Briefwechsel Thurn und Taxis* 322–23).

30. Letter to Nora Purtscher-Wydenbruck, 11 August 1924 (*GB* 5:288–95).

31. Letter to Lou Andreas-Salomé, 21 October 1913 (*Briefwechsel Andreas-Salomé* 315).

32. Letter to Marie von Thurn und Taxis, 27 December 1913 (*Briefwechsel Thurn und Taxis* 345).

33. Although virtually all of his love relationships, with the exception of his early affair with Lou Andreas-Salomé, followed a similar pattern—ardent passion succeeded soon thereafter by emotional distancing—each of Rilke's many romantic liaisons nonetheless bore its own stamp of individuality: his interaction with Benvenuta, for instance, took place mostly through letters, fizzling out almost immediately once the two lovers finally met in person; the affair with Loulou Albert-Lazard was far more long-lasting and more physical in nature (the two even shared a flat for some months) but less sustained emotionally; and the relationship with Merline, one of the most peaceful and fulfilling of Rilke's life, would endure for many years, although Rilke, typically, seldom allowed actual meetings of more than a few weeks or even days at a time.

34. Letter to Lou Andreas-Salomé, 20 June 1914 (*Briefwechsel Andreas-Salomé* 341–44).

35. Letter to Nora Jaffé, 14 November 1915 (Schnack 517).

36. Letter to Nanny Wunderly-Volkart, 30 November 1920 (*Briefe Wunderly-Volkart* 349).

37. Letter to Marie von Thurn und Taxis, 8 September 1921 (*Briefwechsel Thurn und Taxis* 686).

38. Rilke was so impressed and fascinated by Valéry's poetry that he would eventually undertake to translate a good deal of it. For more on these translations and on Rilke's relationship with Valéry, see Bianquis, "Rilke traducteur"; Cox, *Figures of Transformation: Rilke and the Example of Valéry*; Goth, *Rilke und Valéry*; Ryan, "Creative Subjectivity in Rilke and Valéry"; and Wais, *Studien zu Rilkes Valéry-Übertragungen*.

39. In fact, the total number of completed sonnets was sixty-four, of which Rilke decided to omit nine from the published cycle. See Rilke's letter of 25 February 1922 to Marie von Thurn und Taxis, in which he compares the Sonnets' genesis to that of *The Life of Mary*, which unexpectedly came into being alongside the first two Duino Elegies in 1912 (*Briefwechsel Thurn und Taxis* 464).

40. Letters to: Jean Strohl, 7 February 1922 (Prater 347); Marie von Thurn und Taxis, 11 February 1922 (*Briefwechsel Thurn und Taxis* 698); Baladine Klossowska, 9 February 1922 (*Correspondance Merline* 393); Lou Andreas-Salomé, 11 February 1922 (*Briefwechsel Andreas-Salomé* 464).

41. Letter to Nanny Wunderly-Volkart, 18 February 1922 (*Briefe Wunderly-Volkart* 675).

42. Letter to Gertrud Ouckama Knoop, 7 February 1922 (*GB* 5:112).

43. The similarities between this sonnet and Keats's "Ode on a Grecian Urn," in which the lovers are forever trapped within, yet also forever celebrated by, the vase's static surface, are perhaps not entirely coincidental; Rilke had enthusiastically read Keats's poetry, in German translation, in 1911 (Schnack 380). Also apparent here and in all of Rilke's "dancer" poems is the influence of Valéry's "L'Ame et la danse," which Rilke had read only a few weeks before he composed the Sonnets.

Chapter 2

Epigraphs are from D. H. Lawrence, *Study of Thomas Hardy*, 56; and *Fantasia of the Unconscious*, 93.

1. Sherman, "America Is Discovered," review of *Studies in Classic American Literature*, in *New York Evening Post Literary Review* 4 (20 October 1923): 143–44, quoted in Draper 209; Rosenfeld, obituary of Lawrence in *New Republic* 62 (26 March 1930): 155–56, quoted in Draper 335; Eliot, *After Strange Gods*, 59; Bynner, *Journey with Genius*, 2; Tindall, *D. H. Lawrence and Susan His Cow*, 5; Mailer, *Prisoner of Sex*, 157.

2. Murry, review of *Aaron's Rod* in *Nation and Athenaeum* 31 (12 August 1922): 655–56; reprinted in Draper 177. It is interesting to note that Murry's own views regarding what is "good" and "horrid" in Lawrence's work are completely at odds with both past and current critical concensus; Murry hated *Women in Love*, arguably Lawrence's finest novel, but lavishly praised *Aaron's Rod*, which he considered to be a more important work of literature than Joyce's *Ulysses*.

3. Sackville-West, review of *Reflections on the Death of a Porcupine*, in *New Statesman* 27 (10 July 1926): 360–61; reprinted in Draper 260.

4. See also Baker, "Lawrence as Prophetic Poet."

5. Forster, obituary of Lawrence in *The Listener* 3 (30 April 1930): 753–54; reprinted in Draper 345.

6. Blake, *The Marriage of Heaven and Hell* (Perkins 69); Lawrence, "Notes for *Birds, Beasts and Flowers*" (*LCP* 348).

7. Birkin tells Ursula, "What I want is a strange conjunction with you . . . — not melting and mingling . . . but an equilibrium, a pure balance of two single beings:—as the stars balance each other" (*Women in Love* 164). On Lawrence's conception of the Holy Ghost, see "The Crown" (1915), *Phoenix II*, 398.

8. For an exhaustive list of the male and female attributes that Lawrence posits in *Study of Thomas Hardy*, see Daleski 30–31.

9. In a letter of 9 March 1917 Lawrence relayed to Catherine Carswell H.D.'s negative response to the *Look! We Have Come Through!* manuscript: "Hilda Aldington says they [the poems] won't do at all; they are not *eternal*, not sublimated: too much body and emotions" (*Letters* 3:102).

10. Blackmur, it should be noted, was not alone in applying the epithet *hysterical* to Lawrence; H. G. Wells made the same diagnosis when he visited

Lawrence upon his deathbed in Vence, France, in 1930. See Barbara Weekley Barr, "Memoir of D. H. Lawrence," in Spender, *D. H. Lawrence*, 33.

11. "Morality and the Novel," *Phoenix*, 528; quoted in Gilbert, *Acts of Attention*, 16.

12. Letter to Henry Savage, 2 December 1913 (*Letters* 2:115); "Poetry of the Present," *LCP* 185; preface to Harry Crosby's *Chariot of the Sun*, *Phoenix*, 255.

13. Letter to Ernst Collings, 24 February 1913 (*Letters* 1:519).

14. Letter to Henry Savage, 15 November 1913 (*Letters* 2:102).

15. Letter to Arthur McLeod, 2 June 1914 (*Letters* 2:181).

16. Martin Green declares flatly, in his biography of Frieda Lawrence, that "she made him [Lawrence] a genius" (*Von Richthofen Sisters* 132). Emile Delavenay, on the other hand, agrees with Aldous Huxley's denunciation of Frieda as "stupid," implying that she was dishonest and manipulative in her dealings both with Lawrence himself and, after his death, with his estate (Delavenay, "'Making Another Lawrence,'" 80–98). Janice Robinson, searching for evidence to support her extremely tenuous claim that Lawrence had a prolonged affair with H.D., seconds Delavenay's portrayal of Frieda, calling her "immoral, malicious, and slovenly—more of a parasite than a creative source" (Robinson, *H.D.* 164). Delavenay, interestingly, cites as evidence of Frieda's "general intellectual inconsistency" her "many contradictory utterances" (81), a claim that he, as Lawrence's biographer and staunch admirer, would not, presumably, make so quickly in the case of Frieda's equally self-contradictory husband.

17. In chapter 7, "A Literary Trespasser," Simpson both discusses Lawrence's own collaborations, real and planned, with women and reviews other cases of "literary trespassing," exploring the implications, especially for female writers, of such appropriations of material. See also Miles, *Fiction of Sex*, for a discussion of "the assumption that literary creation is in itself a masculine act, a process of exploring and mastering the feminine, unconscious mass of life and material" (49).

18. Letter to Ottoline Morrell, 1 March 1915 (*Letters* 2:297–98).

19. For some twentieth-century female writers' responses to and protests against the negative dimensions of Cassandra's plight, see H.D.'s poem "Cassandra," *CP* 169–71; Christa Wolf's novel *Kassandra*; and Louise Bogan's poem "Cassandra" (Gilbert and Gubar, *Norton Anthology* 1612–13).

20. These stereotypes are, of course, present in many Eastern philosophies as well and have duly influenced Western thought on the subject, encouraging their acceptance as universal "truths." See, for instance, the Chinese opposition of yin and yang (passive female and active male, both of which are necessary to any creative act) and the Hindu yoni and lingam (stylized representations of female and male genitalia, representing the female and male cosmic principles, respectively).

21. Letter to Bertrand Russell, 24 February 1915 (*Letters* 2:294).

22. Letter to Henry Savage, 15 November 1913 (*Letters* 2:101).

23. "Reality," *Phoenix*, 671.

24. See Lawrence's postcard to Frieda Weekley, 11 May 1912: "Now I am in Hennef—my last changing place. It is 8:30—and still an hour to wait. So I am sitting like a sad swain beside a nice, twittering little river, waiting for the twilight to drop, and my last last train to come. . . . It's getting dark. Now, for the first time during today, my detachment leaves me, and I know I only love you. The rest is nothing at all. And the promise of life with you is all richness. Now I know" (*Letters* 1:398).

25. See, for example, Charles Rossman's article, "You Are the Call and I Am the Answer: D. H. Lawrence and Women." Rossman, to be fair, is more concerned with exposing the paradoxes of Lawrence's gender ideology than with tracing a simplistic call-answer pattern of gender relations.

26. See H.D., *Bid Me To Live*, 111–12. The charade, which took place in H.D.'s London flat in late 1917, is also described by Frieda Lawrence in *"Not I, but the Wind . . .,"* 78–79.

27. Letter to Ernst Collings, 17 January 1913 (*Letters* 1:503); letter to Gordon Campbell, 21 September 1914 (*Letters* 2:218).

28. Letter to Bertrand Russell, 12 February 1915 (*Letters* 2:284).

29. Letter to Henry Savage, 15 November 1913 (*Letters* 2:102).

30. See Genesis 18:1–2.

31. Woolf, in her 1931 essay "Professions for Women," argued that women cannot effectively become artists until the ideal of the "Angel in the House" (the phrase comes from a poem by Coventry Patmore) has been overcome (*Virginia Woolf Reader* 276–82). Needless to say, Woolf's vision of how the angel might be evicted differs considerably from Lawrence's.

32. See Kermode, "Lawrence and the Apocalyptic Types." For an account of how Lawrence's later poetry collection *Birds, Beasts and Flowers* also serves as a narrative of descent and return, see Gilbert, "Hell on Earth."

33. For a summarizing discussion of the issue, see especially Spilka, "Lawrence Up-Tight, or the Anal Phase Once Over," and the critical debate that follows in *Novel* 5 (Fall 1971): 54–70.

34. See, for instance, Nixon 10–14 and passim; Moore 83–88, 132–34; Core, "'The Closed Door': Love between Women in the Works of D. H. Lawrence"; and Meyers, "D. H. Lawrence and Homosexuality."

35. For contrasting views to my own, see especially Kiberd, *Men and Feminism in Modern Literature*; and Dix, *D. H. Lawrence and Women*. Kiberd specifically points both to Lawrence's liking for domestic chores and to his friendships with women as proof that "Lawrence never sought to suppress or conceal the female element in himself" (137), while Dix concludes from her reading of *Sons and Lovers* that "Lawrence perhaps lived with the fantasy of being a woman who was loved by a man" (96). Both authors share the enterprise of rescuing Lawrence (and, in Kiberd's case, Joyce and Yeats as well) from the clutches of "partial and wrong-headed" feminists who (like me) have failed to recognize and acclaim Lawrence's "impeccably feminist" credentials (Kiberd 140).

36. Lawrence's reactions to female homosexuality appear to have been sim-

ilarly mixed; in *The Rainbow* (1915) he writes sympathetically of Ursula's love affair with her teacher, but in his 1929 *Pansies*—in which his attack on lesbianism is but one manifestation of his overall misogyny—he lashes out furiously at "ego-bound women," who "are often lesbian, / perhaps always," adding that "of all passions / the lesbian passion is the most appalling" ("Ego-Bound Women," *LCP* 475).

37. Letter to Henry Savage, 2 December 1913 (*Letters* 2:115).

38. Letter to David Garnett, 19 April 1915 (*Letters* 2:320–21).

39. Carpenter, *The Intermediate Sex*, 18; quoted in Delavenay, *D. H. Lawrence and Edward Carpenter*, 211. See also Carpenter, *Intermediate Types among Primitive Folk*.

40. Letter to Arthur McLeod, 2 June 1914 (*Letters* 2:180–81).

41. Letter to Dollie Radford, 29 June 1916 (*Letters* 2:618).

42. Letter to Godwin Baynes, March 1920 (*Letters* 2:618).

43. *The Symbolic Meaning*, 260; first printed in *The Nation and the Athenaeum*, 23 July 1921.

44. *LCP* 990; Carswell, *The Savage Pilgrimage*, 91.

45. "Aristocracy," *Phoenix II*, 480.

46. ". . . Love Was Once a Little Boy," *Phoenix II*, 447, 451.

47. Oates's assessment of Lawrence's poetry is couched in enthusiastically Lawrentian language; she argues, for instance, that "Lawrence is one of our true prophets, not only in his 'madness for the unknown' and in his explicit warning . . . but in his lifelong development of a technique, a fictional and poetic *way* in which the prophetic voice can be given formal perfection" (9). She concludes, tellingly, that only "a spiritual brother or sister of Lawrence himself can understand his poems, ultimately" (14).

48. Woolf, "Notes on D. H. Lawrence," *Moment*, 79.

49. For a defense of Mailer's reading of Lawrence and a critique of the feminist attacks that provoked it, see Balbert, *D. H. Lawrence and the Phallic Imagination*.

50. For more on Lawrence's transformation of the phallus into a religious, ethical, and artistic symbol "adequate to represent the full complexity of maleness" (129), see Simpson, chapter 6, "The Phallic Consciousness" (122–42).

51. Sandra Gilbert, explaining how it is possible to be both "a feminist and a Lawrentian," argues that creative women such as H.D., Katherine Mansfield, and Anais Nin (not to mention Gilbert herself) have admired Lawrence "because, despite his often hectically masculinist rhetoric, they sensed his profound rejection of the cultural metaphysics that would suppress darkness, nature, the body, otherness—and women" ("Feminism and D. H. Lawrence" 92, 98–99).

52. As a postscript, it is perhaps worth noting that Lawrence's death proved to be as self-contradictory as so much of his life and work: he died of tuberculosis, the paradigmatic illness both of such poetic precursors as Elizabeth Barrett Browning and John Keats (Lawrence attributed the latter's fragility to an excess of "male" spirituality) and of the brawny miners—earthily macho men

who were nonetheless associated in Lawrence's mind with the mystery, physicality, and underworld darkness that characterized for him "the feminine principle"—among whom he spent his childhood.

Chapter 3

Epigraphs are from *Notes on Thought and Vision*, 20, 22; letter to Bryher, 15 May 1933; *Hermetic Definition*, 54. The letter to Bryher is held in the Yale Collection of American Literature, Beinecke Library, Yale University (henceforth "Beinecke").

1. *Notes on Thought and Vision*, 20 ("vision of the womb"); *Notes*, 22 (jellyfish); *Majic Ring*, 246 (radio); *Notes*, 26, "H.D. by Delia Alton," 201, and *Majic Ring*, 246 (telegraph receiving station); *Majic Ring*, 238 (Aeolian harp); *The Sword Went Out to Sea*, 56 (switchboard); *Sword*, 62 (battery); *Sword*, 186, *Notes*, 187, and *Majic Ring*, 211 (opera glass); *Majic Ring*, 127 (film projector); "The Dream," 605 (magic lantern); *Majic Ring*, 297 (kaleidoscope). *Helen in Egypt*, 22 ("She herself is the writing"); letter to Bryher, 15 May 1933 (book as penis); *Hermetic Definition*, 113 ("Espérance"). *CP* 569 (inspiration as goddess/muse); *Compassionate Friendship*, 72 (male initiator); *CP* 510 (Spirit); *Majic Ring*, 125 (Daemon).

2. *New York Times Book Review*, 10 December 1972. For more on the critical double standard by which H.D. has frequently been judged, see Friedman, "Who Buried H.D.?"

3. See Friedman, *Psyche Reborn*; DeShazer, *Inspiring Women*; and DuPlessis, "Romantic Thralldom in H.D."

4. H.D. acted opposite Paul Robeson in Kenneth Macpherson's 1930 film *Borderline* and wrote a pamphlet about the film (*Borderline: A Pool Film with Paul Robeson*). For more on the film and its uses of the borderline image, see especially Friedberg, "Approaching *Borderline*"; and Friedman, "Modernism of the 'Scattered Remnant.'"

5. Appropriately, it was at the Hotel du Littoral in London that H.D. and her estranged husband Richard Aldington made a brief but unsuccessful attempt, shortly after the birth of H.D.'s daughter, Perdita, in 1919, to resume their broken marriage (Silverstein 37).

6. If such love triangles are frequently made the subject of H.D.'s poetry, that is in part, no doubt, because they so often occurred in her life. One such triangle—formed by H.D., Frances Gregg, and Ezra Pound—became the subject of H.D.'s novel *HERmione*; another, consisting of H.D., Richard Aldington, and Dorothy "Arabella" York, is immortalized in *Bid Me to Live*. A somewhat less traumatic triangulation occurred in the late 1920s, when H.D.'s male lover Kenneth Macpherson and her lesbian companion Bryher entered into a marriage of three-way convenience. This ménage à trois survived happily for several years, a period of extraordinary creativity that resulted, most notably, in the production of several avant-garde films (*Wing-Beat*, *Borderline*) and the founding of a successful film journal (*Close-Up*). It eventually disintegrated, however, under

the pressures of quadrangulation, as MacPherson began to take up, ever less discreetly, with a series of young men.

7. Although I refer here to the poet's beloved using a male pronoun, there is no reason why this poem, which after all is based on a fragment from Sappho, should not be addressed to a female lover, instead; the preceding poem, "We Two," almost certainly apostrophizes Bryher, as do a number of others from this period. Louis L. Martz, in fact, reads "Fragment Thirty-Six," with its invocation of "two minds," as encoding H.D.'s conflict between "male love" and the "Sapphic lyre" (*CP* xxii). Many other poems of *Hymen* and *Heliodora*, however, particularly those that speak of love in terms of victimization, do specify a male interlocutor.

8. See Morris, "Reading H.D.'s 'Helios and Athene.'"

9. Perdita Schaffner, quoted in Friedman, *Psyche Reborn*, 303 n. 43.

10. H.D.'s romans à clef about her relationship with Frances Gregg include *HERmione* (1927) and *Asphodel* (1921–22) as well as the unpublished *Paint It Today* (1921; Beinecke). For more on H.D.'s conflicted sexuality and the role of her bisexuality in her literary production, see especially Friedman, *Psyche Reborn*, 38–47; Friedman and DuPlessis, "'I Had Two Loves Separate'"; DuPlessis and Friedman, "'Woman is Perfect'"; Buck, "Freud and H.D."; and Jaffe, "'She Herself Is the Writing.'"

11. See Evans, *The God of Ecstasy*, for more on the gendering of ecstasy in relation to Euripides' *The Bacchae* and the cult of Dionysus.

12. See Otto, "The Meaning of the Eleusinian Mysteries"; on H.D.'s appropriations of the mysteries, see especially Burnett, *H.D. between Image and Epic*; and Bruzzi, "The Fiery Moment."

13. See Matthew 6:28–29: "Behold the lilies of the field, how they grow; they neither toil nor spin; yet I tell you, Solomon in all his glory was not arrayed like one of these"; also Matthew 10:29: "Are not two sparrows sold for a farthing? and one of them shall not fall on the ground without your Father."

14. The late 1920s and 1930s also saw the production of numerous novels, short stories, essays, and reviews by H.D., of which the most complete studies to date are Burnett, *H.D. between Image and Epic*, and Friedman, *Penelope's Web*. My discussion, regrettably, for the most part omits not only H.D.'s prose work but also the very important series of long poems, including "The Master," "The Dancer," "The Magician," and "The Priest," that H.D. wrote in the late 1930s.

15. *Close-Up* (August 1927): 35 (cited in Morris 422); *Close-Up* (November 1927): 28 (cited in Burnett, *H.D.* 101).

16. For more on H.D.'s "Projector" poems and her involvement in the cinema, see especially Friedberg, "H.D., Woman, History, Recognition"; Diepeveen, "H.D. and the Film Arts"; and Mandel, "The Redirected Image" and "H.D.'s 'Projector II.'"

17. *Little Review* 12.2 (May 1929): 38; quoted in Morris, "Concept of Projection," 422.

18. Letter to Conrad Aiken, probably written from Vienna in 1933 (Beinecke).

19. Letter to Bryher, 28 May 1933 (Beinecke).

20. Letter to Bryher, 24 November 1934 (Beinecke).

21. Letter to Bryher, 3 May 1933 (Beinecke).

22. Letter to Bryher (Fido was a nickname), 27 November 1934 (Beinecke). In her roman à clef *Nights* (published in 1935 but mostly composed before her meetings with Freud) H.D. portrays her protagonist's autoeroticism not as a creative block but, rather, as a path to spiritual fulfillment, even prophetic revelation: "Her deity was impartial. . . . She was sexless, being one chord, drawn out, waiting the high-powered rush of the electric fervour. . . . She wanted electric power to run on through her, then out, unimpeded by her mind" (51). In her 1933–34 letters home from Vienna, however, H.D. assents without comment to Freud's apparent condemnation of masturbation as a dangerous perversion.

23. Bevan 105–8. For more on applications of *bat qol* to literary criticism (and, as in H.D.'s case, to poetic production as well), see especially Bloom, *Kabbalah and Criticism*.

24. Letter to Viola Jordan, 28 April 1942 (Beinecke). Frequent references to H.D.'s tapestries can be found in H.D.'s wartime letters to Viola Jordan, Gretchen Wolle Baker, and Hattie Howard (Beinecke); see also Perdita Schaffner's introduction to *The Gift* (x).

25. See "Writing on the Wall": "Religion, art and medicine, through the latter ages, became separated. . . . These three working together . . . might be symbolized by the tripod . . . [which] was the symbol of prophecy, prophetic utterance or occult or hidden knowledge; the Priestess or Pythoness of Delphi sat on the tripod while she pronounced her verse couplets" (*Tribute to Freud* 50–51). Like the Pythia's prophetic pronouncements, *Trilogy* is composed almost entirely in verse couplets, except for its opening section, which plays upon the terza rima scheme of another vatic forebear, Dante.

26. Numbers 17:8, 20:11.

27. For more on H.D. and temporality, see Walker, "H.D. and Time."

28. The "new wine" passage occurs in three of the four Gospels (Matt. 9:16–17; Mark 2:19–22; Luke 5:36–39) and refers to the need for new religious forms and rituals to accompany a new faith: "Neither is new wine put into old wineskins; if it is, the skins burst, and the wine is spilled, and the skins are destroyed; but new wine is put into fresh wineskins, and so both are preserved" (Matt. 9:17). Jesus' statement here may be contrasted with Gershom Scholem's description of mystical experience as a dialectic balancing conservative and revolutionary religious elements, like "new wine into old bottles" (7). Scholem's, rather than Jesus', enological model, with its emphasis on the paradoxical nature both of mysticism and prophecy, seems best to describe H.D.'s modernist recovery and rewriting of ancient traditions in *Trilogy*.

29. For reflections on the problematics for female poets of establishing their own Muse figures, see especially DeShazer, *Inspiring Women* (1–44); and DuPlessis, "Family, Sexes, Psyche." See also H.D.'s own statement in *Compassionate Friendship* (1955): "my Muse is an old doll" (62).

30. On H.D.'s use of the worm, shell, and other similar images, see especially Gubar, "The Echoing Spell of H.D.'s *Trilogy*"; and Levertov, "H.D.: An Appreciation."

31. Joan A. Burke devotes three chapters of her dissertation on "H.D. in

Prophetic Tradition" to *Helen in Egypt*, but she does little to show how the poem fits any of the definitions of prophecy that she spells out in her introductory chapters. Indeed, Burke even quotes a letter to Norman Holmes Pearson (25 November 1952) in which H.D. explicitly describes *Helen in Egypt* as "too metaphysical or mystical, I suspect, for most readers" (165).

32. On the "jellyfish state," see "Notes on Thought and Vision," 22; and *Tribute to Freud*, 130, 147–48. (H.D. also refers often to the "Scilly scene" in her letters home to Bryher from Vienna in the spring of 1933.) On the Van Eck incident, see especially "Advent" (*Tribute to Freud* 154–62, 182–87); and *Majic Ring*; also H.D.'s 1935 letter to George Plank (quoted in *CP* xxvi). On the "writing on the wall," see *Tribute to Freud*, 44–56; also "H.D. by Delia Alton," 198–99. On dance scenes, see *Majic Ring*, 195–261; and *Tribute to Freud*, 172–73.

33. Letter to John Cournos [1919?], in H.D., "Art and Ardor."

34. D. Bruce Ogilvie, a former RAF pilot who was close friends with Hugh Dowding, has recently claimed that H.D. and Bryher were involved at least since 1940 with a circle of "Atlantean" initiates including not only Ogilvie and Dowding but also J. R. R. Tolkien and Robert Graves (Ogilvie, "H.D. and Hugh Dowding," 11–12). H.D.'s own memoirs and letters indicate, however, that she did not begin corresponding with Dowding until 1943 and did not meet him personally until February 1945.

35. H.D. muses on the table's significance in *Majic Ring*, *The Sword Went Out to Sea* (the title comes from a William Morris poem), the *Hirslanden Notebooks*, and elsewhere. Her obsession with William Morris and his circle also resulted in an unpublished novel, *White Rose and the Red* (probably 1948; Beinecke).

36. Lord Hugh Dowding, letter to H.D., 24 February 1946 (Beinecke).

37. See my article, "H.D.'s *Majic Ring*" (*Tulsa Studies in Women's Literature* 14.2 [1995]), for a detailed account of H.D.'s spiritualist experiments and her correspondence with Dowding.

38. Friedman notes that *Delia* is "[a]lmost an anagram for Hilda" and "may also encode a layered identity—overtly feminine in its onomatopoeic seductions of dahlias, Delilahs; but also covertly androgynous in its austere etymological meaning, 'she is Delos, i.e., Artemis'" (*Penelope's Web* 43).

39. Letter to Viola Jordan, 28 July 1942 (Beinecke).

40. *Majic Ring*, "Notes" (n.p.). The séance notes are included with, but are not part of, the first draft of *Majic Ring* in the H.D. collection at the Beinecke Library.

41. Up to the end of her life Bryher refused to admit either that she and H.D. had ever taken part in séances or that H.D. was even interested in the occult (Friedman, *Psyche Reborn* n. 318).

Chapter 4

Epigraphs are from Lawrence, *Phoenix*, 630–31; Rich, *Fact of a Doorframe*, 119–20. Charles Segal notes that Rich's poem is a response to Jean Cocteau's film *Orphée* (184).

1. For discussions of these and other accounts of the Orpheus myth, see Schondorff, *Orpheus und Eurydike*; Strauss, *Descent and Return*; Warden, *Orpheus: The Metamorphosis of a Myth*; Lee, "Orpheus and Eurydice"; Segal, *Orpheus: The Myth of the Poet*; and Theweleit, *Orpheus (und) Eurydike*. Orpheus/Eurydice poems by twentieth-century male writers include Paul Valéry, "Orphée" (*Poésies* 6); Yvan Goll, "Der neue Orpheus"; Gottfried Benn, "Orpheus' Tod" (343–44); Lawrence Durrell, "Orpheus" (19); Randall Jarrell, "Che farò senza Euridice" (394); Stephen Spender, "No Orpheus, No Eurydice" (*Poems*, 105–6); Robert Graves, "Eurydice" (*Man Does, Woman Is* 24); and John Ashbery, "Syringa" (245–47).

2. See also Hassan, *The Dismemberment of Orpheus: Toward a Postmodern Literature*, for an explicit association of the Orpheus myth with what Hassan calls postmodernism's "crisis of language and culture" (xiii).

3. See Robbins, "Famous Orpheus," Warden 9–17.

4. The Orpheus/Eurydice story appears in Virgil, *Georgics*, 4:453–527; and in Ovid, *Metamorphoses*, 10:1–85. In both accounts Orpheus descends to the underworld to retrieve his dead wife, Eurydice, who has been stung by a poisonous snake. He charms Pluto and Persephone with his song, so that they agree to let him lead Eurydice out of the underworld but only on the condition that he neither speak to her nor turn around. He breaks the taboo, and Eurydice is forced to return to the world of the dead.

5. For a discussion of Jacopo Peri's *Euridice* (1600) and Monteverdi's *La Favola d'Orfeo* (1607), both of which omit the condition of the turn altogether, see McGee, "*Orfeo* and *Euridice*, the First Two Operas." In Gluck's 1762 *Orfeo ed Euridice*, Eurydice is first lost but then restored to Orpheus in an abrupt deus ex machina happy ending. See also *The Magic Flute*, Mozart's loosely adapted version of the Orpheus myth, in which Tamino successfully leads Pamina through the hellish "trial of fire and water."

6. Some of the many contemporary poems by women about the Orpheus/Eurydice myth include Edith Sitwell, "Eurydice" (267–70); Muriel Rukeyser, "Orpheus" (291–99); Adrienne Rich, "I Dream I'm the Death of Orpheus" (*Fact of a Doorframe* 119–20; see epigraph); Margaret Atwood, "Orpheus (1)," "Eurydice," and "Orpheus (2)" (131–33, 138–39); Kathleen Raine, ["What substance had Euridice"]; and Judith Wright, "Eurydice in Hades."

7. For a sobering overview of modernism's battle of the sexes, its political and historical implications, and its literary consequences, see Gilbert and Gubar, *No Man's Land* (especially vol. 1: *The War of the Words*). On what I call "Eurydicean rebellion and Orphic counter-rebellion" in modernist literature, see Scott, *The Gender of Modernism*; and Theweleit, *Orpheus (und) Eurydike*.

8. H.D.'s poem "Eurydice," first published in *The Egoist* in May 1917, was composed at Corfe Castle, Dorset, in late 1916, at a time when she was exchanging manuscripts with Lawrence (see H.D., "Autobiographical Notes," Beinecke). "Eurydice" bears little resemblance to the rather incoherent free-verse fragments that make up Julia's "Orpheus" poem in *Bid Me to Live*. More impor-

tant in the context of the novel than the fragments themselves, however, are their reception by Rafe (Julia's poet-husband) and Rico; their battle for editorial precedence over Julia's drafts defines the background of gender conflict and critical aspersion against which "Eurydice" must have been written.

9. See especially Firchow, "Rico and Julia: The Hilda Doolittle–D. H. Lawrence Affair Reconsidered"; and Robinson, *H.D.: The Life and Work of an American Poet*. Both Firchow and Robinson share the enterprise of determining, almost solely on the basis of "encoded" novelistic hints, whether or not H.D. and Lawrence were lovers. Firchow concludes that they probably were not, while Robinson argues that they carried on a prolonged and passionate affair and even that Lawrence was the father of H.D.'s daughter, Perdita. For an incisive attack on the methodological shortcomings and factual inaccuracies of Robinson's book, see Gilbert, "H.D.? Who Was She?" For further rebuttals to Robinson's claims, see H.D.'s letter to Bryher (16 January 1935) in which H.D. comments "how grateful I am . . . that I never slept with D. H. L." (Beinecke); and Perdita Schaffner's statement, in her afterword to *Bid Me to Live*, that Cecil Gray was her father (185–94).

10. For two examples of intertextual resonances between Lawrence and H.D., see Burnett, "H.D. and Lawrence: Two Allusions"; and Roessel, "H.D. and Lawrence: Two More Allusions." Both Burnett and Roessel argue, as I do, that the literary relationship between H.D. and Lawrence was characterized as much by adversarial tension as by mutual admiration.

11. Letter to John Cournos, 31 October 1916. Printed in H.D., "Art and Ardor" 139–40.

12. See Lawrence's letter to Arthur McLeod (21 December 1916): "H.D. is good: none of the others worth anything" (*Letters* 3:61); and to Edward Marsh (29 January 1917): "Don't you think H.D.—Mrs. Aldington—writes some good poetry? I do—really very good. I send you an *Egoist* for this month. It is nothing of a paper—but H.D. is good, without doubt" (*Letters* 3:84). Lawrence's praise of H.D., although consistent, is uncharacteristically inarticulate; *good*, it seems, is about the most evocative adjective he can produce.

13. Letter to Cecil Gray, 7 November 1917 (*Letters* 3:179–80). Apparently at Richard Aldington's insistence, the reference to H.D. (Hilda Aldington) was omitted from the early editions of Lawrence's letters.

14. I borrow the notion of sex as a "harrowing of hell" from Kermode ("Lawrence and the Apocalyptic Types"). Kermode's specific reference is not to penile-vaginal intercourse but to the anal sex—a "love-death" that "amalgamates heaven and hell, life-flow and death-flow, in one act"—that Ursula and Connie experience in *Women in Love* and *Lady Chatterley's Lover*, respectively (69).

15. These are Eurydice's responses in Virgil's and Ovid's versions of the myth, respectively. In the *Georgics* (4:453–527) she laments the "madness" and the "cruel fate" that have caused her husband to break the taboo and turn, while in the *Metamorphoses* (10:1–85) she utters no recriminations whatsoever, merely muttering "Vale!" before slipping back to the underworld.

16. For other readings of "Eurydice," see especially DuPlessis, *Writing beyond the Ending* (70–71, 105–10); and "Family, Sexes, Psyche: An Essay on H.D. and the Muse of the Woman Writer." A more general discussion of the feminist, revisionary strategies that H.D. employs in this and other poems is offered by Alicia Ostriker, "The Poet as Heroine: Learning to Read H.D." (*Writing like a Woman* 7–41); and "The Thieves of Language: Women Poets and Revisionist Mythmaking."

17. Unfortunately, little record remains of the Lawrence-H.D. correspondence itself. Lawrence, with his peripatetic lifestyle, did not generally preserve letters written to him, while H.D. recalls in *Compassionate Friendship* that Richard Aldington admitted some time after the breakup of their marriage to having burned Lawrence's letters to her: "'I am sorry, Dooley,' he said" (61).

18. Lawrence, "Nathaniel Hawthorne," *Symbolic Meaning*, 131. The Hawthorne essay, written sometime between 1917 and 1919, first appeared in the *English Review* (May 1919) and was republished in significantly revised form in *Studies in Classic American Literature* (1923).

19. Virgil, *Georgics*, 4:497. In a letter to Catherine Carswell (5 February 1917) Lawrence calls "And now farewell" (*"Jamque vale"*) the "motto" to *Look! We Have Come Through!*, his 1917 volume of love-hate poems about his relationship with Frieda (*Letters* 3:87). H.D., in her 1957 long poem *Vale Ave*, implicitly rejects Lawrence's poetics of abandonment, depicting instead a recurrent historical pattern not only of romantic valediction ("Vale") but also of reunion ("Ave").

20. For an eloquent statement of this position, see Hélène Cixous, "Sorties: Out and Out: Attacks/Ways Out/Forays," in Cixous and Clément, *The Newly Born Woman*, 63–130.

21. H.D. may have been referring to Lawrence's letter of 10 August 1929, in which he wrote, presumably in reply to her request for a meeting: "But now it's more than ten years since we met, and what should we have to say? God knows! Nothing, really. It's no use saying anything. That's my last conviction. Least said, soonest mended; which assumes that the breakage has already happened" (Lawrence, *Collected Letters* 2:1175).

22. H.D. reports in "Advent" that she at first thought Lawrence must have stolen the plot of *The Man Who Died*—"the story of the wounded but living Christ, waking up in the rock-tomb" (*Tribute to Freud* 142)—from her own unpublished novel *Pilate's Wife* (Beinecke). The final draft of her novel, begun in 1924 but completed in 1934 after she had read *The Man Who Died*, serves as her female-centered response to Lawrence's version of the tale.

23. In "Advent," noting that she and Lawrence were born 364 days apart, H.D. comments that "for one day in the year, H.D. and D. H. Lawrence were twins" (*Tribute to Freud* 141); and in the unpublished *Thorn Thicket* (Beinecke) she muses on the mirror image likeness of their initials (39).

24. H.D. herself is referred to as an "Orphic maenad" by Cecil Gray in his memoir, *Musical Chairs, or Between Two Stools*, 133–34. The Maenads, in the early accounts of the Orpheus myth, dismember Orpheus because they are

angry at him for having neglected other women after losing Eurydice. Ovid introduces a homosexual undercurrent by noting that Orpheus spends his time, after Eurydice's death, solely in the company of young boys—an aspect of the story that, given Lawrence's own preoccupations with homosexuality and "male comradeship" during his misogynist phase, suggests some intriguing parallels.

25. H.D., *CP* 461–66; see also Louis L. Martz's commentary on the poem (*CP* xxviii–xxix). "The Poet" was first published in *Life and Letters Today* (13 [December 1935]: 80–83), five years after Lawrence's death.

26. As she describes in "Advent" and *Compassionate Friendship*, H.D. read several books by and about Lawrence after his death in 1930; I have not, however, found any explicit mention in her writings of his *Last Poems*, although it seems extremely likely that she would at some point have seen the book, which was edited by her estranged husband, Richard Aldington, and published in 1932. In any case, whether or not H.D. actually read "Bavarian Gentians" before writing *Bid Me to Live* makes little difference to my argument that both H.D. and Lawrence adopted, especially toward the end of their lives, a conciliatory tone—masking, to be sure, a series of defensive strategies that might still be read as hostile—toward the creative threat that the other embodied.

27. Richard Aldington ("Rafe") is figured as Dionysus in H.D.'s poem "The God" (*CP* 45–47), which was written along with "Eurydice" at Corfe Castle in 1916.

Chapter 5

1. Letter to L. A. G. Strong, 25 June 1925 (Yeats, *Letters*, 709). Yeats dictated the letter, possibly to his wife, who often transcribed his letters (an interesting detail given her role as transcriber of *A Vision*'s mysterious "voices" as well). Nonetheless, given the vagaries of Yeats's spelling, it is likely that the "enunciation" error was his own.

2. The Leda myth finds its homosexual analogue in the story of Ganymede, abducted by Zeus in the form of an eagle and carried off to Olympus to be the god's cupbearer and bedfellow. The myth was a favorite of the ancient Greeks and Romans, largely "because it afforded religious justification for a grown man's passionate love of a boy" (Graves, *Greek Myths* 1:117). In the nineteenth and twentieth centuries, however, Ganymede has enjoyed nothing approaching Leda's popularity as a subject of art and literature.

3. See H.D., *End to Torment*, 185; and H. Moore 375.

4. Stowell, in "Leda" (1988) speaks as an English teacher reading Yeats's poem to a student who has recently been raped (see epigraph). LaRue, in "Leda" (1987), takes on the voice of a skeptical, unenthralled Leda. Van Duyn's (1974) third-person narrator, similarly, presents Leda's point of view (although Leda does try to imagine Zeus's perspective). Fraser, in an excerpt from an unfinished (and subsequently lost) work called "Leda. and Swan" (1981), identifies herself with both Leda and the swan—not as a symbol of domination,

however, but, rather, as one of poetic freedom. Broumas, in "Leda and Her Swan" (1977), feminizes the swan and strips it of its violent connotations, turning the rape scene into a lesbian love affair (5–6). See also Mitchell, "Exploring the Aesthetics of Rape," for a discussion of some contemporary Leda poems by both men and women; unfortunately, Mitchell's analysis never moves far beyond the level of plot summary, as she evaluates the feminist agenda (or lack thereof) of each poem in turn.

5. An earlier draft of the poem appeared in *To-Morrow* in 1924; the final and widely anthologized version was published (with some forty pages of commentary) in *A Vision* in 1925 (Johnsen 81).

6. Leda's iconographic genealogy is so extensive that I can offer only a brief overview here. Though some Greek and Roman art shows a standing Leda resisting the swan, most works from antiquity portray a union of mutual acquiescence. Similarly, representations from the Renaissance through the early nineteenth century—including paintings and sculptures by Leonardo, Michelangelo, Correggio, Veronese, Rubens, Tintoretto, Ammanati, Delacroix, Géricault, and Boucher—generally present a willing Leda who welcomes the swan's advances; Tintoretto's Leda even conceals the swan in her bedchamber (Fletcher pl. 5); paintings after Leonardo portray a peaceful familial scene (Melchiori pl. 5; Fletcher pl. 3); and Coypel shows the swan engaging Leda from the front while an anatomically well-equipped Zeus enters her from behind (Fletcher pl. 11). Although artists of the fin de siècle, including Cézanne, Renoir, Moreau, Albert-Valentin Thomas, Albert-Henri Bramtot, J. M. Heinrich Hofmann, Max Klinger, and Félicien Rops (Dijkstra 314–15), also tend to portray Leda either as passively supine or as actively acquiescent and even orgasmic—Moreau describes her union with the swan as a sacred marriage culminating in the "apotheosis of eternal beauty" (qtd. in Fletcher 96)—the last century has seen a radical increase in decadent, sexually inventive, and sometimes simply perverse variations on the Leda theme: a number of artists, for instance, depict the swan's neck and head in graphically phallic terms (Fletcher 105; Medlicott 19); D. H. Lawrence leaves Leda's head out of the frame so that only her truncated torso is visible (*Paintings* 77); and Sidney Nolan, in one of his seventy-five Ledas, shows the swan treading Leda's bloodied vulva (Medlicott 20). Medlicott, listing dozens of modern artists who have represented the Leda myth, insists that twentieth-century Leda paintings, like those of earlier periods, almost unanimously neglect the theme of rape (20); his claim is belied, however, by the many sinister, even openly violent, works described and reproduced in his article.

For fairly exhaustive discussions of Leda's appearance in art through the ages, including bibliographies and plates, see especially Fletcher; Reid; Melchiori 133–63, 280–82; Dijkstra 314–18; and Medlicott 18–21.

7. I am indebted to Elaine Zickler for pointing out to me the importance of womb imagery in Yeats's poem.

8. "All things are from antithesis," Yeats reminds us in *A Vision*; "from one of [Leda's] eggs came Love and from the other War" (268). Perhaps not coinci-

dentally, the opposed catagories of Love and War—romance versus violence—themselves reflect the two extremes by which artists and writers tend to interpret Leda's rape.

9. Letter to Dorothy Wellesley, 28 November 1936 (*Letters* 868).

10. For further discussion of Yeats's attributions of special visionary powers to women, particularly with reference to "Leda and the Swan" and "The Second Coming," see Keane 62–69.

11. Letter "an ein junges Mädchen," 20 November 1904 (*Briefe* 1:104).

12. "Der Geist fährt so unwirsch aus und ein, kommt so wild und bleibt so plötzlich aus, daß mir zumuth ist, als ging ich körperlich dabei in Stücke" (Thurn und Taxis-Hohenlohe 43).

13. I have endeavored in my translation not only to preserve but to foreground some of the ambiguities of Rilke's original, particularly the confusing abundance of masculine pronouns and the structure of double penetration (see n. 14). For instance, I have translated *Die Aufgetane*—"the opened-up [female] one"—as "the woman, undone" for the sake of emphasizing one of the situation's central paradoxes: Leda, tragically passive, is always already "undone," whether before the rape (in terms of her accessibility) or afterward (through her sexual disgrace).

14. *Betreten*, which literally means "to step into" or "to set foot in," does not have the sexual connotations of the English verb *to enter*, nor does the pronoun *ihn*, referring to the swan, have quite the same gender specificity as the English *him*, since *der Schwan*, in German, is a masculine noun and all swans therefore take a masculine pronoun. The poem's opening, then, might be most literally translated as "When the god stepped into it" rather than "When the god entered him." Even so, my argument stands that the opening line is disorienting and even homosexually suggestive; the title, after all, prepares us for a poem about Leda, not for one about Zeus' relationship to the swan.

15. Both the German and French words for *feather* (*Feder* and *plume*) also denote a feather pen; the English word *pen*, similarly, derives from the Latin word for *feather* (*penna*). In an etymologically unrelated development a *pen* is also a female swan.

16. The swan song, of course, has long served as a favorite metaphor both for the proximity of art to death and for the triumph of art over death; see, for example, Orlando Gibbons's 1612 madrigal "The Silver Swan" (310–12); Alfred Lord Tennyson's poem "The Dying Swan" (36–67); and T. Sturge Moore's 1914 "The Dying Swan" (111).

17. Although the swan is celebrated in more poems than I could possibly list here as a symbol of love, death, poetry, art, the spirit, the soul, etc., a number of modernist poems specifically deromanticize the image of the swan, thus calling into question the very qualities and values that it most traditionally represents. See, for example, Charles Baudelaire's "Le Cygne" (118–20), which links a displaced swan with the spiritual decay of the modern city; Wallace Stevens's "Academic Discourse at Havana" (142–45), which ironizes the Symbolist landscape that Stevens himself so often inhabits; Marianne Moore's "No Swan So

Fine" (19), which hints at the superiority of artifice over nature; and Enrique González Martínez's "Tuércele el cuello al cisne" ("Twist the neck of the swan" [145]), which requires, I think, no paraphrase.

18. See Harrison's *The Reactionaries* for a thorough and sobering account of the problematic political/aesthetic tendencies of these and other modernist writers.

19. In an unpublished introduction to *A Vision* Yeats links divine inspiration and annunciatory experience not only to "Dove or Swan" but also to his pet canary. Owen Aherne, the supposed author of *A Vision*, and Michael Robartes, another fictional character, visit Yeats and ask him to undertake editorship of Aherne's work. When Yeats reveals that he already has copybooks full of diagrams documenting the same mystic system, Robartes exclaims excitedly, "You can only have found that all out . . . through the inspiration of God." Yeats coolly replies: "Is not that a rather obsolete term? . . . It came in the first instance quite suddenly. I was looking at my canary, which was darting about in the cage in rather brilliant light, when I found myself in a strangely still and silent state and in that state I saw with the mind's eye symbols streaming before me. That still and silent state always recurs in some degree when I fix my mind upon the canary" (Yeats, *Letters* n. 700).

20. Edna St. Vincent Millay, in her sonnet "I dreamed I moved among the Elysian fields," does specifically identify herself with Leda, "the Swan's featherless bride," as well as with Danae (inseminated by Jupiter in the form of a golden shower) and Europa (carried off by Jupiter in the form of a bull). The poet wistfully concludes that "Wherefore I was among them well I knew": "All these were mortal women, yet all these / Above the ground had had a god for guest" (85). Her association of her remembered lover with Jove is a double-edged one, of course; Danae, Europa, and Leda, though loved by the king of the gods, were also deceived, seduced, and abandoned by him.

21. See H.D.'s poem "Lethe," which expresses a desire not for forgetfulness achieved through sexuality but, rather, for a forgetfulness utterly free of sexuality:

> The roll of the full tide to cover you
> Without question,
> Without kiss.

(CP 190)

Both "Leda" and "Lethe" were written in Cornwall in 1918, at a time when H.D., distressed by her husband Richard Aldington's infidelities, was unsuccessfully trying to drown her own emotional anguish in a short-lived love affair with the composer Cecil Gray (Guest 107–8).

22. The Leda story evolved from the tale of Nemesis, a nymph-goddess identified with wild swans, who, in pre-Hellenic myth, hunted and eventually devoured the sacred king. For the ancient Greeks swans were the sacred birds of women—"the V-formation of their flight was a female symbol" (Graves, *Greek Myths* 1:126)—and particularly of Aphrodite, the goddess of love; thus, when in the mythology of later centuries a divine male pursues a human

female, Zeus takes on the form of a swan not because it signifies male power but because it offers him the most deceptive means whereby to catch Leda off her guard (Graves 1:126). Other Indo-European versions of the Leda story, incidentally, follow a similar pattern of development: Wendy Daugherty O'Flaherty relates how, "under the influence of a steadily increasing Indo-European androcentrism (or, to put it more bluntly, male chauvinism)," early Indian legends of a swan-goddess who mates with a mortal man later became reversed, so that the once-powerful goddess was eventually "demoted," like the hapless Leda of Hellenic myth, to "ignominious mortality and passivity" (212).

Works Cited

Works by H.D.: dates given in parentheses after the title of a work refer to the probable date of composition; those given without parentheses refer to the earliest publication date, if it differs from that of the edition cited. "Beinecke" denotes unpublished manuscripts housed in the Yale Collection of American Literature, Beinecke Library, Yale University. The list given here represents only those works by H.D. to which I refer in this book; for a full list of published and major unpublished works by H.D., see DuPlessis, *H.D.*, 150–54.

Adams, John F. "'Leda and the Swan': The Aesthetics of Rape." *Bucknell Review* 12.3 (1964): 47–58.

Andreas-Salomé, Lou. *Lebensrückblick: Grundriß einiger Lebenserinnerungen.* Zurich: Max Niehans, 1951.

———. "Der Mensch als Weib. Ein Bild im Umriß." *Neue Deutsche Rundschau* 10 (1899): 225–43.

Arnold, Armin. *D. H. Lawrence and German Literature: With Two Hitherto Unknown Essays by D. H. Lawrence.* Montreal: Heinemann, 1963.

Ashbery, John. *Selected Poems.* New York: Penguin, 1985.

Atkinson, Clarissa. *Mystic and Pilgrim: The Book and the World of Margery Kempe.* Ithaca: Cornell UP, 1982.

Atwood, Margaret. *Selected Poems II: Poems Selected and New, 1976–1986.* Toronto: Oxford UP, 1986.

Baker, James R. "Lawrence as Prophetic Poet." *Journal of Modern Literature* 3 (1974): 1219–38.

Balbert, Peter. *D. H. Lawrence and the Phallic Imagination: Essays on Sexual Identity and Feminist Misreading.* London: Macmillan, 1989.

Barnwell, W. C. "The Rapist in 'Leda and the Swan.'" *South Atlantic Bulletin* 42.1 (1977): 62–68.

Barthes, Roland. *Critical Essays.* Trans. Richard Howard. Evanston: Northwestern UP, 1972.

Baudelaire, Charles. *Les Fleurs du mal.* 1861. Paris: Gallimard, 1972.

Benn, Gottfried. *Gedichte.* Frankfurt a.M.: Fischer, 1982.

Berg, Christine, and Philippa Berry. "'Spiritual Whoredom': An Essay on Female Prophets in the Seventeenth Century." In *1642: Literature and Power in the Seventeenth Century*, ed. Francis Barker et al., 37–54. Colchester: U of Essex, 1981.

Bevan, Edwyn. *Sibyls and Seers: A Survey of Some Ancient Theories of Revelation and Inspiration*. London: George Allen and Unwin, 1928.

Bianquis, Geneviève. "Rilke traducteur." In *Rilke et la France*. Paris: Plon, 1942.

Blackmur, R. P. "D. H. Lawrence and Expressive Form." *Form and Value in Modern Poetry*. Garden City, NY: Doubleday, 1957.

Blanchot, Maurice. *L'Espace littéraire*. Paris: Gallimard, 1955.

———. *La Part du feu*. Paris: Gallimard, 1949.

Bloom, Harold. *The Anxiety of Influence: A Theory of Poetry*. Oxford: Oxford UP, 1973.

———. *Kabbalah and Criticism*. New York: Seabury, 1975.

———, ed. *D. H. Lawrence*. New York: Chelsea House, 1986.

———. *H.D.* New York: Chelsea House, 1989.

Broumas, Olga. *Beginning with O*. New Haven: Yale UP, 1977.

Bruzzi, Zara. "The Fiery Moment: H.D. and the Eleusinian Landscape of English Modernism." *Agenda* 25.3–4 (1987–88): 97–112.

Buber, Martin. "Prophecy, Apocalyptic, and the Historical Hour." *On the Bible*, ed. Nahum Glatzer, 172–87. New York: Schocken, 1982.

Buck, Claire. "Freud and H.D.—Bisexuality and a Feminine Discourse." *m/f* 8 (1983): 52–65.

Burke, Joan. "'In Another Dimension': H.D. in Prophetic Tradition." Ph.D. diss., U of Maryland, 1991.

Burke, Kenneth. "On Motivation in Yeats." In *The Permanence of Yeats*, ed. James Hall and Martin Steinmann, 249–63. New York: Macmillan, 1950.

Burnett, Gary. "H.D. and Lawrence: Two Allusions." *H.D. Newsletter* 1.1 (1987): 32–35.

———. *H.D. between Image and Epic: The Mysteries of Her Poetics*. Ann Arbor: UMI Research P, 1990.

Butler, E. M. *Rainer Maria Rilke*. Cambridge: Cambridge UP, 1946.

Bynner, Witter. *Journey with Genius: Recollections and Reflections concerning the D. H. Lawrences*. New York: John Day, 1951.

Carpenter, Edward. *The Intermediate Sex*. New York: Kennerley, 1912.

———. *Intermediate Types among Primitive Folk: A Study in Social Evolution*. London: George Allen, 1914.

Carroll, Lewis. *The Annotated Alice*. Notes by Martin Gardner. New York: New American Library, 1960.

Carson, Anne. *Eros the Bittersweet: An Essay*. Princeton: Princeton UP, 1986.

Carswell, Catherine. *The Savage Pilgrimage: A Narrative of D. H. Lawrence*. London: Secker and Marburg, 1951.

Cixous, Hélène, and Catherine Clément. *The Newly Born Woman*. Trans. Betsy Wing. Minneapolis: U of Minnesota P, 1986.

The Cloud of Unknowing and Related Treatises. Ed. Phyllis Hodgson. Exeter: Catholic Records P, 1982.

Core, Deborah. "'The Closed Door': Love between Women in the Works of D. H. Lawrence." *D. H. Lawrence Review* 11.1 (Summer 1978): 114–31.

Corke, Helen. *D. H. Lawrence: The Croydon Years*. Austin: U of Texas P, 1965.

Cox, Richard. *Figures of Transformation: Rilke and the Example of Valéry*. London: Institute of Germanic Studies, U of London, 1979.

Curtius, Ernst Robert. *European Literature and the Latin Middle Ages*. Trans. William R. Trask. Princeton: Princeton UP, 1953.

D'Annunzio, Gabriele. "Leda without Swan." *Nocturne and Five Tales of Love and Death*. Trans. Raymond Rosenthal, 153–214. Marlboro, VT: Marlboro P, 1988.

Daleski, H. M. *The Forked Flame: A Study of D. H. Lawrence*. London: Faber and Faber, 1965.

Delavenay, Emile. *D. H. Lawrence and Edward Carpenter: A Study in Edwardian Transition*. London: Heinemann, 1971.

———. "'Making Another Lawrence': Frieda and the Lawrence Legend." *D. H. Lawrence Review* 8.1 (1975): 80–98.

De Man, Paul. *Blindness and Insight: Essays in the Rhetoric of Contemporary Criticism*. Minneapolis: U of Minnesota P, 1983.

Derrida, Jacques. *Marges de la philosophie*. Paris: Editions de Minuit, 1972.

———. *Writing and Difference*. Trans. Alan Bass. London: Routledge and Kegan Paul, 1978.

DeShazer, Mary K. *Inspiring Women: Reimagining the Muse*. Fairview Park, NY: Pergamon, 1987.

Dickinson, Emily. *The Complete Poems of Emily Dickinson*. Ed. Thomas H. Johnson. Boston and Toronto: Little, Brown, 1960.

Di Cesare, Mario A. *Poetry and Prophecy: Reflections on the Word*. Amherst, MA: Friends of the Amherst College Library, 1977.

Diepeveen, Leonard. "H.D. and the Film Arts." *Journal of Aesthetic Education* 18.4 (1984): 57–65.

Dijkstra, Bram. *Idols of Perversity: Fantasies of Feminine Evil in Fin-de-Siècle Culture*. New York and Oxford: Oxford UP, 1986.

Dix, Carol. *D. H. Lawrence and Women*. London: Macmillan, 1980.

Dodds, E. R. *The Greeks and the Irrational*. Berkeley and Los Angeles: U of California P, 1964.

Dowding, Hugh. *Many Mansions*. London: Rider, 1943.

Draper, R. P., ed. *D. H. Lawrence: The Critical Heritage*. London: Routledge and Kegan Paul, 1970.

DuPlessis, Rachel Blau. "Family, Sexes, Psyche: An Essay on H.D. and the Muse of the Woman Writer." *Montemora* 6 (1979): 137–56.

———. *H.D.: The Career of That Struggle*. Bloomington: Indiana UP, 1986.

———. "Romantic Thralldom in H.D." *Contemporary Literature* 20.2 (1979): 178–203.

———. *Writing beyond the Ending: Narrative Strategies of Twentieth-Century Women Writers*. Bloomington: Indiana UP, 1985.

DuPlessis, Rachel Blau, and Susan Stanford Friedman. "'Woman Is Perfect': H.D.'s Debate with Freud." *Feminist Studies* 7.3 (1981): 417–30.

Durrell, Lawrence. *Collected Poems*. London: Faber and Faber, 1960.

Eliade, Mircea. *Myths, Dreams and Mysteries: The Encounter between Contemporary Faiths and Archaic Reality*. London: Harvill, 1960.

————. *The Two and the One.* Trans. J. M. Cohen. Chicago: U of Chicago P, 1962.

Eliot, T. S. *After Strange Gods: A Primer of Modern Heresy.* London: Faber and Faber, 1933.

————. *The Complete Poems and Plays, 1909–1950.* New York: Harcourt Brace Jovanovich, 1971.

Ellmann, Richard. *The Identity of Yeats.* 1954. Rpt. London: Faber and Faber, 1964.

Emerson, Ralph Waldo. "Nature." *Nature and Other Addresses,* 7–10. New York: John B. Alden, 1886.

Engel, Bernard F. "H.D.: Poems That Matter and Dilutations." *Contemporary Literature* 10.4 (1969): 507–22.

Evans, Arthur. *The God of Ecstasy: Sex-Roles and the Madness of Dionysus.* New York: St. Martin's, 1988.

Firchow, Peter. "Rico and Julia: The Hilda Doolittle–D. H. Lawrence Affair Reconsidered." *Journal of Modern Literature* 8.2 (1980): 51–76.

Fisher, Peter F. *The Valley of Vision: Blake as Prophet and Revolutionary.* Toronto: U of Toronto P, 1961.

Fletcher, Angus. *The Prophetic Moment: An Essay on Spenser.* Chicago: U of Chicago P, 1971.

Fletcher, Ian. "'Leda and the Swan' as Iconic Poem." *Yeats Annual* 1 (1982): 81–113.

Fraser, Kathleen. "Energy Unavailable for Useful Work in a System Undergoing Change." From "Leda. and Swan." *Iowa Review* 12.2–3 (1981): 88–96.

Friedberg, Anne. "Approaching *Borderline.*" *Millenium Film Journal* 7–9 (1980–81): 130–39. Reprinted in King 369–90.

Friedman, Susan Stanford. "H.D., Woman, History, Recognition." *Wide Angle: A Film Quarterly of Theory, Criticism, and Practice* 5.2 (1982): 26–31.

————. "Modernism of the 'Scattered Remnant': Race and Politics in the Development of H.D.'s Modernist Vision." In King 91–116.

————. *Penelope's Web: Gender, Modernity, H.D.'s Fiction.* Cambridge: Cambridge UP, 1990.

————. *Psyche Reborn: The Emergence of H.D.* Bloomington: Indiana UP, 1981.

————. "Who Buried H.D.? A Poet, Her Critics, and Her Place in 'The Literary Tradition.'" *College English* 36.7 (1975): 801–14.

Friedman, Susan Stanford, and Rachel Blau DuPlessis. "'I Had Two Loves Separate': H.D.'s Sexualities in *Her.*" *Montemora* 8 (1981): 7–30.

Fuerst, Norbert. *Phases of Rilke.* Bloomington: Indiana UP, 1958.

Gibbons, Orlando. "The Silver Swan." *The Oxford Book of English Madrigals.* Ed. Philip Ledger, 310–12. Oxford: Oxford UP, 1978.

Gilbert, Sandra M. *Acts of Attention: The Poems of D. H. Lawrence.* Ithaca: Cornell UP, 1972.

————. "Feminism and D. H. Lawrence: Some Notes toward a Vindication of His Rites." *Anais* 9 (1991): 92–100.

————. "H.D.? Who Was She?" *Contemporary Literature* 24.4 (1983): 496–511.

————. "Hell on Earth: *Birds, Beasts and Flowers* as Subversive Narrative." *D. H. Lawrence Review* 12.3 (1979): 256–74.

Gilbert, Sandra M., and Susan Gubar. *No Man's Land: The Place of the Woman Writer in the Twentieth Century.* 3 vols. Vol. 1: *The War of the Words.* Vol 2: *Sexchanges.* New Haven: Yale UP, 1987–94.

———, eds. *The Norton Anthology of Literature by Women.* New York: Norton, 1985.

Girard, René. *Deceit, Desire, and the Novel: Self and Other in Literary Structure.* 1965. Trans. Yvonne Freccero. Baltimore: Johns Hopkins UP, 1976.

Gogarty, Oliver St. John. *Selected Poems.* New York: Macmillan, 1933.

Goll, Yvan. "Der neue Orpheus." *Gedichte des Expressionismus,* 159–62. Stuttgart: Reclam, 1966.

González Martínez, Enrique. "Tuércele el cuello al cisne." In *La poesía hispanoamericana desde el Modernismo,* ed. Eugenio Florit and José Olivio Jiménez, 145. New York: Appleton-Century-Crofts, 1968.

Goodheart, Eugene. *The Utopian Vision of D. H. Lawrence.* Chicago: U of Chicago P, 1963.

Goth, Maja. *Rilke und Valéry: Aspekte Ihrer Poetik.* Bern and Munich: Franken, 1981.

Gourmont, Remy de. *Divertissements.* Paris: Mercure, 1914.

———. *Dream of a Woman.* Trans. Lewis Galantière. New York: Boni and Liveright, 1927.

Graves, Robert. *Collected Poems, 1959.* London: Cassell, 1959.

———. *The Greek Myths.* 2 vols. Baltimore: Penguin, 1955.

———. *Man Does, Woman Is.* London: Cassell, 1964.

———. *The White Goddess: A Historical Grammar of Poetic Myth.* London: Faber and Faber, 1948.

Gray, Cecil. *Musical Chairs, or Between Two Stools.* London: Home and Van Thal, 1948.

Gray, John. *The Poems of John Gray.* Ed. Ian Fletcher. Greensboro, NC: ELTP, 1988.

Green, Martin. *The Von Richthofen Sisters: The Triumphant and Tragic Modes of Love.* London: Weidenfeld and Nicolson, 1974.

Gregory, Horace. *D. H. Lawrence: Pilgrim of the Apocalypse.* 1933. Rpt. New York: Grove, 1957.

Gubar, Susan. "The Echoing Spell of H.D.'s *Trilogy.*" *Contemporary Literature* 19.2 (1978): 196–218.

———. "Sapphistries." *Signs* 10.1 (1984): 43–62.

Guest, Barbara. *Herself Defined: The Poet H.D. and Her World.* New York: Doubleday, 1984.

Harding, Anthony J. *Coleridge and the Inspired Word.* Kingston: McGill's-Queen's UP, 1985.

Harrison, John R. *The Reactionaries.* London: Victor Gollancz, 1966.

Hartman, Geoffrey. "The Poetics of Prophecy." In *High Romantic Argument,* ed. Lawrence Lipking, 15–40. Ithaca: Cornell UP, 1981.

———. *Criticism in the Wilderness: The Study of Literature Today.* New Haven: Yale UP, 1980.

———. *The Unmediated Vision: An Interpretation of Wordsworth, Hopkins, Rilke and Valéry*. Oxford: Oxford UP, 1954.

Hartman, Geoffrey H., and Sanford Budick, eds. *Midrash and Literature*. New Haven: Yale UP, 1986.

Hassan, Ihab. *The Dismemberment of Orpheus: Toward a Postmodern Literature*. Madison: U of Wisconsin P, 1982.

H.D. "Art and Ardor in World War I: Selected Letters from H.D. to John Cournos." *Iowa Review* 16.3 (1986): 126–55.

———. *Asphodel*. (1921–22). Durham: Duke UP, 1992.

———. "Autobiographical Notes." (1949). Beinecke.

———. *Bid Me to Live (A Madrigal)*. (1939, 1949). 1960. Rpt. London: Virago, 1984.

———. *Borderline: A Pool Film with Paul Robeson*. London: Mercury, 1930.

———. "The Cinema and the Classics [Three Essays]." *Close-Up* 1.1 (July 1927): 22–33; 1.2 (August 1927): 30–39; 1.3 (November 1927): 18–31.

———. *Collected Poems, 1912–1944*. Ed. Louis L. Martz. New York: New Directions, 1983.

———. *Compassionate Friendship*. (1955). Beinecke.

———. "The Dream." Chapter 3 of *The Gift*. *Contemporary Literature* 10.4 (1969): 605–26.

———. *End to Torment*. (1958). New York: New Directions, 1979.

———. *The Gift*. (1941–43). New York: New Directions, 1982.

———. "H.D. by Delia Alton" ("Notes on Recent Writing"). (1949). *Iowa Review* 16.2 (1986): 174–221.

———. *Hedylus*. (1924). 1928. Rpt. Redding Ridge, CT: Black Swan, 1980.

———. *Helen in Egypt*. (1952–56). 1961. Rpt. New York: New Directions, 1974.

———. *Her [HERmione]*. 1927. Rpt. New York: New Directions, 1981.

———. *Hermetic Definition*. (1960–61). New York: New Directions, 1972.

———. *Hirslanden Notebooks*. (1957–59). Beinecke.

———. *Majic Ring*. (1943–44). Beinecke.

———. *The Mystery*. (1951). Beinecke.

———. *Nights*. 1935. Rpt. New York: New Directions, 1986.

———. *Notes on Thought and Vision*. (1919). San Francisco: City Lights, 1982.

———. *Paint It To-day*. (1921). Beinecke.

———. *Palimpsest*. Boston and New York: Houghton Mifflin, 1926.

———. *Pilate's Wife*. (1924–34). Beinecke.

———. *The Sword Went Out to Sea (Synthesis of a Dream)*. (1947). Beinecke.

———. *Thorn Thicket*. (1960). Beinecke.

———. *Tribute to Freud*. ("Writing on the Wall" [1944]; "Advent" [1948]). 1974. Rpt. New York: New Directions, 1984.

———. *Vale Ave*. *New Directions in Prose and Poetry*. New York: New Directions, 1982. 44: 18–68.

———. *White Rose and the Red*. (1948). Beinecke.

Heschel, Abraham J. *The Prophets*. Vol. 1. 2 vols. New York: Harper, 1969.

Hilton, Walter. *The Ladder of Perfection*. Trans. Leo Sherley-Price. New York: Viking Penguin, 1957.

Hölderlin, Friedrich. *Werke und Briefe*. Vol. 1. 2 vols. Frankfurt a.M.: Insel, 1969.

Homer. *The Iliad*. Trans. Robert Fitzgerald. Garden City, NY: Anchor/Double-day, 1974.

Hough, Graham. *The Dark Sun: A Study of D. H. Lawrence*. London: Duckworth, 1956.

Howard, Richard. "Oracles." *Grand Street* 6.1 (Autumn 1986): 52–72.

Huxley, Aldous. *Leda*. London: Chatto and Windus, 1920.

Jaffe, Nora Crow. "'She Herself Is the Writing': Language and Sexual Identity in H.D." *Literature and Medicine* 4 (1985): 86–111.

James, William. *The Varieties of Religious Experience*. 1902. Rpt. New York: NAL Penguin, 1958.

Jarrell, Randall. *The Complete Poems*. New York: Farrar, Straus and Giroux, 1969.

Jarry, Alfred. *Léda*. Paris: Christian Bourgois, 1981.

Johnsen, William. "Textual/Sexual Politics in Yeats's 'Leda and the Swan.'" In *Yeats and Postmodernism*, ed. Leonard Orr, 80–89. Syracuse: Syracuse UP, 1991.

Joyce, James. *Ulysses*. New York: Vintage, 1961.

Jung, Carl Gustav. *Gesammelte Werke*. Vol 15. 19 vols. Olten: Walter-Verlag, 1971–83.

Keane, Patrick J. *Yeats's Interactions with Tradition*. Columbia: U of Missouri P, 1987.

Kenner, Hugh. *The Pound Era*. Berkeley and Los Angeles: U of California P, 1971.

Kermode, Frank. "D. H. Lawrence and the Apocalyptic Types." In Bloom, *D. H. Lawrence*, 59–71.

Kerrigan, William. *The Prophetic Milton*. Charlottesville: U of Virginia P, 1974.

Kiberd, Declan. *Men and Feminism in Modern Literature*. London: Macmillan, 1985.

King, Michael, ed. *H.D.: Woman and Poet*. Orono: National Poetry Foundation, 1986.

Knowles, David. *The English Mystical Tradition*. London: Burns and Oates, 1961.

Koestenbaum, Wayne. *Double Talk: The Erotics of Male Literary Collaboration*. New York: Routledge, 1989.

Komar, Kathleen L. "The Mediating Muse: Of Men, Women and the Feminine in the Work of Rainer Maria Rilke." *Germanic Review* 64.3 (1989): 129–33.

Kugel, James L. "Poets and Prophets: An Overview." In *Poetry and Prophecy: The Beginnings of a Literary Tradition*, ed. James L. Kugel, 1–25. Ithaca: Cornell UP, 1990.

Laird, Holly A. *Self and Sequence: The Poetry of D. H. Lawrence*. Charlottesville: U of Virginia P, 1988.

LaRue, Dorie. "Leda." *Massachusetts Review* 28.2 (1987): 350.

Lawrence, D. H. *Aaron's Rod*. 1922. Rpt. New York: Penguin, 1980.

———. *Collected Letters*. Ed. Harry T. Moore. 2 vols. New York: Viking, 1962.

———. *The Complete Poems*. 1960. Rpt. Coll. and ed. Vivian de Sola Pinto and Warren Roberts. New York: Penguin, 1980.

———. *The Escaped Cock*. 1929. Rpt. Ed. with a commentary by Gerald M. Lacy.

Los Angeles: Black Sparrow P, 1973. (Later published under the title *The Man Who Died.*)

———. *Fantasia of the Unconscious and Psychoanalysis and the Unconscious.* London: Heinemann, 1961.

———. *John Thomas and Lady Jane.* New York: Viking, 1972. (Previously unpublished second draft of *Lady Chatterley's Lover.*)

———. *Kangaroo.* 1923. Rpt. London: Heinemann, 1950.

———. *The Letters of D. H. Lawrence.* 7 vols. Cambridge: Cambridge UP, 1979–93.

———. *Lady Chatterley's Lover.* 1928. Rpt. London: Heinemann, 1961.

———. *The Paintings of D. H. Lawrence.* Ed. Mervyn Levy. London: Cory, Adams, and Mackay, 1964.

———. *Phoenix. The Posthumous Papers, 1936.* Ed. Edward D. McDonald. Harmondsworth and New York: Penguin, 1978.

———. *Phoenix II: Uncollected, Unpublished and Other Prose Works.* Ed. Warren Roberts and Harry T. Moore. London: Heinemann, 1968.

———. *The Plumed Serpent.* 1926. Rpt. New York: Penguin, 1987.

———. *The Rainbow.* 1915. Rpt. New York: Penguin, 1985.

———. *Studies in Classic American Literature.* New York: Seltzer, 1923.

———. *Study of Thomas Hardy and Other Essays.* (1915). Cambridge: Cambridge UP, 1985.

———. *The Symbolic Meaning: The Uncollected Versions of Studies in Classic American Literature.* Ed. Armin Arnold. London: Centaur, 1962.

———. *Women in Love.* 1921. Rpt. New York: Penguin, 1986.

Lawrence, D. H., and M. L. Skinner. *The Boy in the Bush.* 1924. Rpt. Cambridge: Cambridge UP, 1990.

Lawrence, Frieda. *"Not I, but the Wind . . ."* London: Granada, 1983.

Lee, M. Owen. "Orpheus and Eurydice: Some Modern Versions." *Classical Journal* 56.7 (1961): 307–13.

Leuba, James H. *The Psychology of Religious Mysticism.* New York: Harcourt, Brace, 1926.

Levertov, Denise. "H.D.: An Appreciation." In Bloom, *H.D.*, 7–10.

Levine, Bernard. *The Dissolving Image: The Spiritual-Esthetic Development of W. B. Yeats.* Detroit: Wayne State UP, 1970.

Lieb, Michael. *The Visionary Mode: Biblical Prophecy, Hermeneutics, and Cultural Change.* Ithaca: Cornell UP, 1991.

Lieberman, Laurence. "Leda's Revenge." *South Carolina Review* 6.2 (1974): 4.

Lipking, Lawrence. *Abandoned Women and Poetic Tradition.* Chicago: U of Chicago P, 1988.

Louÿs, Pierre. *Lêda.* Paris: Borel, 1898.

MacIntyre, C. F., trans. *Fifty Selected Poems,* by Rainer Maria Rilke. Berkeley: U of California P, 1940.

Mailer, Norman. *The Prisoner of Sex.* London: Weidenfeld and Nicolson, 1971.

Mallarmé, Stéphane. *Poésies.* Paris: Gallimard, 1945.

Mandel, Charlotte. "H.D.'s 'Projector II' and *Chang,* a Film of the Jungle." *H.D. Newsletter* 1.2 (1987): 42–45.

————. "The Redirected Image: Cinematic Dynamics in the Style of H.D. (Hilda Doolittle)." *Literature/Film Quarterly* 11 (1983): 36–45.

Marks, Herbert. "On Prophetic Stammering." *Yale Journal of Criticism* 1:1 (1987): 1–20.

Marshall, Tom. *The Psychic Mariner: A Reading of the Poems of D. H. Lawrence.* New York: Viking, 1970.

Martin, Biddy. *Woman and Modernity: The (Life)Styles of Lou Andreas-Salomé.* Ithaca: Cornell UP, 1991.

Martz, Louis L. "Introduction." In *Collected Poems, 1912–1944,* by H.D.

McGee, Timothy J. "*Orfeo* and *Euridice,* the First Two Operas." In Warden 163–81.

Medlicott, R. W. "Leda and the Swan—An Analysis of the Theme in Myth and Art." *Australian and New Zealand Journal of Psychiatry* 4.15 (1970): 15–23.

Melchiori, Giorgio. *The Whole Mystery of Art: Pattern into Poetry in the Work of W. B. Yeats.* London: Routledge and Kegan Paul, 1960.

Merrill, James. *The Changing Light at Sandover.* 1982. Rpt. New York: Knopf, 1992.

Meyer, Kinereth. "Visionary Poetry and the Breaking of the Tablets." *Religion and Literature* 19:3 (1987): 1–14.

Meyers, Jeffrey. "D. H. Lawrence and Homosexuality." In Spender, *D. H. Lawrence,* 135–46.

Miles, Rosalind. *The Fiction of Sex: Themes and Functions of Sex Difference in the Modern Novel.* London: Vision, 1974.

Millay, Edna St. Vincent. *Collected Sonnets.* New York and London: Harper Brothers, 1941.

Millett, Kate. *Sexual Politics.* London: Rupert Hart-Davis, 1971.

Milton, John. *Paradise Lost.* New York: Penguin, 1989.

Mitchell, Felicia. "Exploring the Aesthetics of Rape: Leda and the Swan in Selected Poems by Women." *Phoebe* 3.2 (1991): 64–72.

Mitchell, Stephen, trans. *The Sonnets to Orpheus,* by Rainer Maria Rilke. New York: Simon and Schuster, 1985.

Moore, Harry T. *The Priest of Love: A Life of D. H. Lawrence.* London: Heinemann, 1974.

Moore, Marianne. *The Complete Poems.* Harmondsworth: Penguin, 1986.

Moore, T. Sturge. *The Sea Is Kind.* Boston and New York: Houghton Mifflin, 1914.

Morris, Adalaide. "The Concept of Projection: H.D.'s Visionary Powers." *Contemporary Literature* 25.4 (1984): 411–36.

————. "Reading H.D.'s 'Helios and Athene.'" *Iowa Review* 12.2–3 (1981): 155–64.

Morse, B. J. "Rainer Maria Rilke and the Occult." *Journal of Experimental Metaphysics* (July 1945, October 1945, January 1946).

Murray, Penelope. "Poetic Inspiration in Early Greece." *Journal of Hellenic Studies* 101 (1981): 87–100.

Murfin, Ross. *The Poetry of D. H. Lawrence: Texts and Contexts.* Lincoln: U of Nebraska P, 1983.

Nixon, Cornelia. *Lawrence's Leadership Politics and the Turn against Women.* Berkeley: U of California P, 1986.

O'Flaherty, Wendy Daugherty. *Women, Androgynes, and Other Mythical Beasts.* Chicago: U of Chicago P, 1980.

Oates, Joyce Carol. *The Hostile Sun: The Poetry of D. H. Lawrence.* Los Angeles: Black Sparrow Press, 1974.

Oesterreich, T. K. *Possession Demoniacal and Other among Primitive Races, in Antiquity, the Middle Ages, and Modern Times.* 1930. Rpt. Trans. D. Ibberson. New Hyde Park, NY: University Books, 1966.

Ogilvie, D. Bruce. "H.D. and Hugh Dowding." *H.D. Newsletter* 1.2 (1987): 9–17.

Olsen, Tillie. *Silences.* New York: Delacorte, 1978.

Osborne, Charles. *W. H. Auden: The Life of a Poet.* New York: Harcourt Brace Jovanovich, 1979.

Ostriker, Alicia. "The Thieves of Language: Women Poets and Revisionist Mythmaking." *Signs: Journal of Women in Culture and Society* 8.1 (1982): 68–90.

———. *Writing like a Woman.* Ann Arbor: U of Michigan P, 1983.

Otto, Walter F. "The Meaning of the Eleusinian Mysteries." In *The Mysteries: Papers From the Eranos Yearbooks*, ed. Joseph Campbell, 14–31. Princeton: Princeton UP, 1955.

Ovid. *Metamorphoses.* Trans. Mary M. Innes. Harmondsworth: Penguin, 1955.

Perkins, David, ed. *English Romantic Writers.* New York: Harcourt Brace Jovanovich, 1967.

Perloff, Marjorie. *The Poetics of Indeterminacy.* Princeton: Princeton UP, 1981.

Plath, Sylvia. *Collected Poems.* Ed. Ted Hughes. New York: Harper and Row, 1981.

Plato. *Phaedrus, Ion, Gorgias, and Symposium, with Passages from the Republic and Laws.* Trans. Lane Cooper. London: Oxford UP, 1938.

Ponge, Francis. *Le Parti pris des choses.* Paris: Gallimard, 1942.

Prater, Donald. *A Ringing Glass: The Life of Rainer Maria Rilke.* Oxford: Clarendon, 1986.

Prescott, Frederick Clarke. *The Poetic Mind.* Ithaca: Cornell UP, 1922.

Raine, Kathleen. ["What substance had Euridice."] In Gilbert and Gubar, *Norton Anthology*, 1714.

Reid, Jane Davidson. "Leda, Twice Assaulted." *Journal of Aesthetics and Art Criticism* 11.4 (1953): 378–89.

Rich, Adrienne. *The Fact of a Doorframe: Poems Selected and New, 1950–1984.* New York: Norton, 1984.

———. *Of Woman Born: Motherhood as Experience and Institution.* New York: Norton, 1976.

———. *On Lies, Secrets, and Silence: Selected Prose, 1966–1978.* New York: Norton, 1979.

Riddel, Joseph. "H.D.'s Scene of Writing—Poetry as (and) Analysis." In *American Critics at Work: Examinations of Contemporary Literary Theories*, ed. Victor A. Kramer, 143–75. Troy, NY: Whitsun, 1984.

Rilke, Rainer Maria. *Briefe.* 3 vols. Frankfurt a.M.: Insel, 1950.

————. *Briefe an Nanny Wunderly-Volkart*. 2 vols. Frankfurt a.M.: Insel, 1977.

————. *Gesammelte Briefe*. 6 vols. Frankfurt a.M.: Insel, 1936–39.

————. *Sämtliche Werke*. 6 vols. Frankfurt a.M.: Insel, 1987.

————. *Tagebücher aus der Frühzeit*. Leipzig: Insel, 1942.

————. *Das Testament*. Frankfurt a.M.: Insel, 1974.

Rilke, Rainer Maria, and Lou Andreas-Salomé. *Briefwechsel*. Zurich: Max Niehans, 1952.

Rilke, Rainer Maria, and Marie von Thurn und Taxis. *Briefwechsel*. 2 vols. Zurich: Max Niehans, 1951.

Rilke, Rainer Maria, and Merline (Baladine Klossowska). *Correspondance, 1920–1926*. Zurich: Max Niehans, 1954.

Robbins, Emmet. "Famous Orpheus." In Warden 9–17.

Robinson, Janice S. *H.D.: The Life and Work of an American Poet*. Boston: Houghton Mifflin, 1982.

Roessel, David. "H.D. and Lawrence: Two More Allusions." *H.D. Newsletter* 1:2 (1987): 46–50.

Rossman, Charles. "You Are the Call and I Am the Answer: D. H. Lawrence and Women." *D. H. Lawrence Review* 8:3 (1975): 255–328.

Rothenberg, Albert, M. D. *Creativity and Madness: New Findings and Old Stereotypes*. Baltimore: Johns Hopkins UP, 1990.

Rukeyser, Muriel. *The Collected Poems of Muriel Rukeyser*. New York: McGraw-Hill, 1978.

Ryan, Judith. "Creative Subjectivity in Rilke and Valéry." *Comparative Literature* 25 (1973): 1–16.

Saint-Hélier, Monique. *A Rilke pour Noël*. Bern: Editions du Chandelier, 1927.

Schnack, Ingeborg. *Rainer Maria Rilke: Chronik seines Lebens und seines Werkes*. 2 vols. Frankfurt a.M.: Insel, 1975.

Scholem, Gershom G. *On the Kabbalah and Its Symbolism*. Trans. Ralph Manheim. New York: Schocken, 1969.

Schondorff, Joachim, ed. *Orpheus und Eurydike: Poliziana, Caldéron, Gluck, Offenbach, Kokoschka, Cocteau, Anouilh*. Munich: Langen, 1963.

Scott, Bonnie Kime, ed. *The Gender of Modernism: A Critical Anthology*. Bloomington: Indiana UP, 1990.

Sedgwick, Eve Kosofsky. *Between Men: English Literature and Male Homosexual Desire*. New York: Columbia UP, 1985.

Segal, Charles. *Orpheus: The Myth of the Poet*. Baltimore: Johns Hopkins UP, 1989.

Sexton, Anne. *The Complete Poems*. Boston: Houghton Mifflin, 1981.

Silverstein, Louis H. "Planting the Seeds: Selections from the *H.D. Chronology*." *H.D. Newsletter* 2.2 (1988): 4–14.

Simpson, Hilary. *D. H. Lawrence and Feminism*. DeKalb: Northern Illinois UP, 1982.

Sitwell, Edith. *Collected Poems*. London: Macmillan, 1957.

Snukal, Robert. *High Talk: The Philosophical Poetry of W. B. Yeats*. London: Cambridge UP, 1973.

Spender, Stephen. *Collected Poems, 1928–1953*. New York: Random House, 1955.

————, ed. *D. H. Lawrence: Novelist, Poet, Prophet.* London: Weidenfeld and Nicolson, 1973.

Spilka, Mark. "Lawrence Up-Tight, or the Anal Phase Once Over." *Novel: A Forum on Fiction* 4 (1971): 252–67.

Spitzer, Leo. "On Yeats's Poem 'Leda and the Swan.'" *Modern Philology* 51.4 (1954): 271–76.

Stephens, Anthony. "Zur Funktion sexueller Metaphorik in der Dichtung Rilkes." *Jahrbuch der Deutschen Schillergesellschaft* 18 (1974): 521–48.

Stevens, Wallace. *Collected Poems.* New York: Vintage, 1982.

Stowell, Phyllis. "Leda." *New Letters* 54.3 (1988): 88.

Strauss, Walter A. *Descent and Return: The Orphic Theme in Modern Literature.* Cambridge: Harvard UP, 1971.

Swann, Thomas Burnett. *The Classical World of H.D.* Lincoln: U of Nebraska P, 1962.

Tavis, Anna Alexeevna. *Rilke's Dialogues with Russia.* Ph.D. diss., Princeton U, 1987.

Tennyson, Alfred, Lord. *Poems.* London: Oxford UP, 1913.

Theweleit, Klaus. *Orpheus (und) Eurydike.* Vol. 1 of *Buch der Könige.* 1 vol. to date. Basel and Frankfurt a.M.: Stroemfeld/Roter Stern, 1988–.

————. "The Politics of Orpheus between Women, Hades, Political Power and the Media: Some Thoughts on the Configuration of the European Artist, Starting with the Figure of Gottfried Benn Or: What Happens to Eurydice?" *New German Critique* 36 (1985): 133–56.

Thurn und Taxis-Hohenlohe, Marie von. *Erinnerungen an Rainer Maria Rilke.* 1932. Rpt. Frankfurt a.M.: Insel, 1966.

Tindall, William York. *D. H. Lawrence and Susan His Cow.* New York: Columbia UP, 1939.

Trilling, Lionel. "Freud and Literature." In *Psychoanalysis and Literature*, ed. Hendrik M. Ruitenbeek, 251–71. New York: Dutton, 1964.

Tucker, Cynthia G. "Rilke's Eternal Woman and the Translation of Louise Labé." *Modern Language Notes* 89 (1974): 829–39.

Valéry, Paul. *Oeuvres.* Paris: Gallimard, 1957.

————. *Poésies.* Paris: Gallimard, 1958.

Van Duyn, Mona. "Leda Reconsidered." *Quarterly Review of Literature* 19.1–2 (1974): 321–24.

Vickery, John B. "Orpheus and Persephone: Uses and Meanings." In *Classical Mythology in Twentieth-Century Thought and Literature*, ed. Wendell M. Aycock and Theodore M. Klein, 187–212. Lubbock: Texas Tech P, 1980.

Virgil. *The Aeneid of Virgil.* Trans. Allen Mandelbaum. New York: Bantam, 1971.

————. *The Georgics.* New York: Penguin, 1982.

Von Rad, Gerhard. *The Theology of Israel's Prophetic Traditions.* Vol. 2 of *Old Testament Theology.* Trans. D. M. G. Stalker. 2 vols. New York: Harper and Row, 1965.

Wais, Karin. *Studien zu Rilkes Valéry-Übertragungen.* Tübingen: Niemeyer, 1967.

Walker, Cheryl. "H.D. and Time." In *Taking Our Time: Feminist Perspectives on*

Temporality, ed. Frieda Johles Forman and Caoran Sowton, 47–59. Oxford: Pergamon, 1989.

Warden, John, ed. *Orpheus: The Metamorphoses of a Myth*. Toronto: U of Toronto P, 1982.

Webster, Brenda S. *Yeats: A Psychoanalytic Study*. Stanford: Stanford UP, 1973.

Weiskel, Thomas. *The Romantic Sublime: Studies in the Structure and Psychology of Transcendence*. Baltimore: Johns Hopkins UP, 1976.

Weiss, Daniel. *Oedipus in Nottingham: D. H. Lawrence*. Seattle: U of Washington P, 1962.

Williams, William Carlos. *Autobiography*. New York: Random House, 1961.

———. *Complete Collected Poems, 1906–1938*. Norfolk, CN: New Directions, 1938.

———. *Paterson*. New York: New Directions, 1963.

Wittreich, Joseph Anthony, Jr. *Visionary Poetics: Milton's Tradition and His Legacy*. San Marino, CA: Huntington Library, 1979.

Wolf, Christa. *Kassandra*. Darmstadt: Luchterhand, 1983.

Woolf, Virginia. *The Moment and Other Essays*. 1947. Rpt. London: Hogarth, 1981.

———. *The Virginia Woolf Reader*. Ed. Mitchell A. Leaska. New York: Harcourt Brace Jovanovich.

Wright, Judith. "Eurydice in Hades." In *The World's Best Poetry*. Supplement 5: *Twentieth Century Women Poets*, 334. Great Neck, NY: Poetry Anthology P, 1987.

Yeats, William Butler. *The Cat and the Moon and Certain Poems*. Dublin: Cuala, 1924.

———. *The Collected Letters of W. B. Yeats*. Ed. Allan Wade. New York: Macmillan, 1955.

———. *The Collected Poems of W. B. Yeats*. New York: Macmillan, 1956.

———. *A Vision*. 1925. Rpt. New York: Macmillan, 1938.

Index